Enigma Books

Also published by Enigma Books

Ardavan Amir-Aslani

Islam and the West

Wars of the Gods

The Geopolitics of Faith

Enigma Books

Enigma Books
New York, NY
www.enigmabooks.com

First English Language Edition

Copyright © 2013 by Enigma Books

Copyright © 2011 by Nouveau Monde éditions

Translated by Robert L. Miller

Original French title: *La Guerre des dieux*

ISBN 978-1-936274-50-5
e-ISBN 978-1-936274-51-2

Printed in the United States of America

Library of Congress Cataloging-in-Publication Data

For My Mother

Contents

Islam and the West

Chapter 1

The "Clash of Civilizations"

An obsolete idea and a failed doctrine

When both communism and the Berlin Wall came crashing down at the same time the world was at a crossroads: but the shiny future that had been forecast never did materialize. An academic was seduced by that dream: Francis Fukuyama in his book *The End of History* made reference to Hegel's philosophy. The work appeared in 1992 following the disappearance of dictatorships in the West (Spain, Portugal, Greece, Latin America) that had made their mark until the 1970s and 80s. The momentous events in Eastern Europe were thought to herald a new era of democracy and liberalism. War, as Fukuyama implied, was destined to recede: with the coming end of history, while events would still continue to unfold, the basic principles being widely accepted, no great surprises would appear and any additional changes would only be marginal.

The facts have not confirmed whether Fukuyama's vision was correct or not. Never has the world been involved in so many wars having such universal repercussions: Afghanistan, Gulf Wars I and II, the former Yugoslavia, Georgia… while local conflicts remain just as deadly (Somalia, Eritrea, Yemen, Ruanda). Several of these situations are the consequences of 9/11. Democracy was not triumphant in the new era of liberalism and deregulation that has been strongly challenged during the tidal wave that engulfed the world economy from the sub-prime crisis to sovereign debt and the risk of collapse of monetary and financial systems that followed. What kind of world emerged after the Cold War and what was the impact of events such as 9/11?

Before questions are raised concerning the confrontation between the West and Islam that some have dubbed a "clash of civilizations" we must examine the origins of modern history.

Fernand Braudel, in his work *A History of Civilizations*, defines civilization as a psychology, a frame of mind. It is the summing up of many elements (geography, ethnology, religion, political realities) that taken together create a feeling of belonging to the same entity. The idea is that a collective mentality surfaces that cannot be separated from belonging to a specific civilization. Braudel views religion as playing a major role along with today's media, in making its influence felt anywhere in the world, and causing a chain reaction. This happened with the publication of the caricatures of Muhammad in Denmark. It can become a tool to ostracize an entire way of thinking, to ban a whole community or worse, to fan the embers of revolt and rekindle ethnic or religious hatreds.

Following 9/11 Islam ran the risk of being equated to terrorism. Some parts of the media and portions of public opinion sided with that interpretation, in particular the neo-conservative Fox News Network. The description "axis of evil" used by the republican administration of George W. Bush also contributed to ostracizing not just political regimes, but also entire populations. The issues of immigration, the building of mosques and a debate on national identity in Europe may also explain the rise of populism and the far right.

Rather than deploring immigration, it is the risk of the Islamization of societies that is now seen as the main danger.

The importance of religion is clear even though it may be debatable. This is true for every society and civilization. Europe is mostly the product of Christianity and remains identified with Christian civilization even though the Christian faith is not limited to Europe alone. The treaty of Lisbon has preferred to replace the idea of a religious heritage and a reference to Christian roots with that of a cultural and moral heritage.

This concept contradicts the traditional place and the actual importance of religion in society. If no one objects to the idea of Christian roots where Europe and France are concerned, the very notion of Judeo-Christian roots could also have been justifiable. Today the issue is one of recognition of the new religions of Europe such as Islam or Jehovah's Witnesses that will have to petition the French Council of State and the European Court of Justice to obtain the classification as cultural associations. The debate (in France) regarding the compatibility of Islam and the values of the French Republic appears to be somewhat unrealistic if one considers the Muslim community where most of its members are for the most part well integrated. The risk of heading in the wrong direction comes when Islam and secularism are the objects of a national debate…in order to capture the votes of the far right. As Odilon Vallet an authority in the history of religions and civilizations wrote, the initial perception the French people had of Islam was skewed from the start. During the colonial period the French knew nothing about French Muslims who happened to be living on a different continent. During the Algerian war Islam was "associated with the troubles" then later on, Muslim immigrants were often identified with "the deep poverty" of shantytowns of today along with the imagery of violent delinquency and rioting.

Returning to history it is important to understand how Braudel approaches Islamic civilization. He dates its birth at the eighth or the beginning of the ninth century AD or some 150 to 200 years after the death of the Prophet Muhammad and he ends its golden age at the twelfth century. Religion was at the root of that civilization. The dissemination of Islamic civilization and of Islam as a religion spanned about 100 years from Mecca where the Prophet was born until it reached Baghdad, the seat of power of the early religion.

Muslims were to thrive on military and commercial conquests as Braudel explains, using geography for the development of Islam and its civilization. The Near East was a natural crossroads connected to most of the Mediterranean. The central continent is located between two oceans, (the Mediterranean and the Indian Ocean) and three continents (Africa, Asia and Europe). Trade is the traditional activity and the routes of the caravans would also help Islam reach out and cover a vast area from Dakar to Jakarta and from Cairo to Cordova.

Muslim society revolves around the Koran, the Book of Teachings written by the Prophet. It is a diverse society that adapts to indigenous peoples and their customs which enrich it. Christian and Muslim Spain may be compared to Buddhist and Muslim India. In West Africa and Senegal in particular it is filled with Sufi thought and communities practice a tolerant Islam that works well with the Christians in a an atmosphere that both presidents Senghor and Diouf had promoted in the recent past. Persia, contrary to other Muslim countries, stands out as an exception because of its cultural and historical as well as religious heritage. It is the only major state having a civilization thousands of years old and a Shia majority.

From the twelfth to the eighteenth centuries Islam went through a long period without territorial development and even, according to Braudel, the beginning decadence of the whole civilization. At the end of the eleventh century Europe would begin re-conquering what was known as the internal sea, meaning the Mediterranean. During the twelfth century Islam experienced some very dark times with the Crusades and the invasions by Asiatic peoples that prevented its growth and splendor. During the sixteenth century the Ottoman Empire's conquests brought back at least part of Islam's influence. Fernand Braudel doesn't deny the presence of the religious element in lands that were traditionally Islamic, but the same cannot be said for its civilization. In Africa the ties were only religious; in the Arab world Pan-Islamism is social and political but doesn't create a civilization.

The same applies to Pakistan. Such differences point to the absence of an Islamic civilization even though Arabic, the language of the Koran, is common to the various countries of Muslim culture.

From Braudel to *The Clash of Civilizations*

Written by Harvard Professor Samuel Huntington, *The Clash of Civilizations and the Remaking of World Order*[1] was published in 1996. Bill Clinton had been in the White House for three years. The initial attack on the World Trade Center took place in 1993 along with those against American embassies in Africa: Kenya and Tanzania.

Huntington's essay was very controversial as soon as it was published. His thesis hinges on a geopolitical description of the world based no longer on political and ideological cleavages but on less clear cultural oppositions that he dubs "civilizational" where religion holds a key position. According to him wars will have an ethnic component because those states that share the same values (religious, philosophical, customary) are collaborating more and more and support one another. The war in Bosnia-Herzegovina is a case in point. The Bosnian Muslims had the financial and military support of Muslim countries (Turkey, Iran, Saudi Arabia) while Orthodox Serbia could count on its Orthodox brothers in Russia.

The author concludes that we are in the midst of a "clash of civilizations" and has widely drawn inspiration from Braudel's work. The French historian died in 1985 and didn't have the opportunity to observe the growth of fundamentalisms in a globalized society, the consequences of Iran's Islamic revolution or the reactions of the Western and Arab world as they gave their support to those who were to become the Taliban and Al Qaeda. The fact that the Muslim religion has become a main factor in European society because of immigration also doesn't appear in the historian's work. His thoughts and point of view would certainly have been useful as the concept of national identity faces the very idea of civilization.

Another phenomenon is the reappearance of religion in the former Eastern European satellites. While Hungary takes its turn in

---

1. *The Clash of Civilizations and the Remaking of World Order.*

presiding over the European Union the Hungarian parliament under the influence of Viktor Orbán and his Christian fundamentalist allies has passed laws contrary to the basic spirit and texts of the EU. A new constitution was passed on April 18, 2011, that represents a pure and simple return to the millennial Hungary of the sacred Crown of Saint Stephen. The basic law is explicit in that "Christianity is the historical cement of the nation." It also refers to "the protection of life at conception…" which is a rejection of the right to abortion and resembles that position of the Vatican and American pro-life movements.

This growing influence of religion in society doesn't simply become a point of doctrine. Cities and townships in Hungary are increasingly handing over teaching in kindergartens and primary schools to the Catholic Church. If the "clash of civilizations' has been an inspiration for the neo-conservatives one must draw a line between them and Huntington. The neo-cons have a vision that excludes regional and ethnic diversity as well as religious differences, as opposed to Huntington who takes them into consideration. Most American neo-cons are former liberals and should not be confused with the ultra religious right. They provided the inspiration to the Bush Administration on Iraq and Iran, adopting the 'axis of evil' rhetoric even though it is a Reagan era slogan that can have religious overtones.

In the 1996 manifesto entitled *Project for the New American Century*, the neo-cons summarized their principles in a few points: rejection of any thought of a decline in American power because it is the first democratic nation in the world; opposition to allowing the emergence of any rival power; reinforcement of the military to respond to any aggression; an end to any "acquiescence" of dictatorships; moral transparency and benevolent hegemony. This was before 9/11 and the first major terrorist act on American soil that would be used by the neo-cons to justify the American invasion of Iraq without any international agreement, the overthrow of Saddam Hussein and the plan to attack Iran and overthrow the Teheran regime. Just like the Christian Zionists, the neo-cons are also unconditional supporters of Israel.

Obama: The Opening to the Muslims

Nine months into his first term in White House the Nobel foundation awarded the Nobel Peace Prize to President Barack Obama. Lech Walesa, a former recipient, commented that the award was given prematurely. What exactly was the jury attempting to celebrate? In his will Alfred Nobel wanted to reward: "the personality who had best or the most contributed to the coming together of nations, to the suppression or the reduction of standing armies and the progress of peace. Israeli former Premier Menachem Begin, and Egyptian President Anwar Sadat had made peace. During his historic trip to Jerusalem Sadat had given a speech at the Knesset. Nelson Mandela and Frederik de Klerk worked together to abolish apartheid and make peaceful transition. Mandela's party, the ANC, won the elections and its leader became president of South Africa. Barack Obama had little to show other than his commitment to be an agent of change. "Yes we can!" An appeal to America and an opening to the world.

The Nobel Prize was interpreted as an encouragement and the rejection of the Bush years. The speech at Stockholm focused on an idea: that war was a necessary evil. The U.S. president discussed the relationship to religion an implicit reference to Jihad and the Muslim world:

> ...no Holy War can ever be a just war. For if you truly believe that you are carrying out divine will, then there is no need for restraint—no need to spare the pregnant mother, or the medic, or even a person of one's own faith.[2]

In an article in the daily *Le Monde* Antoine Basbous probed the Obama myth. His youth spent in Muslim countries, his middle name Hussein ... all made it possible to foster a climate of sympathy in the Arab countries and among Muslim youth. As he said an open hand to the Muslims stemmed from his own experience: "Part of this conviction is rooted in my own experience. I am a Christian, but my father

---

2. December 10, 2009.

came from a Kenyan family that includes generations of Muslims. As a boy, I spent several years in Indonesia and heard the call of the azaan at the break of dawn and the fall of dusk. As a young man, I worked in Chicago communities where many found dignity and peace in their Muslim faith."

Was that empathy sufficient to carry an entire policy. Were the speeches at Ankara and Cairo media events in a communications strategy or did they actually signify true change and a different view of the Muslim world translated in political terms?[3] Obama didn't want to create false hopes: "A single speech cannot do away with years of suspicion. And I don't have instant answers to all the complicated questions that have brought us to where we are now."

Even though communication is an essential element in the president's strategy we must stick to the facts. The initial moves by the democratic administration were as many breaks in style and in substance. Style and power groups changed (even though new groups simply switched with the older ones) but most of all a policy was altered. Reversing George W. Bush's decisions wasn't only a rhetorical device in response to the expectations of most Americans, it was a new line that was being drawn at the start of the new presidency. It was all the more daring since the incoming president didn't win the election on foreign policy. Disengagement from Iraq had already been decided by the previous administration and Secretary of State Condolezza Rice, was planning an American diplomatic presence in Teheran as early as November 2008 or four months before Obama 's taking office at the White House.

The democratic candidate was elected based on his greater credibility compared to McCain in handling the subprime crisis, to save the banks and prevent the economic failure as symbolized by the problems at General Motors. The election was also one of contrasts: the energy of a 47 year old man compared to that of an ageing Vietnam veteran. Senator Barack Obama would win in every age group except those over 65... The neo-cons were finished, the "clash of civilizations" was a thing of the past; such were the hopes created by his speeches at Ankara and Cairo. A return to the rule of law and

---

3. June 2 and 5, 2009.

sound procedures meant, as the president told the United Nations, accepting a multi polar world with its multiple decision making points.

This was a condemnation of unilateral American intervention in Iraq leading a coalition consisting only of Great Britain with Tony Blair and Spain with José-Maria Aznar that Obama would cautiously identify: "aware of a choice that caused much opposition in my country and the rest of the world". It also meant not using fabricated evidence as Secretary of State Colin Powell had done at the UN Security Council to justify U.S. intervention in Iraq by displaying a small bottle given to him by the Pentagon with a harmless product that had been labeled dangerous when used in creating weapons of mass destruction. The return to the rule of law also meant forbidding the use of torture by the United States and the intended closing of Guantanamo prison by early 2011. But the real world was to cancel the promise made by the candidate: where could the detainees be sent since no state of the United States wanted to have them?

A Return to the Real World

The "new beginning" that Obama was mentioning also required a new way to create democracy in the world. Under George W. Bush, the idea of a "Greater Middle East" where democracy would win at the polls didn't last long. The first election under that doctrine saw the victory of Hamas while the Americans and their allies in the region had been rooting for Al Fatah! As with Guantanamo, the administration had to take reality into account. Former Secretary of State James Baker, expressed the American dilemma at the Council on Foreign Relations as he was commenting on the revolt in Egypt and the fall of Mubarak: "We have to consider principles and values, yes: democracy, human rights, freedom. But we also have to consider the national interest, whether or not the particular entity we're dealing with is aligned with the United States or not. And those two considerations meet head-on in this conflict."

While President Obama was moving toward in engaging the Iranian people in his speech, what would that mean to the regime in

Teheran? First of all the past must not be shoved aside and Iranians do not forget. Washington had instigated the coup that overthrew Mohamed Mossadegh in 1953. Secretary of State Madeleine Albright had offered the apologies of the American people and now the man in the White House recalled that "in the midst of the Cold War the United States played a part in the overthrow of a democratically elected Iranian government." Since the creation of the Islamic Republic in 1979 free elections were always held in Iran and no Arab country can match that record.

The president of the United States is aware of this even though the democratic ideal was not what the West was hoping for. Since 1981 various elections have seen opposing groups come to power and there is opposition within the institutions. Even Iranian government ministers are subject to parliamentary approval before they can take their positions. If we factor in the votes of the regime's true believers in the lower income classes of society living off the subsidies provided by the regime under its control and a good part of society (rural and more conservative) wedded to the edicts of the Supreme Guide, then Mahmoud Ahmadinejad would have been elected with or without fraud. The Americans also agree with this assessment as evidenced by WikiLeaks. Obviously the percentages would have been lower but Ahmadinejad would still have been regularly elected. It was to be expected therefore that the president of the United States should address the Iranian leaders since his predecessor had relegated them to the sidelines of the international community. Barack Obama could then state:

> So in this season of new beginnings I would like to speak clearly to Iran's leaders. We have serious differences that have grown over time. My administration is now committed to diplomacy that addresses the full range of issues before us, and to pursuing constructive ties among the United States, Iran and the international community. This process will not be advanced by threats. We seek instead engagement that is honest and grounded in mutual respect.[4]

---

4. Radio speech for Iran's New Year. The president of the United States has repeated this event every year since he has been in the White House.

His objective was clear: the United States want the Islamic Republic of Iran to take its rightful place within the community of nations. As he often does to make his point on March 20, 2009, the president enlisted cultural themes:

> But let us remember the words that were written by the poet Saadi, so many years ago: "The children of Adam are limbs to each other, having been created of one essence."

This was a reference to the children of the Book and a rejection of the clash of civilizations. When the president addressed the Muslim world he disapproved of those who defend democracy "when they are out of power" and "once in power implacably repress the freedom of others." Many Arab heads of state felt targeted but this was also a condemnation of the policies of other administrations in Washington as much as his own. If Barack Obama had promised during the campaign to turn the page it is clear that once he was elected he had to face reality…and Guantanamo remains part of Realpolitik.

Does the United States Still Count in the Middle East?

None of the great democracies expressed any shock because of the sham elections in Egypt in November 2010 when the party in power practically took all the seats in parliament. It must also be said that the Rais was in a struggle with the Islamists and the Muslim Brotherhood while he remained an ally of Fatah against Hamas and the Arab guarantor of Israel. Following the Arab Spring how must we interpret the attitude of the great powers toward Bashar Al-Assad and the events in Syria? By stating that no nation can impose a system of government on another Barack Obama recognized the right to self-determination. American involvement was minimal in Libya. The president like most world leaders was taken by surprise by history. Nations no one paid much attention to Yemen, Tunisia, Oman, Bahrain, Egypt, Jordan and Libya were all seeking change.

Afghanistan remains an American priority, the largest military theater of operations where thousands of troops are fighting at an enormous financial cost. When Obama entered the White House he followed policies that were the opposite of those of his predecessor. By proclaiming that once you start a war you must also know how to end it, Obama announced the exit from Afghanistan by June 2011. If the electoral calendar makes the intention clear, it also remains a strategic gamble even though the date had to be set back even further. The Taliban also know that they only have to wait for the Americans to leave. Once Washington announced that it would negotiate with the "neo-Taliban" (the good ones as opposed to the mean ones), the Obama administration showed that at some point realism would prevail even if it meant dealing with yesterday's enemies. It was much ado about nothing, in a sense. Soon Afghanistan will be in the hands of the Taliban, and Pakistan will remain a fundamentalist cauldron. Without the "clash of civilizations" we shall be in the realm of coexistence taking a step backward as to the hopes and aspirations of people who are longing to enter the modern world.

Unexpected Support

Washington's support for Israel is traditionally the excuse of a primitive form of anti-Semitism that wants to believe in the existence of a Jewish Lobby manipulating the media and finance. A slice of the French nationalist right-wing believes this with the support of such intellectual icons as Charles Maurras, Louis-Ferdinand Celine, Robert Brasillach and a few others who held similar views. To assess American policy simply through the Jewish Lobby angle is not a serious position. The American Jewish community is the first to worry about the colonization policy in Israel preventing any solution to the Israeli-Palestinian conflict. Israel's best friends today are more militant than the American Jews and come under the general term of "Christian Zionists." A few evangelical ministers have set up a group called Christians United for Israel (CUFI).[5]

Various initiatives such as Christians United for Israel, the International Christian Embassy Jerusalem are of interest because even if they enjoy Israeli support they originate in the United States.

---

5. The countdown for Jerusalem is the last opportunity for peace.

They are different from the support groups led by American Jewish organizations or the Israelis themselves such as AIPAC (American Israel Public Affairs Committee), an official group that is openly dedicated to supporting the cause of Israel in Congress and with the administration. The founder and spokesman of CUFI is Texas fundamentalist minister John Hagee who is something more than a television evangelist. He is a media star and a critically important politician. He started his church in San Antonio in 1975 and claims 18,000 followers. Today CUFI is managed by former secretary of education in the Reagan administration, Gary Bauer, who describes himself as "pro-life, pro-family, pro-free-enterprise." The Reverend Hagee is well known around the world since he published his book in 2005 that became a best seller in the U.S.: *Jerusalem Countdown: A Warning to the World... the Last Opportunity for Peace.*

The countdown is a warning of the apocalypse to come. The reverend states that "the battle for Jerusalem has begun." Evil is personified by the fanatical Islamists who rule Iran. Their accomplices are Russia, France, and Germany all helping Iran prepare to bring about a nuclear holocaust. He announces that Russian and Arab armies will invade Israel but shall be defeated by God, that Israel will then become a battleground between China and the West represented by the anti-Christ which is the European Union. The author predicts that Jesus Christ will return to earth when the final battle is about to begin. If the book is close to a form of ghost-like delirium, Reverend Hagee has some influence and CUFI is given enough attention by conservative republicans and neo-cons.

It is interesting to see which personalities CUFI refers to in its defense of Israel. Shimon Peres said: "it is very important to have you at our side." "In a short time, He [my friend John Hagee] and other Christian leaders were able to create an in important movement in support of Israel," stated Prime Minister Benyamin Netanyahu... and even Senator Joseph Lieberman who sees "the hand of God in Reverend Hagee's efforts."

It's very important to examine the origins of these movements. Following the Six-Day War of 1967 Israel showed interest in the Evangelical Zionists in the United States. The Jewish State became close to Reverend Jerry Falwell co-founder of the Moral Majority, a movement that will have over 6.5 million members. Falwell was received by the highest Israeli leaders, he was also the head of the Thomas Road Baptist Church as well as a small media empire worth 200 million dollars. He describes his struggle as that "of the forces of God over the power of Satan and supported the candidacies of both Bushes and Reagan. The 9/11 attacks were "divine punishment" for a nation "spiritually weakened" by the American Civil Liberties Union (ACLU) that is calling for abortion rights and equal rights for homosexuals. Following the attacks he described the Prophet Muhammad as a "terrorist."

The era of the struggle against "the forces of evil" has begun. Israel must also face another dilemma to break its isolation within the region as well as in the international community. For some American Christian Zionists, "during the 1970s the Lord began speaking to the heart of many believers around the world about Israel and its prophetic role in modern times." In September 1980 the Knesset confirmed that in spite of many UN resolutions to the contrary Jerusalem was the capital of Israel. The last embassies still there left the Holy City and moved to Tel Aviv. Prime Minister Menachem Begin welcomed the creation of the International Christian Embassy Jerusalem by the Christian Zionists.

What the Christian Zionists Want

The International Christian Embassy Jerusalem centers on four main action points:

> Take an interest in the Jewish People and the State of Israel.
> Encourage Christian leaders, churches and associations to become centers of influence in their respective countries for Israel and the Jewish people.
> Participate in God's project to return the Jews to Israel.
> Start new projects or take part in projects in Israel for the benefit of all the inhabitants of the country.

The embassy also has two other projects regarding the Arabs. Its mission is "to build bridges for the reconciliation of Jews and Arabs" and "to contribute to the well-being of all those living in the country." Yet the funding of the embassy is mainly aimed at helping the settlers or Jewish settlements in East Jerusalem. It is very clear that on the eve of a crucial presidential election Obama is not in a position to engage in peace talks in the Near East. The religious right such as the Christian Zionists, join the republicans while on the other side if the democrats want to hold on to the Jewish vote they cannot favor the creation of a Palestinian State.

The preachers and five million American evangelical Christians as do the Christian Zionists can count on large media groups such as Trinity Broadcast Network (TBN) along with support from political groups. During his presidential campaign John McCain took part in a joint press conference with the Rev. Hagee. The Arizona senator said he was "very honored" by the event. His campaign planners saw this support a way for McCain to strengthen his bid for the presidency with the religious wing of republican voters that had been hesitant to follow him until then.

Later on McCain will have to repudiate the support by the Texas evangelical preacher when his statements on Hitler, God, and the Jews became an embarrassment. In a sermon Hagee said: "God sent Hitler to help the Jewish people reach the Promised Land." He had to apologize for calling the Catholic Church the "great whore." In yet another example of his rhetoric Rev. Hagee said Hurricane Katrina, the cause of 1500 deaths, was: "Divine punishment because New Orleans had welcomed a homosexual march!" Rather uncomfortable support for a candidate to the White House! Even though fundamentalist Christians can agree with the views of the neo-cons on some issues, it would be a mistake to say that they are politically close.

Irving Kristol is thought to be the founder of American neo-conservatism. Originally a Marxist and left liberal democrat he moved to the Republican Party. A member of the Young People's Socialist League, he was later sympathetic toward McCarthyism. His magazine *Public Interest*, founded in 1965, remained focused on American politics and began the wave of conservative free market ideas that became dogma under Reagan and Thatcher. Kristol attacked the welfare state and attracted political thinkers such as Samuel Huntington and William Bennett soon to become Reagan's secretary of education. At the time there were as many democrats as republicans among the neo-conservatives. In the 1970s neo-conservatism would change as it turned its sights on foreign affairs and created a sister publication called *The National Interest*. Democrats among the neo-cons feared the policy of detente with the Soviet Union and republican hawks put Ronald Reagan in the White House. With Bill Clinton the movement became the spearhead of those opposed to his health care plan and who later on happened to be in the forefront of the attempt to impeach him.

While the neo-con influence was very real in the republican administration it was led by a few public figures and didn't have the structured appearance of a political movement. As Irving Kristol coined it neo-conservatism is above all a feeling without any religious connection even though he quoted Charles Péguy who wrote: "Everything begins with mysticism and everything ends up in politics."

From *The Clash of Civilizations* to Islam Phobia

The danger is to have intellectuals willingly confuse "Muslim" and "Islamist." Historian Sylvain Gougenheim played his part as he whipped up a furor. Considering *Aristotle and Mont Saint-Michel*, the Greek roots of Christian European civilization, he built the case that the Christian West doesn't owe the discovery and the transmission of Greek thought to the Muslim Arabs but rather to the Oriental Christians. The culture of Latin Europe in the Middle Ages is deeply infused with Greek culture while at the same time Arab-Islamic culture was barely touched by it. Greece is above and beyond all other civilizations. From that starting point as opposed to Samuel Huntington who talks about the clash of civilizations, Gougenheim reaches the conclusion that any cultural exchange between civilizations is simply impossible.

The historian will be reminded of a few key facts by his peers: the contribution by Arab Muslim scientists in mathematics, and astronomy between the ninth and thirteenth centuries and the great medical doctors such as the Persian Avicenna. During the Middle Ages the name "Aristotle" indicated not just the philosopher but also Averroes his commentator (as well as Avicenna and Algazel). Without Cordoba the Enlightenment would never have received the Greek and Roman heritage. Gougenheim says we are Europeans, therefore Christian and Greek, while fourteen centuries of Islam produced nothing. The book review in *Le Figaro* agrees with this analysis: "Let us congratulate Mr. Gougenheim for not hesitating to remind us about a medieval melting pot created by the heritage of Athens and Jerusalem while Islam was not offering its knowledge to the West."

Intellectuals must carefully avoid mixing Muslim fundamentalism and Islamic civilization because to postulate that Arab-Muslim thought is incapable of rationalizing because it is so thoroughly blocked by the Word as revealed in the Koran, can only benefit fundamentalism and Islam-phobia. The refusal of the contribution made by Islamic civilization must be viewed while keeping in mind the importance of Islam as a religion in Europe during the welcomed immigration of the past compared to the organized and limited immigration when it is not refused, taking place today. Intellectual negationism, meaning the rejection of other cultures, can only favor the rise of extremists. The debates on national identity, centered on the burqa or the minarets in Switzerland appear in a context marked by the rise of populism and the far right.

Until now the issue of integrating Muslims was unknown in the United States. Islam as a religion is a small minority in the country and most American Muslims are part of the middle class. A country created by waves of immigrants following one another is open to religious belief and to different religions. 9/11 had little impact on the American Muslim community. Bin Laden, al-Qaeda and the wealthy financiers from Saudi Arabia and elsewhere were the enemy that was in favor of that movement. Proof can be found in Obama's speech to the Muslim world and in his condemnation of legislation that forbids the full body veil as an infringement on religious freedom.

Some people and even entire groups—besides the Christian Zionists—didn't accept a Black president in the White House.

Barack Obama won the presidency of the United States by a landslide but with the crisis his lead in the polls is slipping even though no republican enjoys clear popular support. The campaigns and protests against building a mosque near Ground Zero could be the image of a tree hiding an entire forest. The hostility to Islam then spread to the whole country. The reasons used by those who oppose the mosque are based on the idea that Islam is "a threat to Western Civilization."

It would be beneficial to examine the world in which we will be living in tomorrow. Some initiatives that were destined to be still-born such as the Union for the Mediterranean meant to bring north and south closer together must be viewed in the context of recent expectations revolts and revolutions. Why worry about a potential migratory threat when it was impossible to forecast the movement and supported regimes that denied human rights for decades?

To allow the development of democracy and the economy is a positive response to the "clash of civilizations" and a way to inhibit the Islamic risk tomorrow since it is often the last recourse of hopeless societies without a future. It is important to examine these Arab revolts as Joseph Maila sees the problem:

> For the most part they are leaderless movements, without an ideology that follow no previous model... These are societies in search of themselves and they will need time to find what they are looking for.[6]

---

6. Paris, April 2011, Colloquium, *Institut du monde arabe.*

Chapter 2

American Ambiguities

Voters are fickle and anniversaries can often carry a bitter taste with them. One year after Obama's election the democrats lost the majority in the senate. A republican won Ted Kennedy's old Massachusetts senate seat after the "old lion" died. The president reacted by saying that while he understood the frustrations of the public and was not going to shelve his health insurance reform plan that republicans were equating to more expenses and higher taxes.

The November 2, 2010 midterm elections revamped the House of Representatives, one third of the Senate, 36 governors and many state houses. Those elections are an opportunity for the voters to express their opinions on the president's policies half-way through his term. As it usually happens to the party in power, the democratic administration lost that election and those results are neither a positive or negative sign for Obama 's reelection. Clinton had been through an identical defeat but that didn't prevent his reelection. After the issue of the a cultural center near Ground Zero a poll showed that for a majority of Americans are convinced that President Obama is of the Muslim faith. He will recapture his popularity by giving the order to take down Osama Bin Laden: America has a leader and the man who symbolized terrorism is no longer alive.

While Americans were celebrating the news the United States was pummeled by public and private debt and a huge deficit…a country on the verge of bankruptcy. Democrats and republicans were attempting to find a compromise in order to lift the debt ceiling but Standard and Poor, was about to reduce the country's rating. For the first time in history the world's greatest power was losing its triple 'A' rating. As the primaries begin for the republicans[1] the Tea Party and Middle America are accusing Washington more than ever before. The religious right is sending loud messages while the main worries of most Americans remain the economy and internal policies rather than foreign policy.

In an article published in *The American-Interest*,[2] following the subprime crisis, Francis Fukuyama, a professor at John Hopkins was asking the question: will Barack Obama be able to succeed? He was comparing the president to his three predecessors in the White House. Carter had a negative balance sheet both internally and in foreign matters. Lyndon Johnson was successful internally but failed overseas while Roosevelt achieved great things in both areas. The neo-conservative writer doesn't start from a positive viewpoint. Obama was elected by many centrists and independents who voted for the democrat because they were disgusted with George W. Bush and the Republican Party.

American soldiers are leaving Iraq even though Obama must leave 50 thousand advisors behind. The country is not at peace and there are many deadly attacks still taking place. While coalition troops are beginning to withdraw can the United States end terrorism in Afghanistan without turning Pakistan into a bloodbath and while the Taliban may return to rule in Kabul?

Can Obama open a dialog with Iran while both Tehran and Iraq are supporting Bashar al-Assad and Turkey has taken a position against the Syrian regime, in favor of the Sunnis and the Muslim Brotherhood? Will there be some progress between Palestinians and

---

1. Traditionally the incumbent president is the natural candidate for a second term.
2. January-February 2009.

Israelis while no one can predict the course of events in the Near East? Hostilities with Hamas have flared up again even though the Egyptians served as mediators and a cease-fire has been set between Hamas and Israel.

If Obama manages to stand up to all these challenges, then Francis Fukuyama will be able to call him a new Roosevelt in foreign affairs at least but many signs lead one to think that the opposite will be true.

Next Year in Jerusalem

The changes within the Arab Muslim world have taken Washington and every other government by surprise. The United States could have played a major role in Libya and Syria. The neo-con theories that led to the interventions in Iraq and Afghanistan appear to belong to a distant past of complacency toward dictatorships and moral transparency, with the United States as the first democratic power to impose its system on the rest of the world.

Obama wanted Qaddafi to leave power but he cautiously remained on the sidelines of an involvement that public opinion was bound to reject. Qaddafi fell and American intervention was kept at a minimum: a few air attacks at the beginning, intelligence and logistics support. To die for Tripoli is not an option while there are American casualties in Afghanistan. Perhaps Middle America did have dreams of glory but today retirees worry about the soundness of their pensions and families struggle to pay off their debts as they keep on living day to day. A country entering an election year in the midst of crisis will feel the burden of foreign military engagements and wish to turn sharply inward.

In Syria Bashar al-Assad can shoot his people, place over 10,000 citizens under arrest including young children that are being tortured and murdered, months will go by before any public condemnation is forthcoming.

Within this difficult context American support for Israel and Jerusalem's refusal to recognize the Palestinian State within the 1967 borders is leading to a dead-end. The Arab springs have isolated the

Jewish State a bit more. Time marches on but the city remains divided and the Holy Places remain under the Zahal's control. The moment is not at hand when the historic lands of Cesarea, Judea, Samaria ... will be home to two States living in peace.

The speeches at Ankara and Cairo along with the message to the Iranians for their New Year were the rejection of the "clash of civilizations" and the rhetoric of the "axis of evil" so dear to the neo-conservatives and the Bush administration. Early on in his presidency Obama was able to draw on the low esteem Arab public opinion had for his predecessor.

Yet he was unable to resolve the focal point of the Arab-Israeli conflict. Robert Malley, President Clinton's former advisor for Arab-Israeli matters is rather harsh on the current occupier of the White House. He makes a devastating point that the Palestinians have lost their trust...the Arabs are doubtful...while the Israelis view Barack Obama as an upstart whom they have neither respect nor any regard for. Israel is comfortable with the status quo. Jerusalem's entire policy is bent on undermining the foundation of a future Palestinian State. Its colonization is based on that goal and the whole game plan of the Jewish State is to create a greater split between the Palestinians in Gaza and those in the occupied territories. The calm that exists in those lands is not unrelated to positive economic results. Continued growth is due to the management of Palestinian Prime Salam Fayyad, but also the support of the Jerusalem government known as "economic peace strategy" as opposed to the blockade against Gaza.[3]

Israel has also used the Iranian nuclear threat to place the Palestinian issue on the backburner and refuse the step forward that Washington was hoping for. By focusing all the problems of the region on Tehran, Jerusalem is forcing Washington to turn away from the Palestinian issue thereby relegating it to secondary status. On the American side, after a three year effort and innumerable travels to the region, George Mitchell, the Middle East special envoy has resigned. The traditional American connections: Jordan, Egypt and Saudi Arabia, struggling with their respective internal issues cannot step in. France, with Qatar and the Emirates, is trying to fill

---

3. *Le Monde* January 24 and 25, 2010.

the void. Bin Laden, on 21 January 2010 told Al-Jazeera, what Obama's stakes were:

> The United States cannot hope to be secure before security becomes a reality in Palestine. It is unfair that you should enjoy a quiet life when our brothers are living in the most awful conditions in Gaza [...] our attacks against you will continue as long as you support the Israelis and security is not established in Palestine.

Bin Laden also claimed that the failed attack on the Amsterdam to Detroit flight in December 2009 was an Al Qaeda operation. An Islamist terrorist coming from Yemen tried to blow himself up on the plane. The attempt meant to show that the threat against the United States remained active. Bin Laden wanted to reduce the popularity of the U.S. president in the Muslim world by showing that Obama was simply pursuing the policies of George W. Bush. The failed attack revived American fears that their country was vulnerable to what may be called the "9/11 Syndrome."

Bin Laden's death will not end the terrorist threat. Americans live with the image of the Twin Towers. Some new players that have appeared on the scene with the support of public opinion are exerting pressure on the Palestinian issue seeing their influence increase. This includes Turkey and Iran. Even as the context is changing, Washington cannot bury the past. In a *Time* magazine interview Obama admitted that: "We overestimated our ability to persuade them [the Israelis and Palestinians] to do so when their politics ran contrary..." Was the president admitting the failure of his administration. What will happen next? What will be the results of the elections in Palestine and the rest of the Arab world? One dictatorship should not simply replace another...be it religious or military.

Is There a Religious Right?

It cannot be stressed enough: there was a deep split between George W. Bush's America and the real America. 9/11 had blurred that fact by uniting the people behind the Commander in Chief. The

United States was deeply traumatized since it was the first time that it was attacked on its own territory. However, all Americans do not espouse the thinking of the neo-cons or the preaching of a few fundamentalist ministers that are the heroes of the Christian Right. Yet with those attacks the "clash of civilizations" became a reality for western public opinion. Christian conservatism appeared at the beginning of the 1980s as a force to be reckoned with in American politics.

More than a "Christian Right" the correct term should be "Religious Right" since some Jews were present from the start and remain in the minority within their community. The trend grew in importance with the additional support of the evangelicals (about 25 percent of the population.) Among them are the "Born again Christians" with former president George W. Bush as their most prominent representative. While they used to be close to the Democratic Party, they now vote mostly for Republican candidates. They were far less involved in politics and have become the most active. Their support for the Republican Party was prompted by the values issue, a purely defensive attitude in reaction to the changes in society between the 1960s and '70s.

At that time the Supreme Court legalized abortion, forbade prayers and all religious symbols in all activities that were supported by the government mostly in the public schools. The legal struggle against discrimination has drawn the states into teaching the acceptance of homosexuality in the public schools. Several court decisions have led to same sex unions and now marriage. The army was the last official bastion where homosexuals were subject to discharge if their sexual preference became publicly known. It was only on 18 December 2010 after the mid-term elections that Congress overturned the "don't ask don't tell" rule. Sexual orientation is no longer a reason to impose segregation.

Puritanism and conservatism represent the thinking of an entire religious section of American society that will uphold the defense of moral values. In fighting against every "social deviation" the Christian conservatives found their call to political activism. The neoconservatives it should be noted do not share those moral convictions. They have a different vision of America: a strong, domineering country destined to be the world's policeman…using ideas that are far removed from those of the religious right. While the evangelicals dominate the latter it would be mistaken to view them as a single homogenous and dogmatic group according to the image offered by the mass media. Only part is involved in politics while the majority is driven by the desire to proselytize others to join their faith. The flock should not be identified with a small number of its leaders.

A few like George W. Bush, took their inspiration from that rhetoric: the world is divided in two God on one side and Satan on the other. The prominent leaders and organizations of the Christian Right—Jerry Falwell or Pat Robertson, groups like the Christian Coalition—have created distrust among voters. Even President Bush and the most conservative republicans had to condemn Reverend Pat Robertson when he requested that Hugo Chavez, the president of Venezuela be assassinated. The republican administration under both Bush terms did all it could to ingratiate itself to those portions of the electorate but actual decisions that are inspired by the religious right are very rare. Even though the Christian Right was a key component it didn't actually have a say or determining influence over Bush's policies.

Summing up that presidency the Iraq War, unilateralism, the tax breaks to the rich, the weakening of the commitment to environmental protection can all be pinned on the neo-cons, a few lobbyists and think tanks. While the rhetoric of George W. Bush appears to embrace a religious and more precisely evangelical vocabulary that was not the case if we examine the detail of what he was saying.

A study of his speeches from 9/11 and May 2003, a total of some ninety addresses indicates that contrary to public perceptions the president made very few allusions to religion. The formula "axis of evil" appeared quite often but it shouldn't be viewed as having a religious connotation. The neo-cons who are often former liberals from the Vietnam years had conceived their project of a struggle against the "axis of evil" and action against Iraq and Iran long before 9/11. The demands of the religious right have not been fulfilled in a significant way. Attempts to influence the appointments of federal judges opposed to abortion also remained unsuccessful. The stop put on stem cell research didn't materialize and budget cuts didn't prevent progress in that area. In spite of the presidential promise to oppose same sex marriage some states have made it legal.

While Bush and his advisors managed to gain the support of a part of the religious right they didn't fare so well with other denominations. Even if Catholic bishops could agree on some issues with the Bush administration (the opposition to abortion for instance,) the leadership was always cautious about its faithful joining explicitly political religious groups that were not under the influence of the Catholic Church. Among those Christians who are opposed to the republicans there are many Protestants who are not part of the evangelical movement. This opposition centered around issues such as capital punishment, the government's responsibility to the poor or American unilateralism in world affairs. Bush's America was far removed from the image it had been given. It was not neo-conservative even though the influence of the neo-cons was very real and concentrated in the hands of a small group holding the levers of power.

The Myth of a Christian America

Contrary to most forecasts during George W. Bush's presidency, religion and politics remained separate in the United States. The mistake was to lump together the image of a president with the American right wing and make them the standard bearers of the whole country or at least a majority of Americans. Within the Republican Party and its voters the Religious Right is not the in the majority even though the evangelicals were the part of Bush's electoral base. While in 2000 "traditional moral values" were in the forefront of his campaign, during the second term the issue of religion was totally absent from the political discourse. The same would happen during the mid-term elections. The choice of Sarah Palin as John McCain's running mate was an attempt to rally the votes of Middle America: white, Christian, pro-life and therefore conservative.

Barack Obama was elected with 52 percent of the popular vote to 46 percent for his republican adversary. It was the first time a democrat won the presidency and the popular vote since Jimmy Carter in 1976 and Obama had the best margin since Lyndon Johnson in 1964. Even though the Christian evangelicals who were Bush's mainstays voted for McCain it wasn't enough to make up for the loss of centrist voters that are the only way elections are won in western democracies. If Obama won those states where he obtained a majority remain unclear. Traditionally liberal California voted for president and on the same ballot approved a neo-conservative referendum to reject same sex marriage.

Even though there is a reference to God on the greenbacks (In God we trust), the U.S. Constitution is secular. The fact that President Bush began White House meetings with a prayer remains a personal choice. If every speech ends with "May God bless America" it is a tradition and not part of the Constitution. The same is true for the swearing in of the newly elected president. He does this on the Bible, a tradition that comes from the British Parliament started by George Washington, and that is also not in the Constitution. In November 2006, Minnesota a elected Keith Ellisson, a democrat, and the first Muslim to the House of Representatives, thus becoming the top elected official of that faith. He swore to uphold the Constitution on the Koran. "I put my hand on the book that is the foundation of my faith, Islam and I think this is a marvelous thing for our country." Said the 43 year-old African-American lawyer. In Cairo Obama recalled that moment: "When the first Muslim-American was recently elected to Congress, he took the oath to defend our Constitution using the same Holy Koran that one of our Founding Fathers— Thomas Jefferson—kept in his personal library."

Islam is not an issue in the United States which is multiethnic country of mixed races. There are some 8 million Muslims out of a population of 310 million. By comparison there are 53 million Muslims in Europe for a population of 500 million. The U.S. Muslim community is very diverse in New York in particular where one million people represent every Muslim country in the world.[4] Religion

---

4. The United States Mission to the European Union, June 21, 2006.

cannot be understood in the United States in the same way as in Europe. It must be recalled that in the name of equality and a true religious pluralism Thomas Jefferson and James Madison agreed to forbid any kind of public financing of Church and abolished the official status of the Anglican Church in the state of Virginia. The first amendment[5] prohibits an official religion but doesn't extend to the local level. While the founding fathers wanted a secular America they also agreed with Tocqueville that "a free and civilized society cannot survive without religion." While Americans believe in God they cannot be called religious as such. Membership in a Church is a social matter. You change churches after getting married or moving to another town. 28 percent of Americans left their original faith to join a different religious group or are not part of any religion. Among Protestants, 44 percent have changed denomination. Such changes are the result of the mobility and fluidity typical of American society.[6] Italian immigration is revelatory in this context since contrary to the Protestants that came from Plymouth on the Mayflower in 1620 religious practice among Italians was practically forgotten. It was only once they made progress socially, moving to middle class neighborhoods that Italians began sending their children to private religious schools and support their local parish churches.

America remains an essentially white society with a community spirit that allows it to limit persistent racial tensions. Obama can therefore say that he rejects a certain western idea that women who choose to cover their hair is in some way less equal, and that a woman who is denied education is a victim of discrimination. The president's words may have seemed shocking to Europeans, and in France in particular where the debate on secularism is always very charged with controversy but they may not have been well received

---

5. "Congress shall make no law respecting an establishment of religion, or prohibiting the free exercise thereof; or abridging the freedom of speech, or of the press; or the right of the people peaceably to assemble, and to petition the Government for a redress of grievances."
6. Investigation 2007, Pew Forum on religion and public life, February 25, 2008. According to the report, 78.4 percent of the U.S. population identifies itself as Christian and as Protestant, 51.3 percent among which are Evangelicals (26.3 percent), Baptists (17.2 percent) Methodists (6.2 percent), Lutherans (4.6 percent), Pentecostalists (4.4 percent). Roman Catholics are the largest single unified religious group (23.9 percent). Mormons make up 1.7 percent of the population as do the Jews. Buddhists of all factions are 0.7 percent, Muslims 0.6 percent, Hindus 0.4 percent. Those without religious affiliation are 16.1 percent of the total, but Atheists are a minority among them with 1.6 percent.

by Middle America. Obama justified his position because freedom cannot be separated from the freedom to practice one's faith, which is why there is a mosque in every state of the union and more than 1,200 in the whole country. It is also the reason why the United States government went to court to uphold the rights of women and girls to wear the hijab and punish those who would refuse them that right.

Reality and Realpolitik

Will America continue to be the top power in the world? Will she withdraw to its shores under the blows of the economic crisis and the calls for smaller government coming from some quarters? The truth is that America must accept her past and the future can only reflect that history. Barack Obama met with the Dalai Lama twice in the White House. A Nobel Prize winner was bound to meet with one of his colleagues. Beijing condemned those talks as the first took place a few weeks after the sale of American weapons to Taiwan. The visit of a religious leader will change nothing to Chinese-American relations. Reality is far simpler: China is the leading world power holding American treasury bonds. The American economy is highly dependent on Beijing and economic growth has moved from the industrialized countries to emerging economies. Chinese economic growth dictates certain partnerships while the West needs China as much she needs the West.

The Chinese are buying oil and gas in Venezuela, Sudan and Iran…the "axis of evil" countries. If the West wants to do business with Beijing would rather remain silent concerning those connections as well as concerning human rights or religious freedom that are regularly trampled by the Middle Kingdom. To understand Chinese realism one must examine their positions at the UN Security Council: constant support for Iran, Venezuela and Sudan much backtracking before agreeing to intervention in Libya and silence on Syria. The West must now consider Beijing's choices!

The American president has very little room to maneuver. He is duty bound to accept UN and Security Council resolutions where the

Chinese and the Russians have veto power. George W. Bush's plan was to make NATO the world's policeman under American guidance. The president is subjected to a changing public opinion at home as well that of his allies. Military operations in Iraq alone have cost the United States 642 billion dollars, according to the GAO,[7] to which one must add 24 billion to equip and train the Iraqi army. All this as senior citizens have to go back to work and 39 percent of Americans are convinced they will end their days in poverty against 29 percent asked the same question in 2007. America can only turn inward because she no longer has the funds to be the world's policeman. The end of the Berlin Wall signaled the end of the Cold War and East-West antagonism. 9/11 symbolized Islamic terrorism and the new century faces the unknown factor of the Arab countries. Withdrawals from Iraq and Afghanistan have not put an end to the recurring problems of those countries and the region.

Iraq is a case in point regarding the problems America is facing in disengaging from a conflict and could serve as model for Afghanistan the day the Americans leave Kabul. In spite of American intervention the stability of Baghdad and its security depend in large measure on Tehran and its influence on the large Shia community. The withdrawal of American troops at the end of 2010 was not a good omen. Insecurity is everywhere and the country is torn between the Kurds who want independence, the Sunni and the Shia. The king of Saudi Arabia became involved in the political campaign for parliamentary elections in 2010. He didn't want Shia Prime Minister al-Maliki to win and used the kind of pressure that Tehran didn't appreciate. The results showed strong margins of the Sunnis in the victory of the secular coalition of the Iraqi national movement with 25.8 percent closely followed by the Coalition of Prime Minister Nuri al-Maliki a Shia with 25.7 percent.

It is not a nuclear Iran that is a danger to Washington but rather a combustible mix of Iranian nationalism, the theocracy that pervades the country and the messianic certainties of Mahmud Ahmadinejad. If Israel cannot attack Iran militarily and uses cyber-attacks, to prevent communications then a nuclear Iran is no longer an issue for

---

7. May 2011.

the West. Sooner or later normal relations will have to be established between Washington and Tehran.

Another example will demonstrate how in Washington realism always takes the lead. For the first time in October 2009 North Korean diplomats were given visas to travel to the United States. Realpolitik becomes necessary because by themselves the United States are nothing. In the region they must deal with local powers such as India, Pakistan, Turkey and Iran. In December 2010 at Bagram air base Obama was predicting difficult times ahead for the American forces. India complained about the danger that Pakistani Islamists represent. But history weighs in stronger than ever. The high price of the partition of India, the creation of Pakistan, the issue of Kashmir, are the causes of future conflicts based on religious violence. This remains a challenge to America while its troops are stationed in Afghanistan.

Flag, Family, and Faith

A. J. Jacobs is a New York newsman. He grew up in a secular family and decided to spend one year as an observant Jew following the precepts of the Bible.[8] In his book he offers his analysis of American society. "Millions of Americans say they take the Bible's teachings as the letter of the law. A literal interpretation of the Bible—both Jewish and Christian—influences American policy in the Middle east as well on homosexuality, abortion all the way to regulating beer sales on Sundays. But I suspected that almost everyone has a selective concept of what the literal interpretation is. People quote those pages that best reflect their beliefs."

The fundamentalist reading of the Book can be found in almost all the religions that are connected to the Bible: orthodox Jews, evangelical Christians, traditionalist Catholics and some Muslims. The choice to follow the letter of the faith is not just an American characteristic and can be found everywhere. The movement develops within all religions at every level of society. Believing that the Bible must be taken as the word of God the fundamentalists reject the

---

8. *L'année où j'ai vécu selon la Bible*, Odile Jacob, 2008.

theory of evolution and fight to exclude Darwin from science text-books used in schools

The fundamentalists believe in the letter of the sacred texts and some of those ideals are shared by non-fundamentalists in the name of tradition or morality and the concept of man and society. One issue remains beyond partisan divides, the right-to-life and abortion debate on one side and assisted suicide or euthanasia on the other with the natural appeal by some to the religious texts. In the United States the history of the Religious Right cannot be understood without the pro-life component. Since the banning of abortion in the nineteenth century until the election of Barack Obama and from Ronald Reagan to George W. Bush, it remains a recurring focal point of American politics.

In June 2009 George Tiller, a doctor who performed late term abortions was killed during a church service in Kansas. He had already been the target of anti-abortion groups and the outcry condemning his murder was unanimous from President Obama to pro-life groups fearing the negative backlash.

The 1973 Roe vs. Wade Supreme Court decision allows for abortion on a voluntary basis in the United States. This decision legalized abortion even where local laws still made it illegal or restricted. The decision divided the country into pro-life and pro-choice groups and in 1992 the Supreme Court gave the states the right to limit the conditions of abortion. Therefore some states enacted restrictive legislation (parental approval for minors) or simple shut down abortion clinics. On the other hand regulations to limit the legal abortion time frame beyond 12 weeks were rejected by the Supreme Court.

The appointment of Sonia Sotomayor to the Supreme Court by Barack Obama was viewed as dangerous by the pro-life groups and the Religious Right. The first Hispanic woman to reach the Court she is considered favorable to Roe vs. Wade. Following eight years of the Bush presidency and with a new president in the White House the most conservative elements of American society are on the defensive. Yet only three judges out of nine were appointed by democratic presidents. The conservative Clarence Thomas is the second African

American appointed to the court by George H. W. Bush in 1991. Chief Justice John G. Roberts is the youngest person in that position in 200 years and was only fifty when George W. Bush appointed him in 2005 and a devout Roman Catholic.

Middle America and the Religious Right have trouble accepting a black democrat in the White House. Bill Clinton had to endure the attacks of the neo-cons and the Religious Right as well as special prosecutor Kenneth Starr. Either because of perjury or even private conduct, the Monica Lewinsky case could have led to an impeachment procedure. A moral crisis and political harassment set the tone at the end of the Clinton era while Obama took over a country that was in full recession. Main Street is far more concerned with its retirement benefits or the cost of Afghanistan and Iraq that the civilizing mission embraced by George W. Bush, the neo-cons and the republican administration.

With Obama's election, the Tea Party suddenly made its appearance. Prior to the midterms every by-election were carried by candidates having the support of the far right. On April 15, 2010, the Tea Party stopped in Washington on the day income tax returns must be filed when a huge demonstration was organized in the capital. The Religious Right was present in force along with all those who view Washington as the center of federal power responsible for all the ills America is suffering from.

Republicans had to radicalize their message to ride the tea party wave since 43 percent of those in the movement are independents that the party would like to bring back into the fold. Many share the conservative views on religion and social issues but they all agree in rejecting "big government" that interferes on every issue (bank bailouts, capital positions in the stock of some companies) what the average American sees as "socialism". The Tea Party has forced republicans to change their rhetoric and platform and to pay attention to its positions during the primaries. Sarah Palin is one politician who clearly understood this. Will the 3 Fs: Flag, Faith, and Family, be at the White House in 2013? Some people are convinced this will happen. Yet for the former vice presidential candidate times have changed since the publication of her book *Going Rogue: An American*

Life,[9] sold over de 2.2 million copies and the former governor has become a celebrity and a commentator on Fox News owned by Rupert Murdoch.

The Tea Party and other movements in favor of the free sale of firearms had political consequences in January 2011, when Gabrielle Giffords the first Jewish woman elected in Arizona was wounded in Tucson. Giffords was a Democrat who was going against the majority of her party by opposing the right to bear arms that is guaranteed by the second amendment to the Constitution. Sarah Palin's initial comments displaying indifference probably cost the republican former governor her candidacy. The following day she was dropping in the polls! Before that incident she had put on the web target bull's eyes on a map showing Democratic Party candidates' faces. She since dropped out of her party's primaries.

Michele Bachmann then became the Tea Party's new darling. A congresswoman from the key state of Minnesota, with many conservative Christian voters she set up a Tea Party caucus in Congress. A mother of five children she claims to have had her revelation at the age of sixteen and with her husband has created a "Christian Clinic." In August she won the Iowa caucuses, putting her temporarily ahead to take on Obama in 2012.

Like Sarah Palin, she is also a media hound. Both women stand out more for the extremism of their rhetoric than the ideas and proposals they put forward. The Tea Party also spread the rumor that Obama was not a real American forcing the president to show his birth certificate to prove that he really was born in Hawaii.

Michele Bachmann's contribution in congress is nil. And worse of all she embarrasses republicans in condemning the "un-American thinking" of President Obama. While she has no chance of occupying the White House she can influence voters as the spokeswoman of Middle America and the republican grass roots while women count for 55 percent of the Tea Party. She upholds the values of the Founding fathers and she is obviously opposed to abortion and gay marriage.

---

9. Harper Collins, 2009.

Fiercely opposed to government intervention the Tea Party has made reduction of the budget deficit and taxes its signature issues. Michele Bachmann was naturally against lifting the debt ceiling thereby placing the party leadership in Congress and the Senate in an awkward position since they were fully aware what a default would mean. Senators and congressmen accustomed to the subtle games of compromise and negotiation saw themselves as the "reasonable" right wing ready to take charge of the executive branch and opposed to the fanatical Tea party leaders whose representatives in congress had no government experience. The problems encountered by the republicans to secure a compromise with the democrats and the White House was one of the reasons behind the U.S. losing its top rating. The internal disagreements within the Republican Party made any compromise very difficult.

Michele Bachmann is resolutely opposed to the "almighty government." She is for doing away with the minimum wage a federal measure to reduce unemployment. Fundamentalist Christians while in the minority are the ones to hold the narrative. Even Rick Perry, governor of Texas after George W. Bush and easily reelected in 2000, 2006 and 2010 with a good record for job creation (48 percent of the 8 percent created since the Obama election were in the state of Texas) fell in line with religious rhetoric in spite of being a pragmatist. A Methodist and born again southern Baptist he called for "three days of payer for rain" in the midst of the drought. On August 6, 2011, he held a national penance day to save America in Houston. The old line GOP leadership sees many risks in the excesses of the Tea Party that might help reelect Obama.

Chapter 3

The Return of Holy Mother Russia

What if the Kremlin suddenly flaunted its power by building cathedrals and churches throughout the world?

What may sound as fantasy is actually true. For example the project to build a Russian Orthodox cathedral close to the Eiffel Tower in Paris. The French government has sold to Russia and not to the Russian Church the Paris headquarters of Meteo France. According to *Newsweek*'s Russian-language edition, Saudi Arabia was eyeing the same location to build a mosque and apartment houses.[1] Paris already has a Russian Orthodox cathedral: Saint-Alexander-Nevsky. But the issue for the Kremlin was that it was affiliated to the Patriarch of Constantinople a rival of the one in Moscow. The Moscow Patriarch's desire to have a presence in Europe has the support of the Russian government. The Russian government has also obtained after years of haggling and legal procedure the property of the Cathedral of Saint Nicholas of Nice. An even better symbol of the close connection between the Russian State and the Patriarch is the construction and dedication of the church of Saint Catherine in Rome in 2007. It is located inside the grounds of the Russian embassy residence a few steps away from the Vatican. In Europe the Russians are eager to show their presence through the state as well as the church and act the same way in other parts of the world.

---

1. January 30, 2010.

A few days prior to the election of Barack Obama, a symbolic event took place in Cuba when the church of Our Lady of Kazan was inaugurated in Havana.[2] Raul Castro was present at the religious ceremony. Like his brother Fidel, he was to receive the Orthodox Church's decoration of the Order of Prince Daniel from the Metropolitan Bishop Kiril (and now Patriarch), then deputy to the patriarch of Moscow. Russian Deputy Premier Igor Setchin offered an icon of the Virgin to the new church. In 1991, during the collapse of the USSR, relations between Havana and Moscow were tense. The Kremlin had dropped Cuba. The construction of the church in 2004 followed by its inauguration four years later symbolized Russia's return to the region. It was the first time the Russian Orthodox Church was present in that part of the world. Since then Hugo Chavez, the president of Venezuela, has authorized construction of an Orthodox church in his country. Metropolitan Bishop Kiril at the inauguration in Havana made a statement that neither Vladimir Putin, or Dmitri Medvedev would have denied: "We have regained our strength and we are once more a great power." While Russian-American relations were poor after the fighting between Russia and Georgia, the Bishop was showing Russia's determination to regain its position in the region.

Vladimir Putin and Dmitri Medvedev have understood the importance of the Orthodox Church, the faith of a majority of Russian citizens and they intend to protect it. The very liberal 1990 law on the freedom of conscience was replaced by a far more restrictive law in 1997 that privileges so-called traditional religions and curtails the work of foreign missionaries. The aim is to protect and expand the monopoly of the Russian Orthodox Church. Political power and the Orthodox hierarchy are closely allied, Alexis II was delighted when Dmitri Medvedev was chosen as Vladimir Putin's successor. The Patriarch praised the then prime minister's views as having "an understanding of the problems the Church is facing" and was convinced of Medvedev's "desire to follow the joint goals of the Church and the State."[3] He viewed the partnership of Medvedev president

2. Prensa Latina, Cuban Press Agency, October 19, 2008.
3. Interfax, March 3, 2008.

and Putin premier as "a blessing for Russia."[4] Putin symbolizes Russia in a sense, describing himself as an Orthodox Christian while accepting the full Soviet and imperial past. He reintroduced Stalin's 1944 national anthem and gave the Russian Army the red banner with the Soviet star as a flag.

With such a double heritage both Tsarist and Communist, Russia doesn't neglect to play the religious card in international affairs.

Close Relations

2010 was the year of Russia in France. An impressive exhibit at the Louvre museum, 'Holy Russia' traced the history and conversion to Christianity at the time of Peter the Great. Patriarch Alexis II said in Moscow that "the spiritual rebirth taking place now in Russia proves that Holy Russia is not a thing of the past but lives on very well today."[5]

Except for a limited time from the creation of the Moscow patriarch (1589) to the schism of the Old Believers (1654) Russian history is marked by the complete subordination of the church to the state. This became the norm with the accession of Peter the Great to the throne when he abolished the patriarchy early in the eighteenth century and replaced it by the Holy Synod headed by a layman appointed by the tsar. The church then was turned into a kind of lay ministry completely subservient to the tsar.

In the communist era there were various periods where the hierarchy named by the government was not involved with the millions of priests and faithful that rejected any political compromise and paid for their faith with torture and martyrdom. The Great Purge years of 1937-1938 saw innumerable executions, deportations, and the shutting down of seminaries and churches. Religion to the communists was the "opium of the people" and the church was a threat to their power. The Soviet regime attempted to manipulate the Orthodox Church by creating the living church that was then called "modernist."

---

4. Solemn statement by Patriarch Alexis II broadcast on Russian television on December 13, 2007.
5. March 6, 2008, RIA Novosti.

The patriotic attitude of the Church during the Second World War led to a relative amount of tolerance from the government. A few churches and seminaries were allowed to reopen. The period was called the Stalin religious NEP as a replay of the 1921 partial economic liberalization. Fidel Castro would later salute the Orthodox Church: "It is a spiritual force. In critical moments in Russian history the church played an important part. When the country was compelled to launch its patriotic war after the treacherous Nazi attack, Stalin sought the help of the church to support the workers and peasants that the October Revolution had made the masters of the land and the factories and in recent times when the USSR collapsed imperialism didn't find an ally in the church."

This helped the Russian Orthodox Church to survive even though many priests and the ranks of the faithful were to rebel against the regime. The patriarchal leadership was completely loyal to the Soviet system. During the Cold War the Orthodox Church took part in the Kremlin's international peace drives. The Soviets were also anxious to have the Baltic Orthodox support the regimes set up by the USSR. In the former eastern Polish region the church and the state were pressing the 2 to 3 million Uniates to convert to the Orthodox faith.[6] The Soviet constitution recognized the freedom to worship and it upheld the right to disseminate anti-religious propaganda.

Like any religion the Orthodox also have factions. Moscow and Constantinople are at odds. The Kremlin, under Stalin and Putin, supports the Moscow patriarch which is nothing new. In *The Brothers Karamazov* Father Paissy says that the Russian Orthodox Church and not Rome should transform the government and the world into a future universal church on earth

Dostoevsky, Solzhenitsyn, Putin: A Vision of Russia

Glasnost and perestroika improved the position of the Orthodox Church. A new era begins with the return of the church to the

---

6. Christian oriental rite Church, the Uniates are under Rome's jursidiction. In countries such as Pologne or the Austrian Empire the faithful came under a special statute whereas the Orthodox were considered second-class citizens.

forefront of public life. With Gorbachev's reforms that began in 1985, the Russian Orthodox Church emerged from years of persecution as a new cultural and ethical force. Adults were getting baptized by the tens of thousands that was more often the expression of patriotic feeling than one of deep seated faith.[7] Alexander Solzhenitsyn was given back his Russian citizenship and left Vermont to return to Russia in May 1994. He decided to reenter at Magadan, a far eastern port city in Siberia some 5000 miles east of Moscow and a major prisoner transit point into the Gulag. His return coincides with the moment when Russian society was in transition and effervescence under Boris Yeltsin. The people were being tempted by the proselytizing of some Catholic groups and American religious sects. Later on Putin and Medvedev would condemn those attempts as intrusions into Russian life.

Russians were fascinated by western culture and the Salvophiles were warning against the "rotten West." An identity crisis began and the Russian Church faced with the temptations of modernity was split. Was Solzhenitsyn's choice to return to his native land as the author of *The Gulag Archipelago* a testimony to the millions of innocents that perished in the camps or was it nostalgia for a past inherited from Dostoevsky and Holy Russia? Both writers share a common history: the Gulag and the Tsar's forced labor camps.

After the fall of communism the Russian church managed to strike a balance between conservatives and modernists. Professor Olivier Clément, of the *Institut orthodoxe Saint-Serge* (in Paris), stated: "Right-wing nationalists and neo-communists in today's Russia are mostly nationalist and anti-Semitic! They have an almost autistic view of Russian history: as a Jewish-Masonic plot, the alliance between Catholicism and Islam to destroy the orthodox religion, the debunking of the reformers who are denounced as western spies. Some would like to see the orthodox faith become an ideology that replaces Marxism and attempts to influence the patriarch and the bishops. The former KGB is behind this attempt since it is far from having lost its power."

---

7. Olivier Clément, *Le Monde*, June 10, 1998.

At that point Solzhenitsyn returned and until 1998 he would appear on national television twice a month. Nostalgic for the days of Holy Russia that he was seeking: a mythical country in the distant past. He was ideologically opposed to capitalism and private property, to pluralism and freedom of the press "the unbearable tide of useless news." More of a nationalist than a patriot, a reactionary rather than a traditionalist, the author of *The Gulag Archipelago* was a man of faith. The Nobel Prize winner had a Russian messianic vision and a single truth: his personal Holy Russia, in the Russian intellectual tradition. As Dostoevsky wrote the Russian people "carries God: the only one of its kind."

In their semiotics of Russian culture, Yuri Lotman and Boris Uspenski explains that sixteenth century Moscow named itself the third Rome since Jerusalem had been tainted by the Saracens. This tradition revived by many intellectuals nurtures Russian nationalism, its claim to hegemony, rejection of democracy and its corollary namely anti-Semitism… Solzhenitsyn calls Russia corrupt and amoral in his 1990 essay published four years before his return when he was demanding that the frontiers of Russia be redefined within the USSR. He wanted to keep most of Russia, Ukraine, Byelorussia and part of Kazakhstan (the historically Russian territories) and expel everyone else whether they liked it or not. The Russians in the other republics were to return to Russia. In another essay *The Russian Question* he offered his view of his country's history. He knew that the Russian people are the product of ethnic mixing the consequence of wars and annexations and this is something he deplores because it brought a multitude of tribes into the Russian ethnicity. He feels that "Russian man was sullied."

Before the war in Chechnya (1994-1996), he would write: "Was it not also our duty to evacuate the Russians from Chechnya where they are held in ridicule and where plunder, violence and death threaten them all the time?" The writer opposed the first war while he would support the second one that Putin began as soon as he took over in 1999. He views the Muslim rebels as a threat to the Orthodox faith. Alexis II took a similar position as he condemned the 1994 intervention and a more ambiguous position in 1999 aligning himself on the new master of the Kremlin who was justifying his policy as the struggle against terrorism.

Solzhenitsyn was obsessed by the purity of Russian man: "We have offered hospitality over the years in Russia to 40 thousand Meskhetian Turks whose crops were burned in Central Asia and had been thrown out by the Georgians; to Armenians fleeing Azerbaijan; to the Chechens even though they declared their independence; even to the Tajiks who have their own country..." His conclusion is very clear: "We need to build a moral Russia or no Russia at all and must preserve and grow all the good seeds that have fortunately not been trampled in Russia."

Solzhenitsyn shared anti-Semitism with Dostoevsky, and was in favor of a strong executive and a local form of democracy. He supported Putin in his struggle against the oligarchs. Kremlin authorities say that seven out of eight top richest oligarchs have Jewish origins a statement that reminds us of the "Doctor's Plot." In 1951, a group of mostly Jewish doctors were accused of having murdered two Soviet leaders and getting ready to kill more. The false conspiracy had been set up by Stalin's secret police and those accusations were dropped after the dictator's death in 1953.

The oligarchs were held responsible according to the law but clearly their fortunes were amassed with the blessing of Yeltsin's Kremlin. Anti-Semitism remains a constant factor of Russian life.

Since the sixteenth century when there were fewer Jews, the Orthodox Church encouraged the tsar to banish them. Under the tsars while Tbilisi was the official capital of the Caucasus, the large Jewish cities were Odessa and Kiev where the bureaucracy assembled the Jews in a "pale of settlement." By bribing high officials many were able to move to other parts of the empire like the Ukraine and Azerbaijan where they were more readily accepted.

During the reign of Catherine the Great and with her conquests Russia appeared unable to integrate "the Jewish element." The Jews increased in numbers by half a million with the conquered Polish territories (1772, 1793, 1795). They were forced to remain where they were and couldn't move, thus creating the largest ghettos in history. Alexander I wanted them to convert and in 1817 he set up the

Society of Christian Jews that turned out to be a failure. Napoleon had attempted something similar without trying to proselytize provide the Jews in France with representation to the authorities. The tsar and his opponents all had projects to settle the issue of the "foreign elements" meaning the Jews. Count Pestel, an aristocratic free thinker in 1820 proposed the creation in Central Asia of an independent Jewish state that would include all the European Jews. Konstantin Pobedonostsev, the advisor to the last two tsars had an even more radical suggestion: emigration for one third of the community, conversion of another third and death by hunger for those remaining.

With Stalin and the Soviet regime the Jews were exposed to acts of vengeance by the government. When Alexis II became patriarch in 1990 he would vigorously condemn anti-Semitism: "This archaic attitude that still weighs down on the Russian Church." While neither Putin nor Medvedev can be accused of anti-Semitism, incidents against the Jews are common and those responsible enjoy a kind of immunity with the authorities.

Rereading History

One symbol that best expresses Russia and its ambitions today is the state seal chosen by Boris Yeltsin. Red as the color of Greater Russia and the double eagle for the empire extending over two continents Asia and Europe. The eagles hold in each claw a scepter and a golden sphere that represent the power of the tsar and of the Church. In the center is the shield of Saint George the patron of the Slavs! Sergei Filatov is a professor and politician who is critical of the Orthodox Church and was one of Boris Yeltsin's close advisors. From 1993 to 1997 he was in charge of the presidential administration in the Kremlin where his duties included relations with the Orthodox Church.. In an article published in 2005, he is skeptical about the patriarch's ability to accept democracy.[8]

---

8. *Russian Review*, Keston Institute, Center for the Study of Religion and Communism in Eastern European countries, May 2005.

"The Russian Orthodox Church is in fact the only important Christian religion in the world that remains impervious to democracy and human rights." He also worries about the reinterpretation of history to be found in Alexis II's statements when he was patriarch of Moscow tending to minimize the authoritarian and repressive nature of the Stalinist regime and turns the Russian involvement in World War II into a crusade when he states: "Examples of military confrontations with the West in the course of Russian history are the mark of the eternal struggle between Russian Orthodox civilization and the Anti-Christ." He portrays the great Red Army generals as part of the faithful and in his speech to the ninth Russian world congress Patriarch Alexis II will praise the Soviet takeover of Eastern Europe: "Victory allowed the assembly of the Orthodox people in Europe, increasing the authority of the Russian Church and allowed for the creation of churches in Poland and Czechoslovakia." This return to the past makes Russia what it is today. Even the FSB, the heir to the KGB now has its very own patron saint Prince Alexander Nevski, Saint Alexis for the Orthodox Church. Policemen now honor the defender of Russia's borders against the Mongol Khan on the holidays and in a religious ceremony.

The Russian armed forces also have their patron saint. In April 2007 another step was taken when the Orthodox Church in response to a request from the Kremlin renewed the tradition of "military priests" of the tsarist armies. Rabbi Aaron Gurevitch, the first Jewish chaplain since 1917 "Imams and Rabbis should be able to officiate in every military district." One Russian soldier out of six is Muslim. The religious factor is compelling in Medvedev and Putin's Russia and in some ways we are close to the American Religious Right with the difference that the United States are a country of laws. In Russia there is an Orthodox work code on top of the official regulations. The Russkoye Moloko company gave an ultimatum to its employees: it gave a two month time frame to those married civilly to get married in the church otherwise they would be fired. The owner could be an American pro-life militant when he says: "If a woman has an abortion she can no longer work in our company. Abortion is murder we don't want to work with murderers."

The Orthodox Legacy: Russia vs. the West

On February 17, 2008, Hashim Thaci declared that Kosovo was "independent, sovereign and free" when 109 Kosovar deputies voted unanimously for a unilateral declaration of independence. Since June 10, 1999, Kosovo was under UN administration. The Security Council had set up the UN Interim Administration Mission in Kosovo to administer the territory having legislative, executive and legal power. The funds come mostly from the EU. The armed forces—KFOR and NATO—were there to ensure stability in the area that was the source of tensions with Moscow and Serbia. After Georgia and Ukraine the Kremlin couldn't accept Kosovo's close relations with the EU and NATO. The Kosovo declaration of independence had the support of the United States and France while Germany and others remained cautious. Riots broke out in Belgrade with the American embassy a target of the demonstrators. Several Serbian radicals in Kosovo demanded that the territory be part of Serbia. Vladimir Putin said that the independence of Kosovo was illegal and immoral while the Kremlin feared a domino effect that could break away the territories of the former USSR to "separatists" seeking independence. Putin saw independence as a "horrible precedent" that would lead to "unforeseeable consequences." In 2010 the court of justice in The Hague confirmed the legality of Kosovo's independence.

The Moscow Patriarch spelled out the Orthodox Church's position in March 2009 in a letter to Patriarch Paul of Serbia reiterating his intention to defend the orthodox in Kosovo. His message was perfectly clear:

> In the future the Church will use every possible means to express itself in the defense of God's truth, the defense of our orthodox brothers and sisters living in Kosovo a region of Serbia, the defense of all those who have been banished, the defense of victims of violence and injustice.

2010 was the first time a Russian president visited Serbia coinciding with the anniversary of the liberation of Belgrade by the

Red Army on October 20, 1944. Russia and Serbia had a long history of friendship and Moscow was one of the rare supporters of the Milosevic regime. Dmitri Medvedev was the first foreign leader to speak before the Serbian parliament and his message was all the more difficult for the Kosovars to hear after Moscow's agreement in 2008 to give independence to Georgia, Abkhasia and South Ossetia. During an international conference $5.5 million dollars—$2 million of which came from Russia—were collected for Kosovo's cultural legacy consisting of churches and monasteries since, according to Serbia, over 150 Serbian religious buildings were damaged or destroyed. Unesco was responsible for the distribution of those funds. Vuk Jeremic, Serbian minister of foreign affairs called on Unesco and the international community to preserve and protect the Serbian cultural legacy in Kosovo and to prevent that the issue be used for political ends. "It is out of the question that Serbian monasteries should become pawns in a dangerous identity game." He warned Pristina that to pass on the orthodox medieval legacy to the Albanians of Kosovo would be an attempt to "change history."

Kosovo and Serbia are revelatory of the geopolitics that followed the collapse of the Soviet empire. Serbia needs Moscow's support to reject the independence of Kosovo and yet Belgrade would also like to join the EU. The Serbian and Russian orthodox churches are part of the conflict using the religious factor to defend their space even if that means becoming instruments of their respective governments. At the same time they both encourage a dangerous game of nationalist revival.

Ukraine and Russia After the Orange Revolution: Church and State in Conflict

Natural gas was the weapon used in the "war" the Kremlin waged on its neighbor. If Gazprom was one of the actors in this conflict, other unexpected players surfaced using their influence in a tense situation.

The economic crisis and the dependence of Ukraine on Russia are the best trump card of the Kremlin and after many incidents political changes have effectively buried the European dream of the Ukrainians. Following the Orange revolution, voters picked the pro-Russian candidate for the presidency in February 2010. While the result was a product of the political and economic situation of Ukraine one must examine the strategy and geopolitics of the Moscow patriarch and its implications. Beyond Ukraine the Moscow patriarch also uses his influence over a number of autonomous or independent churches.[9]

The various orthodox churches and the influence they have on one another is rather complex. In Belarus and Estonia, there are two orthodox churches, one attached to Moscow, the other to Constantinople. In Moldavia, the two churches live side by side one turned toward Moscow and the other to the patriarch of Romania. In Ukraine various orthodox churches have been organized: the orthodox Ukrainian church linked to Moscow, the western Ukrainian and foreign of Kiev, and the Ukrainian orthodox. The latter having been created in 1992 by separatists from the other two is called "national." The rough geography of the various churches places east and south—namely Odessa is faithful to Moscow—while the west includes Roman Catholics, Greek Catholics and orthodox Ukrainians. This division corresponds to the political map of the country.

At a NATO-Russia meeting in April 2008 in Bucharest Putin described Ukraine as being "an artificial entity carved out of lands given by the USSR and Russia." This was Anton Denikin's idea when he spoke of Russia as "Greater Russia" and the Ukraine as "Little Russia." The Orange Revolution of November 2004 ended with the election of Viktor Yushchenko on the third round of the presidential election. The Ukrainian Orthodox Church linked to Moscow didn't hesitate to support Viktor Yanukovich. The Patriarch of Kiev and the Greek Orthodox Church openly backed the pro-western opposition

---

9. The autonomous churches of Bielorussia (Metropolite of Minsk and Sloutsk), Estonie (Metropolite of Tallinn and all of Estonia), of Latvia (Archdiocese of Riga and all Latvia), of Moldavia (Metropolite of Chisinau and all Moldavie), Ukraine (Metropolite of Kiev and all Ukraine) and the Russian Church outside Russia (since 2007) are all connected canonically. There is also the case of the Russian Orthodox Church beyond the borders (Metropolite of New-York) that was placed under the Moscow Patriarchy in 2007 after pressure from the Kremlin. Some parishes of the Russian diaspora abroad have not accepted the decision and two new Orthodox Churches have recently been created: the Russian Orthodox Church in exile and the Russian Orthodox Church beyond the borders.

candidate. During pro-Yanukovich rallies some participants held up icons to show the religious links between Ukraine and Russia.

The conflict between western and eastern Ukraine that is traditionally oriented toward Russia was described by some observers as a religious feud but this must be viewed with the greatest caution. The Orange revolution has past even though the country's candidacy to the EU has not officially been questioned, Ukraine is practically back in Moscow's camp. In 2010, the new president Victor Yanukovich gave his first speech in Russian. The Orthodox Church contributed to the last election: while the western part was closer to the West the east which is more industrialized was leaning toward Russia. In the uncertainty that gripped the eastern region more that the west, the church provided a pro-Russian element that helped the Kremlin's candidate. The West made a mistake in judgment since Ukraine has always been on the periphery of Russia and for the Russians Ukraine's relations with Europe were treason. The westerner countries were only attempting to cause problems for Russia. The promise made by George W. Bush to bring Ukraine into NATO could not be kept.

The Kremlin Engages Its Muslims

In the course of a visit to the diocese of Arkhangelsk, Patriarch Kiril of Moscow discussed the role of the church in society. Responding to a question about building many more non-Orthodox places of worship (synagogues and mosques) he responded unambiguously: "Our multinational country must not be beset by ethnic or religious strife." And Judaism and Islam are official religions alongside the Orthodox faith.

While the Kremlin nurtures its Muslims in every possible way but Putin Solzhenitsyn, and even the patriarch view the Chechens as terrorists that the Russians call "black asses." Moscow and other Russian cities have seen renewed violence targeting foreigners or people from the Caucasus. African students are often the butt of extreme behavior that can also turn criminal. Anything can spark violence as at a Moscow soccer match where 6000 fans, many of them ultra-nationalist supporters of the Spartak club, were chasing non-Slavs. They cried out slogans such as "Russia for the Russians" in full view of a tolerant police as the young people attempted to lynch Caucasians and others from Central Asia unlucky enough to stand in their way.

What is happening in the Caucasus? The Chechen religious radicalization stems from the tough line taken by Moscow authorities refusing to negotiate with the separatists while only part of the Chechens have chosen radicalization. After having been weakened by Russian attacks in 1999-2000 they managed to reconstitute their forces. As Gennadi Gudkov, a colonel in the reserves and deputy to the Duma, said: "The Russians can eliminate Chechen warlords they kill one and three more come and take his place." Daghestan is also a powder keg ready to explode because of radical Islam and an economic and social crisis: it is one of the poorest republics within the federation. Ethnic tensions could lead to an explosion and yet Islam is multi-faceted in Daghestan mainly in the Sufi tradition and the brotherhoods are represented now at the official institutions of the republic unlike during the Soviet era. Wahhabism is spreading perhaps because it has been outlawed since 1999.

Moscow's main fear would be that these small republics[10] should revolt giving rise to a caliphate in the northern Caucasus. Two approaches have been proposed by the Kremlin leadership. Putin favors a forceful repressive approach while Medvedev is betting that social and economic development will extinguish the Islamist phenomenon. The Arab revolts have not become a source of inspiration in the Muslim republics of the Caucasus thanks to the efficient security system. Yet sooner or later issues of human rights will appear. The Russians fear the spread of these revolts particularly in the southern border states that remain within Russia's "sphere of influence" President Medvedev stated "We may be up against explosive situations and the spread of extremism in the future." In discussing the attacks in the Moscow metro in April 2010 Alexander Bastrykin, a lawyer confirmed that the perpetrators had been trained in religious institutions in the Near East. They then became the

---

10. Chechenia, Ingushtia, Daghestan, Kabardino-Balkaria, Karatchaevo-Cherkessia.

ideologues of terror in the Caucasus and in Russia, a situation that Putin will address, having been reelected to the presidency.

In Russia the Kremlin is being friendly toward "its" Muslims in many initiatives in the region: building new clinics for the population and restoring mosques. Moscow is seeking to improve its image abroad especially with its Muslim commercial and political partners. Many Muslims responded positively in the voting booth: during the last elections they had a group called "Muslims for Putin." On December 9, 2007 the first Muslim clinic was opened in Moscow: an establishment that handles its patients in accordance with Sharia law meaning that it follows the "strict rules of religion." Russia has some 20 million Muslims out of a population of 142 million, making Islam the second religion in the country. One million Muslims live in Moscow.

Back on the international scene Russia decided to compete with the American presence using a policy of cooperation with Muslim countries. This strategy is based on the old Soviet republics of Central Asia that are mostly Muslim but also in Near Eastern countries that remain necessary partners.

Russia has nine Muslim republics and therefore was able to have observer status at the Organization of the Islamic Conference (OCI). President Medvedev confirmed to Ekmeleddin Ihsanoglu (March 2009), the secretary general of the conference Russia's desire to increase cooperation especially to resolve the Near East crisis. Presenting Russia as a multi-confessional country where the believers in Islam also live, Dmitri Medvedev wished to have a conference in Moscow to resolve the Middle East conflict. The president justified Moscow's role in the Middle East saying that some 20 to 25 million Orthodox live in the area (Christian Arabs, Syrians, Lebanese, Palestinians, Iraqis, Egyptians and Jordanians) and because of the ties between Russia and the 5 million Jews that have emigrated to Israel.

Medvedev at first wanted Russia to have a full and equal relationship with the OCI but then in a switch the Kremlin stated that it wanted no full membership in that organization. Such a status is for countries with a Muslim majority which is not Russia's case. Until the 2008 U.S. presidential election Medvedev and Putin reaped the benefits in the Arab and Muslim world of an unpopular Republican administration mired in the Iraq, Afghanistan and Iran issues. After Obama's election and his opening to the Muslims, Russia and America were risking competition in the same territory. For the first time since the exit from Afghanistan, Russia is no longer involved in any military conflict. What could be viewed as a weakness of the Kremlin in international affairs has to be placed in perspective. With Gazprom serving Putin as a "state within the state" Russia's gas weapon gives it more power and influence than most western countries. Moscow is feeding Europe and can close the tap at any time as it did with Ukraine.

Putin and Medvedev don't have to manage Afghanistan, Iraq, Yemen, or Pakistan, giving the Russian leader an advantage over Obama. Putin after reelection could remain president until 2024, which would be a return of the Romanov dynasty!

Iran: Diplomacy, Religion and Commercial Interests

Even though it is not an Arab country the relationship with Shia Iran allowed Russia to assert a presence in the region and with Muslim countries. In return, Moscow's support for Tehran especially at the UN Security Council is a case of pragmatic quid pro quo. The Bushehr nuclear facility built by the Russians is the first large scale project they have built abroad. Moscow wants to see Iran return as a strong regional power.

Relations between Iran and Russia go back to the sixteenth century: in 1521 an emissary from King Ishmael of the Salafid dynasty paid a visit to Tsar Vassili III. The question of commercial exchanges was already at the center of those initial diplomatic contacts even though they came as part of a triangular relationship between Russia, Europe and Iran facing their common enemy: the Ottoman Empire.

The close relations between Russia and Iran have several advantages that must be seen in the context of the fall of the USSR in 1991 and open a new era in Russian-Iranian relations. At the time the main issues were the new countries in the Caucasus and Central Asia that were tempted by the West. Moscow's intent on maintaining its influence in the post-Soviet sphere converged with Tehran's will to resist the United States. Both countries are energy rich with the world's largest gas reserves and every interest in a common stance on those issues. Tehran saw in a Russian-Iranian partnership the only way to break its isolation: the ostracism in which Iran was being held in by the sanctions policy of the West opened the way to a strong partner.

Moscow stepped into the breach by taking part in Iran's nuclear projects and the same applies to China that sees in Tehran a strategic ally. Iran sells China energy and the Chinese help in the exploitation of gas and oil concessions. Since both Russia and China are permanent members of the UN Security Council Iran always benefited from their support. All three are members of the Shanghai Organization, a sort of all-purpose structure that is more or less a counterpart of NATO without a fixed organization. Observers include Afghanistan and Pakistan that are supported politically by the United States.

The other element that justifies a rapprochement between Russia and Iran is the issue of protecting the Caucasus in Russia's sphere. Iran's influence in the Muslim world allows it to limit fundamentalist extremism in those republics and Iran always opposed the Sunni fringes that dabble in terrorism. Turkey also plays a role in the Turkic speaking republics of Central Asia and the Caucasus in its rivalry with Iran. Russia finds it essential to thwart those Turkish ambitions. The area was historically subjected to Ottoman or Persian influence but contrary to Iran the Turks display an ostentatious attitude by financing networks of mosques, sending preachers and inviting the faithful to come and be educated in Turkey. They also attempt to create cultural and economic cooperation. By playing a role in the region where it has an historical legitimacy that is also political and religious, Iran can help its own policies while supporting Russia.

The ties of the Caucasian fundamentalists to Al Qaeda and the uncertainties that lie ahead for Afghanistan and Pakistan are of great importance to the Kremlin. Dmitri Medvedev's invitation to Pakistan's president to meet with him in his summer residence along with

President Karzai indicates the seriousness with which Moscow intends to play a regional role. The Kremlin doesn't intend to leave the Pakistan-Afghan issue to the Americans to solve because it remains an area of turbulence that can only increase the problems that exist in the Caucasus by giving credence to Islamist forces that oppose Russia. On the Afghan and Pakistan issues nothing can be done without Iran's consent.

This geopolitical context encouraged the Kremlin to favor a religious dialog between the Orthodox Church and the Shia clergy. A joint Russian-Iranian commission in 1997 was set up and meets alternatively in Tehran or Moscow. The objective being, according to Patriarch Alexis II, to define areas of agreement as for example the opposition to "secular values that are imposed from foreign countries that contradict religious values."[11] The commission is a signal by Russia to the Muslim world as to its interest in pursuing a dialog while it continues the war in Chechnya. If militants find resonance among the population it is not so much a matter of religious faith as of resistance against the occupying power in the name of fundamental freedoms including self-determination a project that is in contradiction with the Kremlin's desire to see a rebirth of the "Greater Holy Russia."

Moscow must recapture in the Arab world and the Muslim countries the influence it had in the past. The Russians would have liked to take the initiative of a broad peace conference on the Near East that could only succeed with the blessing of the other great powers that rejected the project. During the great pan-Arab moment the USSR had a powerful influence in the Middle East: Syria, Egypt, Iraq were all allied to Moscow. The Near east also includes Israel and the very old relations between Moscow and Jerusalem improved because of the fall of communism and the large Russian immigrant community in Israel that includes Nathan Sharansky who was close to Andrei Sakharov one of the founders of the Refusenik movement and several times a member of the government of Israel.[12] Prime Minister Benjamin Netanyahu believes in Putin as a moderator of

---

11. Statements by Alexis II during the Moscow visit by the President of the Iranian Parliament, Gholam Ali Haddad Adel in December 2005.
12. Those to whom the government was denying an immigration visa.

Iran than Obama and his attempt at engagement. Moscow continued to support Bashar al-Assad and the Russians continued to deliver weapons to Syria.

Up to the Rafters

Another illustration of the power of the Church in Russia's life and the conservatism of the society is found in its relationship with art and artists. Contemporary art criticism is commonplace in any society but in Russia art is under the attentive scrutiny of the church that doesn't exclude a certain amount of anti-Semitism. Often art exhibits are ransacked by fundamentalist orthodox militants and covered with anti-Semitic graffiti. Gallery directors and exhibit stewards are sued for inciting religious hatred and demeaning human dignity which may end up with a maximum sentence of five years in prison. Others are found guilty of "sowing religious and interethnic discord." Very often the nationalist and Orthodox fundamentalists who persecute the exhibits and their organizers as well as the artists are well known to the authorities and are never called to task because their leaders are close to the politicians.

As reported in *Le Monde* the exhibition "Forbidden art 2006" was organized in March 2007 at the Sakharov museum in Moscow and included works that had been rejected by various museums and galleries fearful of the reactions of the Church and the government. Demonstrations opposing this event were organized with the quiet approval of the authorities and the security forces.

Andrei Erofev, the director, was held under house arrest and couldn't leave the country; he also fears for his life and the safety of his family. Yuri Samodurov Sakharov Center director is the object of a legal action for "inciting religious hatred and threatening human dignity" that could bring up to five years in prison. On July 12, 2010, Erofev, an art historian and internationally well known collector, was found guilty of inciting religious hatred and sentenced to pay a fine of 150,000 rubles. While these new Moscow trials were underway, France and Russia were opening the great exhibit at the Louvre that launched the year of Russia in France.

Chapter 4

Israel Torn Apart

Israeli soldier Gilad Shalit had to be saved. He had been captured by Hamas on June 26, 2006, and his freedom had become a cause for the whole nation. Prime Minister Netanyahu was faced with a dilemma: on one hand save the life of the French Israeli soldier by negotiating the liberation of Palestinian prisoners, and on the other witness the stronger opposition from victims of suicide attacks and extreme right wing rabbis who view any prisoners being granted freedom as an encouragement to further terrorism.

Massive liberations did take place in the past but 6,000 Palestinians remain in Israeli jails and the current context is very different from the earlier situations. Jerusalem must now negotiate both with Hamas and Fatah. With the fall of Hosni Mubarak in Egypt the part played by the Muslim Brotherhood and the threats to the Jordanian regime by Islamists and some Bedouin tribes has increasingly isolated Israel. After five years of imprisonment of Shalit by Hamas, Netanyahu agreed to free 1,000 Palestinians for the return of the Israeli soldier.

Even though Hamas is the number one enemy for the Jewish State it was originally set up by Sheikh Ahmed Yassin, the founder of the Islamist movement with Israel's support. At the time Hamas was seen as a counterweight to the OLP and Yasser Arafat. The death of Hamas' spiritual leader in an air strike in March 2004 that was supervised by Ariel Sharon, then prime minister, became a declaration of war for the Islamists.

Without unity, legitimacy and any kind of authority within Fatah, Palestinian President Mahmud Abbas, had threatened to retire from politics if he couldn't have even a semblance of unity within his own family. Israel was worried that the Fatah leader's departure would leave it, forcing only the Islamists of Hamas to negotiate. Thanks to friendly pressure from the West Mahmud Abbas remained at the helm of the Palestinian authority even though his term limit has passed and no elections have been called.

The fate of those being detained is central to Palestinian society and their positions are of great importance. Marwan Barghouti a member of the OLP serving a life sentence in Israel and a historical figure in the Palestinian resistance is a problem for both Israel and Mahmud Abbas. He is not among the prisoners that were freed. Even though Barghouti describes himself as secular he will owe his freedom one day to Hamas rather than Fatah.

As a symbol of resistance against the Jewish State and the oldest Palestinian prisoner held by the Israelis, he will have to lean toward the Islamist movement even though this will reduce the authority of Mahmud Abbas or his successor even more. The Palestinian movement would take a conservative Islamic line closer to a more secularized Iran or Turkey. The restructuring of Islamic forces in the region can only support this development while the Muslim Brotherhood is showing its strength in Egypt, Palestine, Jordan and even Syria. For now Barghouti remains in jail.

During the last ten years there has been the war between Israel and Lebanon, the "Cast Lead" operation in Gaza, humanitarian boats into Gaza and huge changes in the Arab Muslim world. A re-launching of the peace process between the Israelis and the Palestinians in the short term is difficult to envisage. Israel rejected

Obama's proposal to create two states on the 1967 borders and a peace conference was not to the liking of the White House.[1] No one can predict the fate of the latest Fatah—Hamas rapprochement anymore than the fate of the Arab Spring in Egypt and Syria[2] Observers try to interpret any small event as a sign of change. For the first time since the 1979 revolution—in February 2011—two Iranian warships were authorized by the Egyptians to navigate through the Suez Canal bound for Syria. The Rafah crossing is more than a symbol and according to the promise made by the Egyptian minister of foreign affairs the only exit to Gaza that is not under Israeli control has been reopened albeit selectively by Cairo. In the Golan Heights tensions with Syria caused several deaths. A Sunni close to Hezbollah is now the prime minister of Lebanon and in December 2010 the president of Iran was given a hero's welcome in the streets of Beirut. Ahmadinejad used the trip to provoke the Israelis and claim the area as his own by giving anti-Israeli speeches. Syria, armed by Russia and an ally of Tehran remains largely unknown. What would happen should the Syrian leader be driven from power? What would the attitude of Iran, Hezbollah or Hamas be?

All these developments have isolated Israel. To Aaron David Miller, former State Department official and Middle East specialist the Hamas-Fatah closeness is a gift to the Israelis that will complicate the recognition of a Palestinian State.[3] But everything in the orient is complicated and unpredictable

A conservative Islamic regime that would be acceptable to Palestine would run the risk of increasing internal tensions and drive wedges in Israeli society.

Israel as an Exception

The Jewish State is exceptional in more than one way in current history. Since 1948, it is the focal point of the problem of peace in

---

1. Alain Juppé, June 2011.
2. The consequences of the events in Egypt and the determination to introduce a resolution at the UN recognizing the Palestinian State encouraged this rapprochement in the summer of 2011 as much as the clashes between Hamas and Israel that also caused three deaths among Egyptian policemen.
3. *Le Monde*, May 11, 2011.

the Middle East. Events of the twentieth century and the Holocaust in particular give all the issues relating to Israel a strongly emotional connotation. Aside from those issues, the geographic and geopolitical elements that orient the policies of Israeli governments confirm the complexity of the issues that the Jewish State faces. Israel is located on a very small strip of territory compared to the Muslim countries that surround it. At the level of Jerusalem the country is a mere 70 kilometers wide where the Arab world extends from the Atlantic to the tip of Arabia over 7,000 kilometers. It s also surrounded by enemies whether Palestinians, Syrians or Lebanese Shia.

Since the founding of the State of Israel and beyond the Jewish-Arab antagonism which is a product of history for the most part, the complications come from the refusal of the Jerusalem government to apply the decisions and resolutions of the international community in the name of the defense of Israel. The refusal to return the farms in Chebaa in Lebanon or the Golan Heights to Syria, the opposition to a Palestinian State all have a share in keeping this antagonism alive. Public opinion is opposed to the Jewish State across the entire Arab-Muslim world and only a political solution between Israel and the Palestinians can solve that problem.

Operation "Cast Lead" is a new development in the war against Gaza when a flotilla of a Turkish Islamist group having Turkey's tacit approval was boarded by Israeli troops. Israel lost the image and communications war with that action. The pictures of the assault and the behavior of the IDF was dramatic for the Jewish State and the sympathy shifted from the assailants to the supporters of the Gazans.

Jerusalem can undertake almost any kind of action to defend its security and the Israelis are convinced that their actions are subject to impunity even when most of the international community opposes them. When South African Judge Richard Goldstone speaking for the UN published his report where Israel and Hamas are both accused of "war crimes" Jerusalem rejected the document saying it was the victim and shifted the responsibility to its opponents. Yet the facts are undisputable and even part of Israeli public opinion was worried about those initiatives. Surprisingly enough Goldstone withdrew his report and in March 2011 at the UN he exonerated Israel for its actions during the "Cast Lead" operation.

When the ships attempting to break the blockade of Gaza were sailing toward Palestine, Haaretz called the seven members of the war cabinet who made the decision to board the vessels in international waters unwise. The Israeli government rejected any international inquiry commission and preferred its own investigators made up of eighty year olds who while honorable have no true investigative power. Israel's image come out damaged but the government doesn't seem to care.

Yet if relations between Israel and its neighbors—Hamas, Hezbollah, Syria, Iran—are a long term problem for Israel, the Israelis also need to worry about internal issues stemming from the urban development of Jerusalem, the Israelization of East-Jerusalem, the protective wall, the settlement policy and the creation of new settlements. These are as many time bombs for the governments that will follow. If security issues can explain these decisions in the short term they can only weigh heavily on the future since Palestinian demographic and sociological realities are unfavorable to the Israelis and create an explosive set of circumstances.

While President Obama was conferring with Benjamin Netanyahu on July 6, 2010, B'Tselem, an Israeli human rights group issued a report on the settlement policy on the West Bank. The report stated how various Israeli governments failed to keep their promises and end illegal colonization of the West Bank including the road map adopted by the Quartet in 2009.[4] Obama was unable to reach an agreement with the Israeli prime minister when he came to Washington, on an international inquiry regarding the intervention to stop the ships or a relaxing of the blockade of Gaza by both Israel and Egypt. Two months later the Israeli government published a list of goods that would be allowed into Gaza. Construction materials will be authorized if they are to fulfill international projects or if they are approved by the Palestinian authority. Since the EU is the first among lenders to the Palestinians this would justify Catherine Ashton's proposal for Europe to have control of the passage points

---

4. United States, Russia, UN, and EU.

between Gaza and Israel…which was rejected by Jerusalem. Obama also failed to obtain the end to settlements in the West Bank. In another friction point the democratic administration accepted the UN request asking Israel to ratify the non-proliferation agreement.

By giving an answer to this request Jerusalem would have been acknowledging de jure for the first time that it did indeed possess nuclear weapons. Washington's position could mean a change in its doctrine toward Tehran and backing away from Israel's intention to bomb Iran's nuclear installations

The Basic Laws: a Jewish State or a Democracy?

The issue of religion in the State of Israel is not new. It was debated from the start of Zionism and the end of the nineteenth century when rabbis and religious groups joined the movement. Theodor Herzl (1860-1904), the founder of political Zionism and the precursor of the Jewish State had a clear model in his mind as to the kind of society he envisioned. His project was not to create a state that would inherit Jewish culture and be filled with religious values. He wanted a modern state similar to any other, the difference being that Jews would constitute the majority. His answer to theocracy was unambiguous: "While faith gives us our unity, science frees us. We will not allow the theocratic impulses of our religious leaders to emerge." He was in favor of a separation between the state and the rabbinate and rejected any religious interference in public affairs because it would cause internal and external problems.

Three groups faced one another at the creation of the State of Israel. The Zionist majority was secular and was seeking a modern and non-religious state. The religious Jews wanted Jewish tradition to occupy an important place refusing any separation between the state and religion. Finally the Haredim that were ultra-religious wanted no state at all. Israel was created on the basis of a compromise between those three tendencies as Ben Gurion engineered it but that was not to last. The Basic Laws of the State of Israel define the country as "A Jewish and democratic State." For sixty years the very nature of the state is an issue being debated. Must the Jewish character be declared or should Israel be a democratic country among many others? The principles of the Basic Laws cannot handle demographic pressures or the consequences of an electoral system that increases the segmentation of society by encouraging minority groups that include the far right. While Jews represent 6.5 million citizens the Palestinian Arabs about one million and the Palestinians of East Jerusalem 230,000, demographic projections indicate that by 2050 Israel will have a population of 12 million including 4 million Arabs and Palestinians.

The latter could become the majority in East Jerusalem. If the secular and moderately religious Israeli birth rate is close to Western standards 2.5, that of the ultra orthodox at 7.6 and that of the Israeli Arabs at 4.5 have a much higher rate. The ultra orthodox birth rate stems from strict religious observance (rejection of contraception and opposition to abortion) as well as ethnic customs such as early marriage. Should the demographic progress of the ultra orthodox remain two and a half times higher than the average they would represent 11 percent of the Jewish population in 2011 and 17 percent in 2050.

In today's Jewish state secular Jews and moderates represent 75 percent of the population vs. 18 percent for the orthodox and 7 percent ultra orthodox. The identity issue (a Jewish State or a democracy) cannot be seen only in demographic terms or as a moderate—secular issue since other problems (settlements, East Jerusalem) can blur those divisions. The rise of the far right is not just a religious issue. The arrival in Israel of ethnic groups such as the Russian Jews contributes to increased nationalism and the political parties that represent it.

While the 1967 war allowed the Jews to conquer the Holy City the Israelis were unable to expel the Muslims. East Jerusalem only represented 38 square kilometers in 1967 but the construction of Jewish settlements increased that part of the city to 108 square kilometers. The policy has been to encircle Arab neighborhoods through systematic expropriations and at the same time the government encouraged settlements forming a circle around the city. Greater Jerusalem (East, West and settlements) is altogether 900 square kilometers. The security barrier or separation wall as it is called by the Israeli government is meant to protect the settlements located 11 kilometers from Jerusalem.

Nothing is simple in Israel and even less in Jerusalem. Some neighborhoods (the term "new cities" would be more appropriate) such as Piscat Zeev or Neve Yaacov in the north east house almost two thirds of the immigrants from the former USSR. They are mostly non religious secular Jews that reject the intolerance displayed by the orthodox. The secular-religious cleavage is both socio-economic and cultural.

Due to the heavy symbolic value of the city of Jerusalem considered holy by three religions of the Book is the focus of many passions and its status is not only a matter of politics and law. Every UN resolution since 1947 condemns Israel for making the city the capital of the Jewish State: no foreign country has its embassy in Jerusalem, all diplomatic representatives are located in Tel Aviv along with the Defense Ministry. The Holy City is a religious center where all traditions come alive and this creates a "paranoia and increased fundamentalism" in all the three religions. Jerusalem is a Jewish city to some, while others see it as being Christian or Muslim. Besides the internationalization of Jerusalem as the Vatican recommends there is no peace since each of the three religions of the Book is a "defender" of the Holy City and if there is a God it is the same for each of the three monotheistic faiths. The symbolism of Jerusalem and its universality is confronted with the political issue of sovereignty. Zionists and Muslim fundamentalists wish for a single identity for the city: either Jewish or Muslim.

In the settlements relations between Jews and Arabs became more complicated in the 1970s because of the beginning of small Israeli colonies that multiplied over time. Half a million Israeli settlers live on the West Bank of the Jordan River which they call by its biblical name "Judea Samaria." They are beyond the "Green Line" of the 1949 cease fire and were 241,000 in 1993 during the Oslo Peace Agreement. Today over 300,000 settlers live in 121 settlements and 100 outposts that even the Israeli government considers illegal. With these settlements and colonies Israel controls 42 percent of the West

Bank while other settlers numbering 185,000 live in 12 suburbs of Jerusalem that were annexed by the mayor's office with government approval.

The initial colonies were created by Zionists and the newer ones by ultra religious groups. Israeli law considers some of them illegal even though the international community views all of them as such. The intifada compelled Israel to build the "security barrier" that required the expropriation of Palestinian land and homes since the wall is 85 percent located on the West Bank and creates a new separation between Jews and Arabs. In spite of this the religious and ultra religious Jews are against the barrier since it calls into question the idea of the "Greater Israel" they both want. The expropriation policy affecting Palestinian property can only increase radicalization in favor of Hamas. Through "requisitions for military reasons" like the reclassification as "State land for public purposes" Israel can use any number of methods besides the settlers to take over Palestinian land illegally.

President Obama asked the Israeli prime minister to "limit" the settlements.[5] But building shall continue on the West: Pinhas Wallerstein, council director of Yesha the settler organization, made it very clear: "Who would vote in the Knesset in favor of a law forbidding any building? Impossible!"[6] The settlers brought down Netanyahu's first government in 1999 and that threat remains for any government.

Netanyahu had then agreed with the U.S. Administration on freezing of new construction in the "administered Palestinian territories." Even the "Peace Now" movement leaders acknowledged that: "Freezing construction became effective once Benjamin Netanyahu came to power." This didn't stop the prime minister from announcing plans to build 500 dwellings in various locations beyond the green line. That announcement didn't change his policy and was only meant to provide comfort for the Likud members of the government. His policy to slow down settlements created a break with the right and the fall of his government. There was another

---

5. September 2009 meeting with Benjamin Netanyahou.
6. *Le Monde*, September 25, 2009.

reason for his failure: on October 23, 1998 at the White House Netanyahu and Yasser Arafat signed the Wye Plantation Agreements, in the presence of Bill Clinton and King Hussein of Jordan.

The broad smiles from the Israeli and the Palestinian along with the warm handshakes became intolerable to Likud militants and the partisans of a Greater Israel. Six months after the Wye Plantation, Netanyahu was out and six months later, in 2005, the Likud broke up after the withdrawal from the Gaza Strip, a decision made by another hawk: Ariel Sharon. Netanyahu was finance minister at the time and didn't know what position he should take voting for withdrawal twice in the Knesset and during the cabinet meeting. Later on he would condemn a decision he had approved. Ariel Sharon then created the Kadima party and during the elections of March 28, 2006, the Likud was defeated in the worse results in its history with only 12 deputies in the Knesset.

Regarding President Obama's plea to Benjamin Netanyahu about limits to the settlements we are reminded of Henry Kissinger's remark: "Israel has no foreign policy, everything is conditioned by internal politics." which still stands today. The settlement strategy and the East Jerusalem policy must also be viewed in the light of economic reality. The early 2000s saw a recession with heavy unemployment (2003). The recovery came about because of the free market reforms of Netanyahu as finance minister and a massive lowering of taxes, reorganization of pensions and health insurance and drastic cuts in social programs. Public expenditures that were 77 percent of gross domestic product in 1985 became 49 percent in 2006 in spite of funds allocated to the war in Lebanon pushing many families of Arabs and ultra Orthodox Jews into poverty. It is one more difference that increases tensions among Israelis.

During the summer of 2011 some 300,000 Israelis protested about their diminished purchasing power and social inequalities but also against the relationship between politics and money and a system where corruption has become commonplace. Politicians like Ofer Bronchtein of the International Forum for Peace assert that beyond social and economic protest Israelis seek a deeper kind of change. In order to satisfy the demands –lower prices, better housing, salaries and jobs as well as an improved health care system---the country will need to make some choices. According to Bronchtein the cost of a plane would allow to pay for 60 000 students for one year, the price of a tank would give 10, 000 high school students free tuition, a machine gun would let a young couple increase their revenues by 10 percent. His solution is peace and naturally an end to the settlements where the state picks up the salaries of the settlers.[7]

An Institutional System that Favors the Extremes

Ultra religious influence on politics is not proportionate to their real weight in the country and yet they are able to influence policy. In Israel the electoral system is very much criticized for contributing to the fragmentation of politics and society. Every government is based on a number of bargains to form a coalition. Some observers assert that it ends up cheating popular sovereignty by factions that represent a small part of the electorate. The electoral system may be described as fundamentally proportionate.[8] For the founders of the Jewish State it was intended to allow representation of all Jews of any origin or opinion. At the same time Arab citizens that have equal rights could also be represented in the new institutions.

While the minimum required to have deputies in the Knesset has been recently increased it still remains very low: 1 percent before vs. 1.5 percent today. The 1.5 percent requirement with Israel being a single district voting on the basis of a list also increases the importance of the smaller parties making it necessary to have coalitions. The system creates its own perversions. During parliamentary elections on February 10, 2009, the Kadima list led by Tzipi Livni received the highest number of votes. Israelis went to sleep with a progressive future prime minister (at least described as such) and woke up the following morning with a right-wing government formed by ultra religious parties and ultra-nationalists. The proportional system allowed Benjamin Netanyahu to be designated prime minister neither Ben Gurion (Labor) or Menachem Begin (Likud)

---

7. THE "ISRAELI SPRING" IS ON THE MARCH! CORRUPT POLITICAL ELITES ARE HECKELED, *Le Monde*, August 9, 2011.
8. *Pouvoirs*, Ilan Greilsammer.

could reach the barrier of 61 seats out of 120 in the Knesset and be able to govern Israel alone.

When circumstances call for it the politicians come up with a government of "national unity." The Netanyahu government is supported by a coalition including the prime minister's Likud (27 deputies), Yisrael Beiteinu (Israel Our Home), of Foreign Minister Avigdor Lieberman, (15 deputies), the labor party of Ehud Barak (13 deputies), Shass, the ultra-orthodox Sephardic party (11 deputies) and Habayit Hayehudi, on the extreme right (3 deputies).[9]

Avigdor Lieberman, the foreign minister is among the most controversial politicians in Israel. Originally from Moldavia, he immigrated some twenty years ago, and fashions himself as a "savior of the country" and lives in a small isolated settlement south of Bethlehem. In his book *My Truth*, he preaches a total settlement policy and favors population exchanges between Israel and the Palestinian Authority to create two ethnically homogeneous states. In 2006, he demanded capital punishment for Arab Israeli deputies that celebrated the day of Nakba (the catastrophe) the name given to the forced removal of 700,000 Palestinians when the State of Israel was proclaimed in 1948.

The statements of this right-wing populist are extremely clear: during operation "Cast Lead" against Gaza, he deplored the fact that they "didn't finish the job." According to Lieberman Israel should fight Hamas like the Americans fought the Japanese in World War II. Even a portion of the right and the prime minster fear the man who was not informed of and didn't take part in the secret meeting between the Israeli prime minister and the Turkish foreign minister in Brussels on July 2, 2010, in order to improve bilateral relations and give more credibility to Israeli diplomacy. But the troublesome foreign minister of Israel cannot be ignored politically; on several occasions at the end of 2009 and 2010 a summit organized by the Mediterranean Union had to be cancelled because several Arab ministers refused to take part in a meeting that included Avigdor Lieberman. The U.S. Administration doesn't consider him as a valid partner since Lieberman refused to get involved in the peace process

---

9. August, 2010.

when Obama's Middle East envoy George Mitchell was trying very hard to re-launch the discussions.

The political situation wasn't clear in 2010 and it explained Netanyahu's lack of flexibility. The prime minister saw three Labor ministers resign from the government while Ehud Barak left his party to create a new political group and keep his portfolio as defense minister. For the first time Netanyahu headed a homogenous government of right-wing and ultra-orthodox parties.

Orthodox and Liberals: the Religious Break

Regarding other religions Judaism is multifaceted. In France liberal Judaism claims to be part of the contemporary religious movement. Jewish life should adapt to the modern world without abandoning moral spiritual and religious principles that are part of traditional Judaism while remaining fully engaged in society on ethical and social issues. Liberal Jews base their faith on the traditional scriptures and their classical interpretation while accepting a critical and academic explanation. They recognize both the divine (inspired) and human (written) dimension rejecting the literal reading used by orthodox Jews similar to fundamentalist Christians and some Islamic groups.

When Jews came out of the ghettos at the start of the nineteenth century the issue of the compatibility of civil society and traditional Jewish law came up. To avoid the choice between assimilation and tradition some Jewish thinkers in Germany created liberal Judaism. At the close of the nineteenth and the early twentieth century Jewish immigrants found in the United States a country open to relations with other religions where Reform Judaism was welcome. The liberal segment now includes over half of all American Jews. In Europe it extends mainly to the United Kingdom and the Netherlands, reaching France in the early twentieth century where Jewish institutions were to acknowledge it in the 1970s. Without entering into the detail of ritual or doctrine a few examples will serve as an illustration as to its nature.

Everyone is expected to understand what is said during the ritual therefore bilingual texts are used where liberal Judaism has cut many psalms and prayers that didn't fit with the content for example the return to sacrifice, the exclusion of women and of non-Jews. Prayers and texts by contemporary authors are also included and men and women pray next to one another in the synagogues where some women are rabbis. In Israel liberal Judaism has complicated relationships with the state and the rabbinate. Liberal rabbis are not on the state payroll and many of the acts they perform are not recognized.

The state doesn't recognize religious marriages performed by liberal rabbis and the progress of the last few years has come mostly from Supreme Court decisions. Since February 2002 the interior ministry must recognize persons converted in Israel by non-orthodox rabbis as Jewish without the need for confirmation by the orthodox rabbinate.

Can the Break Destroy the Zahal Myth?

The one Israeli institution that enjoys the greatest prestige is the army. One issue that comes up in Israeli society is the ultra orthodox rabbis' influence on that institution. In the summer of 2006 Israelis found out that the Zahal could also be defeated or at the very least stopped by the Lebanese Hezbollah.

This became a traumatic event for Israelis made worse by two other occurrences: the operation against Hamas and the removal of certain Jewish settlers from areas not undertaken by the police. Both operations were given to the army that is a mirror of society.[10]

The unity of the military is becoming increasingly fragile: on one hand religious or right wing soldiers are more radicalized, but a minority faction is worried about its leadership and human rights violations as demonstrated by some draftees during the last offensive against Hamas in Gaza. Today the danger comes from religious fundamentalism rather than pacifism.

Most Israelis were in favor of the operation in Gaza at the beginning backing the government and the army. The peace block

---

10. The Israeli army has some 161,000 soldiers and 425,000 reservists (2006).

thought that 10 percent of Israelis were opposed to military action along with 20 percent of Israeli Arabs. Among those opposed the "Courage to Refuse" movement that was created when some fifty officers and enlisted men of Zahal refused to serve in the occupied territories. In a letter signed by 628 reservists the war was condemned saying that revenge was not security and the Gaza operation brought no solution to the conflict. They refused to take part in a campaign for the "destruction of Gaza." Eight soldiers were sent to prison for 14 days for refusing to serve in Gaza.

In 2002, a petition was signed in the ranks of the military refusing to serve their annual time in the occupied territories because of the abuses by the army on the West Bank. The army rotated the signers out before punishing them to avoid their gaining a following. Since 2002 many soldiers have refused to serve for reasons of health, travel abroad or work.

Even though these may be isolated cases they show the mood among some Israeli officers. The Israeli army offered the soldiers to buy T-shirts after the Gaza victory showing a pregnant Palestinian woman in the gun sights with the words: "One bullet = Two dead." Haaretz conducted an investigation to find out whose bad idea this was manufactured by the Adiv fabric-printing shop company in Tel Aviv. The initiators were low ranking IDF soldiers. This incident coincided with the Goldstone report accusing both Israel and Palestinian armed groups of "war crimes" in Gaza leading to the deaths of 1,400 Palestinians and 13 Israelis from December 27, 2008 to January 18, 2009. For the first time since 1948 the percentage of young men and women seeking draft deferments for religious reasons was over 10 percent. These are orthodox religious students. The orthodox population is quickly increasing and the numbers of those deferred in coming years is destined to grow. The support given by the orthodox to the settlers encourages the rabbis to call for civil disobedience.

Manhigut Yehudit embodies this movement; the movement was founded in 1998 and has become a faction of religious Zionism inside the Likud now in power. In 2007, 12 soldiers of the Duhifat battalion refused to take part in the evacuation of settlers from

Hebron with students from various Yeshivot Hesder, the Talmudic schools with ties to the army. The killer of Yitzhak Rabin, Ygal Amir, came from a Yeshiva Hesder. In 2009, 1,300 students were drafted into Zahal with 80 percent of them asking to serve in fighting units. These schools –there are about 40 of them—were set up to let about 7,500 religious soldiers to organize their military service. They spend eighteen months in the service (instead of three years) and continue Torah studies while they are in uniform.

On October 27, 2009 during the swearing-in ceremony at the Western Wall 750 soldiers of the Shimshon battalion a few men waved a banner saying "The Shimshon battalion will not evacuate Homesh."[11] An illegal settlement evacuated in 2005 and partially reoccupied. In December 2009, Defense Minister Ehud Barak, attempted to limit the influence of the ultra-orthodox rabbis who were encouraging soldiers to disobey orders to evacuate the settlers. Barak decided to cancel the Talmudic school subsidy (134 000 Euros or 20 percent of the school's yearly budget), located at Har Bracha, a settlement south of Nablus that was considered "hard" under the supervision of Rabbi Melamed. While religious Zionism was developing within the army beyond these monk soldiers of the Yeshivot Hesder, the defense minister attracted the wrath of many "moderate" rabbis who opposed the ideas of their extremist colleagues. The government's main fear is that the Israeli army could also have a religious army within made up of the far right under the influence of Yeshivot Hesder.

Two Places and Two Symbols

In Israel they say: "In Tel Aviv they work and in Jerusalem they pray." As far as pious Jerusalem is concerned Tel Aviv has become Sodom and Gomorrah. For the Ashkenazy orthodox party the secular liberal Jews that eat pork in Tel Aviv or Haifa are the enemy that must be defeated.

During the night of November 4, 1995 the Israelis and the world had to face the unthinkable Prime Minister Yitzhak Rabin, the man

---

11. *Le Monde*, December 17, 2009.

of the Oslo agreements was killed not by a Palestinian but by an ultra orthodox Jewish fanatic. The rabbis that called for Rabin's death were never questioned. Incidents did oppose the ultra orthodox to the rest of society in Israel. Jerusalem and its suburbs saw multiple incidents of tension between Jews. Yet a secular Jew was elected mayor during the last elections. After five years of ultra orthodox administration Holy City businessman Nir Barkat became mayor with 52.4 percent of the vote. Politically close to Netanyahu the new mayor had campaigned on the unity of Jerusalem ruling out any concessions to the Palestinians on East Jerusalem.

But in the Holy City more than anywhere else in Israel nothing is simple. The two main candidates were close on many issues such as Israeli control of Jerusalem and continued settlements in East Jerusalem. These positions gave the new mayor part of the ultra orthodox vote representing 27 percent of the population. His main opponent, Rabbi Meir Porush, received 43.4 percent of the vote. As a member of the Knesset since 1996 in a small religious party he presented his candidacy as the heir to the former mayor, also a rabbi. Only 42 percent of those eligible took part in the vote due to a Palestinian boycott.

On May 20, 2008, *Haaretz* reported the following incident: messianic Jews—they number about 10,000 in Israel and consider Jesus as their savior, they are also known as "Jews for Jesus"—had handed out hundreds of copies of the New Testament and missionary brochures. The books were piled up and burned not far from a synagogue, according to the daily *Maariv* hundreds of students at a Talmudic school took part in that *autodafé*. To many Israelis the thought of Jews burning books is intolerable due to the association of such acts to the Nazis when they burned books by Jewish authors and religious books during the Second World War. Yet this burning did happen.

Last year arsonists entered a church in Jerusalem used by some messianic Jews and set the building on fire. No one claimed responsibility but the same church had been burned twenty five years before by ultra orthodox Jews. Some confrontations between secular and orthodox can also seem strange to the outside observer and

Israeli reporters have called recent events the "Sabbath War." One thousand orthodox Jews demonstrated on August 1, 2009, in Jerusalem for several weeks against the opening of a parking lot on the Sabbath. Some 700 demonstrators blocked the entrance of the lot near the old city of Jerusalem because the Saturday opening offended the sacred day of rest and caused the protest.

The protesters that displayed passive resistance were evacuated by the police and mounted units that made several arrests. A second demonstration that included a few hundred pious Jews dressed in traditional garb took place without incident in the ultra orthodox area of Méa Shéarim, in West Jerusalem. The ultra-orthodox that represent over one third of the Jewish population viewed the parking lot as blasphemous and encouraging car traffic and the opening of Jewish-owned stores.

Some ultra orthodox groups go so far as to oppose the State of Israel in the name of religious tradition. During the summer of 2009 in the Jewish neighborhoods of Jerusalem one could read slogans such as: "The Holy Land will expel the Zionists and their friends in the country." The Haredim or "Those fearful of the Almighty" have their neighborhoods, schools, cities, stores and political parties. They live under the guidance of the rabbis that provide the only legitimate source of power.

A book published in 2009 and quickly banned called for the legitimate preventive killing of "Gentiles" including women and children in case of war. If Gentiles is the word that describes non-Jews in the book entitled *Torah Hamelech* "The King's Torah" the author was designating the Arabs for the most part. Two ultra nationalist, Dov Lior of Kiryat Arba[12] and Yaakov Yossef, support the book and offer a justification of the "preventive murder" of non-Jews. Only in July 2011 would they be briefly detained and after many hesitations, Benjamin Netanyahu finally stated that "the law applies equally to all," rabbi or not.

The matter was revelatory of the influence of religious groups in Israeli society…and the editorial in *Maariv* "Rabbi Lior embodies the

---

12. The rabbi is a follower of Baruch Goldstein, responsible for the massacre of 29 Palestinians praying at the Cave of the Patriarchs in 1994.

creeping change we have witnessed for years; the transformation of a democratic state into an eschatological kingdom." A former Israeli ambassador also notes the importance of religion in public life. Freddy Eytan, writes: "in Israel the ministry of religious affairs was abolished but rabbis and civil servants were not fired, a unique occurrence that takes place only in Israel." The only democracy in the region where civil marriages are not authorized and agnostic burials are not possible…It is high time to do away with religious diktats and the rabbis from the affairs of the Jewish state and avoid the confusion of religion and politics that threatens freedom.[13]

---

13. *Sharon, le bras de fer*, Jean Picollec éditeur, 2006.

Chapter 5

Turkey Between East and West

Conservative Islam or a New Ottoman State

Since 2002, the country of Mustapha Kemal Atatürk has been run by a conservative Islamic government. Recept Erdogan used European style reforms to marginalize the army within the institutions. The army attempted but failed to prevent Erdogan 's political ally Abdullah Gül from being elected president. In June 2011 for the third consecutive time the AKP (Party of Justice and Development) won parliamentary elections with improved margins. One month later the army chief of staff and the heads of the three branches (air force, ground troops and navy) resigned. Some 250 military men including 14 generals and 58 colonels were incarcerated for "plotting against the government."

Modern Turkey has a secular constitution and some feel that the foundations of the Kemalist republic have been endangered. The conservative Islamic government has been the target of the army and of the staunch followers of the founder of the republic. Yet the government is now the guarantor of fundamental rights.

Turkish ties to Brussels have long been in place and Turkey's candidacy to the EU has brought about deep changes within the country. The membership procedure forces the candidates to harmonize its laws and conform to the other members. Under the military dictatorships Turkey enforced the death penalty and encroachments on fundamental rights were condemned by Brussels. The Erdogan government intends to align the legal system and practice to the European laws.

While remaining a candidate to the European Union, and attached to its Muslim roots between East and West, Turkey has come a long way. Where will Recept Erdogan take it? Abdullah Gül's term will end in 2014. Should Recept Erdogan be elected, he would have guided Turkey from 2002 to 2021, while the AKP membership expects the Islamization of society.

Religion was excluded from public affairs while Mustapha Kemal was in power.[1] This represented a break with the Ottoman Empire that had been the standard bearer of Islam for six centuries with the Grand Caliphate. The choice of such a forced westernization to enter modernity and create a constitutional secular state also helped usher a pluralist parliamentary system. In the course of six decades Turkey has become a democracy in spite of three interruptions when military juntas seized power. Differentiating between public and private spheres, the creation of a civil society founded on a dynamic market economy are the elements that have created contemporary Turkey as a NATO member and a candidate for the EU. Movements in the Arab Muslim world gave an aura to the Islamists governing in Ankara. Without specific form of influence some Tunisians as well as the Muslim Brotherhood in Egypt refer to the Turkish model as the ideal regime of conservative Islam.

From Islamism to Conservative Islam

The Islamist political movement had already been part of government coalitions in the past: in 1974 it had won the mayoral

---

1. 1923-1950.

elections in large cities and in 1994 its candidates were elected in Istanbul and Ankara.

The Islamist political movement was based on the party that had decided upon a legalist attitude thereby excluding the radical Muslims. In 1997 the army forced the resignation of the Islamist Prime Minister Necmettin Erbakan who had decided upon a legalist strategy. During parliamentary elections in 1999, the party was defeated because of the ambiguities in its program. The leadership attempted to reconcile nationalism while calling for fraternal relations with the Kurds; displaying democratic aspirations and a return to religious values. They claimed their attachment to a liberal economy while promising to enforce a "just" Islamic social system to take over the state through local government and by taking part in coalitions. This stance transformed the movement into a moderate well integrated political force.

The AKP now holds the presidency with Abdullah Gül, it also heads the government with a majority in parliament after modifying its program and describing itself as democratic, conservative and pro-European—the party may now be called conservative Islamic. On November 3, 2002, with 34,3 percent of the vote AKP obtained the absolute majority (363 seats to 178 for the CHP) as it came to power. The West viewed that result as the political Islamization of Turkey but nothing could be farther from the truth and at first the AKP received a protest vote. The new party was built on the ashes of the Islamist party and represented an alternative to the discredited left that had no program and a right that was closer to the people but without an electoral base. Turkey went through serious economic problems for two years and was facing a political crisis. The CHP led coalition created instability leading to new elections.

Recept Erdogan, the future prime minister and leader of the AKP was able to draw on the lessons of history. Sultan Abdulhamid II (1876-1908) had attempted a pro-Islamic policy to stave off the crumbling of the Ottoman Empire but ended in failure. Religion couldn't be the basis of a political structure. Erdogan used a rational approach instead and focused on unity where neo-fundamentalist Islam would have gone into fragmentation and splits in the social and political structures. He was reassuring when he declared himself in favor of Turkey's candidacy to the EU.

The Turkish situation appears to indicate that in a democracy taking power can transform political Islam into a position closer to nationalism. Turkish political scientists equate the AKP to the Bavarian CSU under Franz Josef Strauss a Christian Nationalist supporting the CDU. The AKP is seen as such by a majority of Turks thereby distancing it from Islamist non-political movements that act in society but not within the institutions. Because of the Kemalist heritage moderate governmental Islamism never did work well with the existing institutions. The first attempt to destabilize the government would be the issue of the scarf.

Democracy vs. Government of Judges

The AKP passed an amendment in parliament authorizing wearing the scarf because: "the prohibition of the scarf imposed after the military putsch of 1980 went against freedom of conscience and the right to education." In June 2008 the Constitutional Court ruled against wearing the Islamic scarf inside the universities. After a seven hour debate on the motion by the secular opposition the eleven judges voided the amendment passed by the national assembly since it violated the fundamental laws that describe the secular nature of the republic of Turkey. The verdict had caused a lot of criticism since it appeared to be outlawing the conservative Islamic party in power. The prosecutor of the court of appeals demanded the punishment along with the political banishment of 71 accused AKP members including Prime Minister Recept Erdogan because of the party's actions against secularism.

The matter took on a different dimension because the president of the republic, the prime minister, 38 deputies some of them cabinet ministers, and local politicians were all democratically elected officials. The vote of the president of the constitutional court was to make the difference. The party would not be dissolved but would have to pay fines to allow the court to save face. International public opinion and American and European governments were apprehensive following a verdict that would ban the AKP and push the country into a hard line Islamic regime with the risk of a military coup d'état. At the same time former high ranking military leaders were being indicted for conspiring with right wing groups to overthrow the president and the prime minister.

In July 2009 the High Court attempted to block the trials of the military leaders thereby obstructing the judicial process. The council wanted to organize the appointments and career rotations so that the prosecutor and judges would have to drop the case. The Ergenekon affair was the first time retired generals and other officers had to testify in court about "putsch projects" from the 2003-04 period, following the AKP's election victory. After many meetings Erdogan secured an agreement from the army chief of staff to allow the trials to take place.

Turkey was the symbol of NATO against the Communist bloc and its army was always the second strongest in the alliance with 600,000 men. But the Turkish government in Ankara still has some old issues to resolve: the occupation of Cyprus, the struggle against the Kurds and the responsibility it refused to acknowledge in the Armenian genocide. Yet Turkey remains the necessary ally for the United States even after the fall of communism. It has common borders with Iraq and Iran and is close to Afghanistan. It is the destination of the BTC (Baku, Tbilisi, Ceyhan) oil pipeline that brings oil from Azerbaijan. The terminal is a symbol of Turkey's importance to the West located close to a NATO military base. Turkey is also in line to join the European Union.

Relations between Islam and the state are all the more important since the country is undecided about its place on the international scene. Should she lean toward Europe or the Turkic speaking republics of the Caucasus? The Arab world in revolt is turning increasingly to Turkey as a model of democracy within Islamic conservatism and the Turks aspires to play a dominant role in the Arab Muslim world.

Kemal and the Limits of the Secular Myth

Mustapha Kemal also known as Atatürk, meaning "Father of the Turks" remains the myth of modern Turkey. Even though he set up a republic the power he created wasn't anywhere close to being a democracy. As a military man he marched Turkey on the double to a model of society without any prior debate. Mustapha Kemal wanted to be a revolutionary and historians call the period the "Kemalist revolution." The Kemalist party today even in decline intends to act as the guardian of that heritage. Recently it still could count on the army General Yasar Büyükanit, army chief of staff,[2] reminded everyone that the military played a major role as guardians of the Kemalist heritage:

"The Turkish armed forces position on secularism has not changed. Neither before me, nor with me or after me." His successor Ilker Basbug (2008-2010), repeated the same ideas. Favorable to a strong alliance with NATO and Israel he is considered a euro skeptic. When Brussels complained that the army was slowing down the democratization of the country, he answered in 2006: "The Turkish armed forces always have and always will defend the nation state, the unified state and the secular state."

In 1908, the Turkish revolution intended to overthrow an old political order. Kemal wanted to transform the Empire into a modern nation state, putting an end to the medieval theocracy and replacing it with a constitutional republic while transitioning from a feudal bureaucracy to a modern capitalist economy. His original project was to separate the Sultanate from the Caliphate where the caliph would be an Ottoman prince having exclusively religious powers. This "compromise" was intended to appease the religious opponents to change.

Once in power Kemal did away with Koranic law and separated Islam from the state in a quest to end the power of religion and religious leaders. In his vision of a modern state anything linked to politics, the economy, social and cultural affairs had to be subjected to secular political power. The criminal code of 1926 draws the line between politics and religion (article 263): "It is forbidden to create political associations based on religion or religious feelings." That same code (articles 241 and 242) provides for the punishment of religious leaders and preachers that while ministering to the faithful

---

2. 2006-2008.

discredit the administration, the laws or regulations passed by the executive branch.

While relegating religious practice to the specific locations of worship—all processions were forbidden—and therefore to the private sphere he still didn't create a truly separate system. A control and tutelage of religion by politics was set up with two new administrative entities: a presidency of religious affairs—appointed and responsible to the prime minister that administers the mosques, monasteries, appoints the imams and the preachers. The head of the religious foundations administers the organizations that the state has taken over such as land and buildings and after 1931, the compensation of religious employees.

The issue of religious training also comes under the authority of the state and a theological college was created at Istanbul University where the education and training of the clergy were part of the state's responsibilities. In 1928 Turkish became the language of worship and all prayers and homilies were no longer given in Arabic but in the national language. This decision led to a vote in parliament to translate the Koran and the teachings of the Prophet into a national edition having the government's approval. But that project would never be completed. In 1929 the teaching of Arabic and Persian, the cultural language, were forbidden in secondary schools.

Faced with protest and a drop in students in theology (in nine years they went from 264 to 20), the state had to close the Istanbul school. Arabic was reintroduced in the mosques and in 1933 to prove to the public that its political line had not changed the government ordered that the call to prayer switch from Arabic to Turkish with a new melody composed by the Ankara conservatory of music.

Kemal achieved his real revolution in 1924 with two decrees: on April 8 he did away with Koranic courts of law and on September 11 a commission of jurists adapted the Swiss civil code to Turkey. Its work was approved by parliament on February 17, 1926, and the new code was adopted in October of the same year. What had changed was at the heart of the Muslim religion meaning family rights: polygamy and repudiation were forbidden and replaced by civil marriage and divorce. A Muslim woman was allowed to marry a non-Muslim man.

While in 1924 the constitution specified that "Islam is the religion of the Turkish State" on April 10, 1928, Kemal felt strong enough to have it amended and erased the mention of religion thus transforming Turkey into a secular state. On December 26, 1926, he decided to adopt the Gregorian era and calendar. In Kemal's Turkey as in today's conservative Islamic regime, the fate of religious minorities was not at all enviable. Only the Christian and Jewish minorities were recognized by the Constitution. If Christians were the victims of violence or injustice these were at the initiative mostly of nationalists and the far right. Another religious minority, the Alevis representing about 25 percent of the population has always been excluded from national life and is not recognized as Muslim. Since they are part of a branch of the Shia, the Sunni do not recognize them as true Muslims therefore the Alevis are politically often members of left wing parties and suffer from religious, cultural and social discrimination. In a secular republic as in the conservative Islamic regime it is best to belong to the Sunni majority than to a minority and better be Christian or Jewish rather than a Shia Alevi.

The Kemalist revolution wasn't only intent on creating a secular society and the fundamental objective was to westernize Turkey. The visible signs of the Ottoman tradition and culture were Kemal 's main focus and he imposed western forms of dress in a decision to break with the past. In October 1927, Kemal explained: "We had to abolish the fez that stood on people's heads as a symbol of ignorance, negligence and hatred of progress and civilization to replace it with the hat as used by the civilized world and demonstrate that the Turkish nation in its thinking and in other ways is not at all outside civilized social life." Kemal proceeded step by step: in September 1925 he made western dress and hats mandatory for government workers. Two months later the law of November 25 made hats mandatory for all men while wearing a fez became a crime.

Then came the issue of the veil: on August 30, 1925, in a speech at Kastamonu, he offered his views on women's dress: "Should the mothers and daughters of a civilized nation wear these strange things

and look so uncivilized? It makes the whole nation look ridiculous."
He ended his appeal with an urgent call to action that would go
unheeded: "We must change this immediately." Only in 1935, at the
People's Party congress would the issue of lifting the veil reappear
but without any resolution.

The Return of Religion After Kemal

In 1938 at the time of Ataturk's death did Turkey experienced a
return to religion? With the ratification of the Charter and its
membership in the United Nations accompanied by a multiparty
political system, Turkey entered a new era. The fact that Turkey like a
large part of the Muslim world and the Grand Mufti of Jerusalem
during the Second World War sympathized with the Axis was quickly
forgotten.

A slow evolution began following Kemal's death that changed the
nature of the imperial institutions that had shaped him. In 1940 the
government decided to reintroduce Muslim chaplains to army units
and the renewed freedom of expression and democracy allowed the
religious representatives to express their opposition to secularism.

Parliament took up the issue of religious education.[3] Several
deputies from the majority were in favor of religious education in the
schools. After the prime minister refused, a compromise was reached:
in 1949 the government proposed two classroom hours on Saturday
afternoons for children having their parent's consent. An over-
whelming majority of children enrolled in the program and the
ministry of education and the presidency of religious affairs published
a textbook about Islam. In October 1950 another step was taken
when religious education became compulsory.

In 1949, in order to train more clerics the government reestablished the theology school at the university which was moved
symbolically from Istanbul to Ankara, the new capital. A chair in
Islamic art and another in the history of religions were also created.
The other significant and conspicuous change was the heightened
attendance in the mosques where sound was piped to those outside

---

3. December 24, 1946.

indicating a return of religion in public spaces. Publishing and religious newspapers also reappeared. Even when the government was refusing to allow any foreign exchange 9,000 Turks were able to travel to Mecca in a pilgrimage in 1950.

The reality of Islam deeply implanted into Turkish society and not simply in the traditionally religious layers of the population such as merchants and the peasantry is obvious. While religious practice is weaker among intellectuals and university students it has made strong inroads among civil servants in the army and in parliament. In broad terms, religion is more attractive to the generations that had experienced the early years of Kemalism than among westernized and educated youth. It is found more in remote rural areas than in Istanbul on the western side and on the Black Sea.

The return to religion has its roots in the reaction to Kemal's decision and, as Thierry Zarcone has shown, in 1925 when he shut down the Sufi brotherhoods he deprived the population of the simplest signposts of Islam very much removed from Islamist rigor. Sufism represented an alternative to fundamentalist Islam and was the main vehicle of sociability for the Muslims in the Ottoman Empire in the nineteenth century. In 1895 there were 350 tekkes (convents) in Istanbul and the Sufi brotherhoods reappeared in the 1950s.

Sufism is multifaceted with millions of followers and the largest brotherhoods such as the Mehlevis are Sunni while the Bekhtasi are originally Shia. Beyond these differences some brotherhoods have tribal origins for example the Nakchibandiye included many Turkish politicians among them Turgut Ozal (who was president from 1989 to 1993) and the current Prime Minister Recept Erdogan. As for the influence of Sufism today a novel explanation comes from researcher Ural Manço, at the Free University at Brussels: "The Islamism of the brotherhoods doesn't appear to be a threat to Turkey but rather a challenge. Their evolution may reinforce tolerance, individual freedom and the movement of ideas and favors the cultural globalization of Turkish society."[4]

---

4. Riva Kastoryano / *Cahier d'études sur la Méditerranée orientale et le monde turco-iranien*, January-June 1992.

Change was palpable within the country, the population since the early years of the republic had greatly increased (13,5 million in 1927, 18 in 1940, almost 19 in 1945) and with it greater urbanization. Literacy was also on the upswing (10,6 percent in 1927, 30,2 percent in 1945). The parliamentary elections of 1950 with newspapers and radio were the first democratic vote held in the country: 88 percent participation elected 408 deputies of the Democratic party, 69 of the Popular Republican party, 1 national party and 9 independents. Atatürk's Popular Republican party was defeated. Turkey joined NATO in 1952 becoming a front line ally of the West in the Cold War facing the Soviet threat.

The Turks as Europeans

Because of Germany's manpower needs it signed a bilateral convention with Turkey in 1961 while other countries already had similar treaties: Italy in 1955, Spain and Greece in 1960, Portugal in 1962 and Yugoslavia in 1968. Through immigration the Turks entered Europe and in 1963 Brussels and Ankara entered into an association agreement between Turkey and the EEC. Between 1961 and 1973 foreigners living in West Germany went from 686,000 to 3,966,000 of which 2,595,000 were actively employed. During the 1973 worldwide recession due to the oil crisis Germany closed its borders and encouraged unemployed foreign workers to return home. Just before reunification in 1989, that would trigger immigration to Germany from Eastern Europe, there were 1,613,000 Turks in the Federal Republic representing the largest foreign contingent in West Germany. The original immigration came mostly from the western part of Turkey including people who had been completely secularized with a higher cultural and educational standard than the waves of Turks that were to follow.

Those Turks were atypical and ready to be flexible to adapt and assimilate, a process that was interrupted in spite of children born in Germany during the initial immigration and educated in that country's schools. As an indication of that first wave, the fertility rate of Turkish women in Germany fell between 1975 and 1984 from 4.3

to 2.5 children per woman. In France by comparison, the number of children per immigrant woman was higher (Algerians: 4.2; Moroccans: 4.5; Tunisians: 4.7). Between 1971 and 1985 the tendency to marry outside the clan was lower from 49 to 24 percent among men and 28 to 7 percent for women among the Turks living in Germany.

Another phenomenon contributing to this change was the law on nationality that was passed as of January 1, 2000, replacing the old legislation. There were several ways to acquire German nationality including filiations.

> The filiations principle states that a child acquires German nationality at birth if at least one of the two parents is a German national. Being born on German territory is a new way to acquire German citizenship. A child born of foreign parents automatically acquires German nationality at birth if one of the two parents resides legally and habitually in Germany for at least eight months and has permanent residency or has a resident's permit for undetermined time for at least three years. This child usually also acquires the nationality of his parents as well. Once he comes of age and until 23 years he may choose one nationality or the other. If he declares wanting to keep his parent's nationality he will then lose German citizenship.[5]

While the law encourages integration few Turks in Germany took advantage of it. The real or perceived exclusion of a large community often ends up with a return to its original cultural and religious identity as well as the tendency to look inward. The small number of "mixed" marriages limited the importance of the law meant to encourage the naturalization of foreign children but on the margins of German society the young man of 23 responding to the pressure of his environment would give up German nationality and opt for that of his parents.

In the Hesse region with an estimated 200,000 adults of Turkish origin only 40,000 requested German citizenship and became part of the voters' lists. While the multi cultural debate has sharpened the religious identity of the community has also been redefined. Among

---

5. *Le Monde*, July 9, 2010.

younger Turks even though the future bride and groom may live in Germany, most decide to return to Turkey to get married as a way of restating their national and religious identity. There are other factors in the inward tendency of Turks in Germany: the reduction of exogamy translates into a growing segregation within society. Marriage outside the ethnic group fell from 24 to 10 percent in 1990 for men and from 7 to 2 percent for women. Two more elements accentuate the isolation of the community: lower school performance compared to German children and other immigrant communities from the former Yugoslavia and a higher unemployment rate.

Studies made of Turkish immigrant workers and their social groups in France and Germany point to ethnic, regional and village connections in the formation of communities and local societies in the host countries. Such organizations favor the transmission and maintenance of traditional values and religious beliefs. Between 1965 and 1985, Muslim fundamentalism increasingly became the dominant religious and ideological characteristic among Turkish immigrants. A direct consequence was the growing fertility rate among Turkish women in Germany after 1990 that rose to 3.4 children per woman.

At the end of the 1980s the Islamist organization Milli Görüs became dominant among Turks in Germany while the closely related Prosperity Party[6] only obtained 16,9 percent of the vote in the 1991 elections in Turkey. Distance from the homeland increased the degree of fundamentalism which also appears in France where Alsace-Lorraine has been a welcoming region for Turks that is closely related to immigration in Germany and recently on the increase. The problems relating to the veil have been more acute in those areas and the first criminal case due to a crime of honor was in the French city of Colmar.

The Turkish government has always been interested in maintaining contact with immigrants that represent the largest Muslim group within Europe with religion playing a leading role. The organization of religion abroad is an area that the authorities were very much concerned with and the imams are appointed by the government in Ankara. This situation existed long before the current con-

---

6. Islamist party founded in 1983 opposed to Turkey's entry into the European Union.

servative Islamic government and was handled by the Turkish embassies since the 1970s. The imams are connected to the associations that are managed directly by the religious affairs diplomatic representatives. The Turkish state is the most efficient organizer of the cultural life of its citizens: today, every two weeks, Ankara sends out by email the themes for the homily at the Friday prayer to the appropriate official in charge of religious affairs. Even though fundamentalism is the main characteristic of Turkish immigration it should be viewed in proper perspective.

As with all religions those most attached to tradition are more visible and more apt to proselytize than others. The immigrants had no role in the rise of political Islamism in Ankara and Turkish law doesn't allow voting by mail or by proxy. The voter must be physically in the precinct where he or she is eligible to vote. Unlike Algeria and Morocco where elected officials represent the immigrant populations, the Turks have no such elected officials. The Turkish population outside the country is both ethnically and religiously diverse and ideologically divided: the Turks are opposed to the Kurds, the secular are against the religious, Sunni against Shia and the right is opposed to the left.

A Regional and Strategic Power

When Iran lived through its Islamic revolution the risk of contagion to Turkey did not come up.

The country is mostly Sunni and the Turkish army and the United States would not have accepted the spread of the Iranian revolution to the country. In any case there was no reason for the influence to extend into Turkey as much for economic and sociological reasons even though there is a strong Alevi Shia population. A majority of the population including the military is opposed to them as heretics. However the changes in Iran sparked a political awakening among the most traditionalist Muslims in Turkey. In Istanbul in the 1980s the veil reappeared in the poorest sections and among the lower classes.

The best way for the international community to reduce the fundamentalist threat was for Turkey to be part of NATO and to join the European Union as proposed by Erdogan. While the prime minister has not given up on the project the obstacles to his candidacy require for him to go in a different direction and extend Turkey's influence and authority in the Muslim world.

Erdogan and the AKP: Neo-Ottoman Politics

The influence game led to competition between Tehran and Ankara. Both countries are seeking to become the main power in the region. Until now Iran remains isolated among the nations and Turkey has not yet recognized the Armenian genocide and must face the Kurd problem. Its proximity to Israel that was an advantage in the recent past could become a handicap. Turkish diplomacy wanted to act as a mediator because of its good relations with Israel until public opinion showed growing support for the Palestinians. Erdogan understood the winds of historical change and the wishes of the people: in January 2009 he criticized Shimon Peres at the Davos Forum and received an enthusiastic welcome when he returned home from Switzerland.

It signaled the beginning of a long series of incidents with Jerusalem. As a consequence to the attack on the Gaza flotilla—a ship under the Turkish flag being used by a Turkish Islamist NGO—was boarded by Israeli commandos, Ankara decided to cancel joint maneuvers with Israel. Turkey thereby became the nation that had peacefully opposed Israel showing solidarity with the Palestinian people.

In the summer of 2010 Turkey took an initiative that further reinforced its stature as a regional power. Ankara became the main player in an agreement on the enrichment of Iranian uranium signed with Brazil and Iran. As the wall of fear is falling in the Arab world and people demand more freedom and justice, Ankara is staking its claim to the Arab Street that was held by Tehran.

To the Arabs Iran represents an exception in the Muslim world. There are two sides to the confrontation: Arabs vs. Persians and Shia vs. Sunni. In Saudi Arabia, besides the fear that Saudi Shia who are the majority can inspire in the highest leaders of the kingdom, they call the Shia heretics and condemn the efforts at proselytizing by their neighbor. King Abdullah in July 2010 was calling for the disappearance of Israel and Iran and revealed the deep fears that influence the keeper of the Muslim holy places. In Bahrain as well the majority Shia are victims of the Sunni minority: the kings and princes of the Persian Gulf prefer Ankara to Tehran. In spite of the historical antagonism between Arabs and Ottomans to Arab governments a Turkish leadership of the Arab-Muslim world is seen as the lesser of two evils. Regarding Israel, the Arabs willingly admit their inability to find a solution to the Palestinian conflict and their fear of an arrogant Iran threatening the Jewish state. The question is whether Turkey, conservative Muslim and Sunni, and Shia Iran intend to find out who will be the leader in the region.

For Turkey the objective is to conquer the Arab Street as spelled out by Foreign Minister Ahmet Davutoglu. It must act in its natural environment that is both Arab and Islamic in the Near East and among the Turkic speaking republics of Central Asia. Ankara is attempting to strengthen its ties to all Muslim countries in the region including Syria and Iran; becoming a mediator as in the nuclear deal with Brazil; and trying to become the policeman in Syria but without much to show for it for the moment while turning its back, relatively speaking, to Israel. A complete break with Israel is not part of this move and not a serious possibility. The wind of revolt that has swept the Arab world makes it necessary for Israel to consolidate its alliances in the region.

The resetting of Turkish foreign policy was made necessary by history: the role of NATO has changed with the demise of the Soviet Union and Ankara is no longer the western outpost against the red menace. Turkey has attempted to show its value in the alliance against the green threat, on the border of Iran and Iraq and its proximity to Afghanistan; also as a terminal for oil and gas to the West as opposed to Russian imperialism.

The other issue is Ankara's keen interest in joining the EU which has been delayed if not barred by France whose attitude is misunderstood not just in Turkey but also in the rest of the Arab world. The secular groups that mostly represent the business community see the position of the French as politically aberrant and economically self defeating. Joining the union is a way of channeling Islamism in Turkey and avoiding future excesses. On the other hand the Turkish Street and most Turkish immigrants in Europe see this as an anti-Islamic position. France's attitude toward Turkey has deteriorated even more after the Arab revolts. The Union for the Mediterranean promoted by Nicolas Sarkozy was a device to stop Turkey from joining the European Union. Both Arab promoters of the Union for the Mediterranean Ben Ali and Mubarak were vice presidents of that short-lived group and are no longer in power so the project is now defunct.

Turkey's candidacy will find a new supporter in British Prime Minister David Cameron. During an official visit to Ankara in July 2010, he stated; "When I think about what Turkey has done to defend Europe as a NATO ally and what Turkey is doing today in Afghanistan alongside our European allies, it makes me angry that your progress towards EU membership can be frustrated in the way that it has been. My view is clear: I believe it is just wrong to say that Turkey can guard the camp but not be allowed to sit in the tent."

While Ankara and Tehran both try to dominate the Arab Street the question is who will sign a "Yalta" type agreement and take the leadership of the region to use the expression of Antoine Basbous.[7] Will the winner be a resurgent Persia or a new Ottoman empire? Events in the Arab Muslim world and the need to identify with a leader or a country offer a new perspective to this race. While Ankara was close to Israel as an intermediary between Damascus and Jerusalem, everything has changed with the Syrian revolt.

Turkey has become the discreet supporter of the opposition to Bashar al-Assad and while Jordan and Lebanon refused to allow the opposition to hold meetings, Turkey agreed. In April 2011 Syrian groups that are close to the Muslim Brotherhood held a meeting; later in June all those opposed to the regime in Damascus met at Antalya to prepare for the regional Yalta. Faced with the madness in

---

7. See *Le Monde*, reported by Guillaume Perrier, June 8, 2011.

Damascus the Muslim world woke up. On August 9, 2011, King Abdullah of Saudi Arabia the strongest financial supporter of Syria decided to recall his ambassador while Erdogan was clearly telling Bashar al-Assad that the situation could not last. The following day he sent the foreign minister to tell him as much.

In the race for leadership Turkey is very well positioned to increase its power and influence in the region. Iran is a victim of its isolation but is starting to secularize and the regime knows it must change. While Turkey has undeniable regional power status its internal situation is not as clear after many leaders of the Arab spring referred to the Turkish political model: the relationship between Islam and politics is changing. Today we can see the hegemonic tendencies of the Islamic party in power.

By reintroducing religion into politics the AKP has provided greater social exposure to Sunni Islam. Turkish society is filled with religion that coincides with the weakening of the secular old guard represented by the Kemalist party that lost its credibility during the scandals of the electoral campaign in June 2011 that included the taping of the sexual trysts of its leaders. The AKP managed to control the army and the legal system and this strengthening of the executive comes as Islam reestablishes its identity. As Europe rejects Turkey, Ankara tries to assert itself among its neighbors and in the Arab world as the regional power.

After the June 2011 elections and a new success for the AKP what will Erdogan 's choices be for Turkey?

Beyond the respectability of Turkish leaders and a prosperous economy, the leadership must take into account the aspirations of the political base. Turkish Islamism is not a homogenous movement. Besides the hardening of the religious ideological position of the prime minister's party, according to the media, the religious fraternity of Fethullah Gülen represents the fundamentalist wing of Turkish Islam: with 3 million members, a banking and media empire and an entrepreneurs' association of over 30,000 businessmen, it comprises 30 of the 200 largest companies in the country. It is basically a state within the state with the power to serve the interests of the AKP.

The Fethullah Gülen community can count on having someone in every decision making agency (government, secret service etc.) and within society (teachers, imams, government officials, and businessmen) that is the result of an easy access policy. The business leaders of the community organize the visits of the head of state overseas lately to Indonesia, Gabon or Ghana. As the president of Tükson said "Our strategy follows that of the state." This is similar to all leadership groups around the world but the difference here is that the initiative is more sophisticated and includes ulterior motives: the Turks are becoming the new Chinese in Africa. Businesses have found new markets and exports have grown to 140 million Euros in 2011 or five times what they were in 2005. As of the end of 2011 Ankara had 30 embassies abroad vs. 6 in 2006.

There are also other tools the community uses to increase its influence: since the 1990s it was present in Central Asia with its "missionaries" and its schools. The Turkish government attributes the greatest importance to the Turkic speaking parts of Central Asia. Called the "Jesuit of Islam" by the faithful, Gülen requests that they build schools rather than mosques; a first school was opened in France at Villeneuve-Saint-Georges.

Fethullah Gülen was living in exile in the United States ever since legal proceedings were opened against him in 1999 because of the risks he represented to the Turkish government. In 2008 he was given amnesty and his dream was to have enough influence to reform the constitution. His right hand man announced their strategy which is to support the AKP so it obtains the relative majority and those elected with Gülen's support can proceed to the Islamization of the constitution. His supporters find Erdogan unreliable and weak; while Shia Iran becomes more secular, Sunni Turkey the country of Kemal could go in the other direction. Another development that could be ominous: when Libyan authorities allowed free internet access, the government in Ankara decided to limit and control its access.

Chapter 6

The Rise of the Muslim Brotherhood in the Middle East

In 2009, at al-Azhar University, the president of the United States spoke of a new beginning. America was holding out its hand to the Muslims. Eighteen months later at the beginning of 2011 the world was watching Tahrir Square. Every television network was broadcasting the images through al Jazeera. Once the Rais was gone what was the Egyptian revolution all about? Unlike the jasmine revolution in Tunisia the events in Egypt were to reverberate throughout the entire region.

In the sub consciousness of public opinion, Nasser's Egypt represented pan-Arabism and the greater Arab nation. With the Camp David Accords, Anwar Sadat and Egyptian diplomacy were given a mission by the West and a role in the affairs of the region. The final years of Mubarak's long tenure signaled the end of Cairo's influence.

With Facebook and Twitter, youth was at the center of events but with time reality forces us to conclude that it differs from the hopes and aspirations of the protesters. The army that was once praised is now criticized and the new Tahrir Square slogan is clear: "The people

want the demise of Marchal Tantawi" Cairo's new strongman and
defense minister since 1991. Even before Mubarak's fall, another
officer had the favor of the Americans had there been the candidacy
of Gamal Mubarak and Mohammed el-Baradei at the presidential
elections in 2011. The former was not acceptable at the time since the
opposition rejected it and the latter had little chance since the former
head of AIEA had no political base in his country.

That man was General Omar Suleiman. Washington saw in the
head of the secret service a fighter against Islamic Jihad and a man of
authority who wouldn't question the peace treaty with Israel.

Following Mubarak's departure there was order in Cairo. While
Egyptians hailed the army for a time, that institution remained neutral
during the protests. The officers, the military courts guaranteed the
transition and the powerful state security an institution that was hated
by both the people and the military that used to be controlled by the
police is no more and the army has occupied its offices. Egyptians are
asking questions as they find that a true democracy is very long in
coming.

The future of Egypt is filled with uncertainty and question marks
as much as its effect on the rest of the region. Will the Muslim
Brotherhood take power in Cairo soon? What will the Palestinians in
Jordan or Gaza do since the Brotherhood already had a sizeable
influence among them? Does the revolution mean even greater
isolation for Israel. Will Iran wield its influence in Lebanon in
support for Bashar al-Assad? Will there be any Christians left in
Egypt and the near east? What will happen to the Arab African world
after the partition of Sudan and the appearance of two blocs while
Christians and Muslims are staring at each other?

It was on January 28, 2011, that the Muslim Brothers and not the
fraternal organization itself, called the people to protest in Tahrir
Square, that the movement gathered its momentum. The position of
the Islamists is complicated. Some of them are prepared to accept a
"temporary military democracy" with the understanding that in due
course a regime similar to the AKP will take over in Egypt. Others
refuse to take part and call for an ideal Islamic State. Finally the
Brotherhood stated that it "opposed a religious state" and favored a

"civilian state with a religious reference." The brotherhood must also deal with competition from a powerful Salafist group that is rigorist, inflexible and violently anti-Christian.

The movement that has the support of Saudi Arabia is opposed to any action against the state as long as it remains "normally" Muslim. The Salafi groups have a bona fide political party called al-Nour (The Light).

The Jihadist movement that General Suleiman had effectively suppressed and whose true strength is unknown remains a question mark for the future. The Brotherhood played the card of constitutional legitimacy and contributed to an orderly transition since it wishes to have deputies elected to parliament but will not have a candidate for president. After some sixty years in the opposition or having been outlawed it waits for its moment. It was also affected by the wind of change in Tahrir Square and its younger militants were disappointed that the leadership didn't call on everyone to demonstrate against the Rais's regime during the early hours of the movement. They felt closer to the reformers that had been eliminated. They reject the fact that Bureau of Guidance which is the supreme decision making organ concentrates all power and is therefore cut off from the base. New personalities such as Mohammed Morsi have emerged as president of the Brotherhood students and today head of "Freedom and Justice" the new political party of the Brotherhood as he directs the television channel called symbolically "25 January" the date of the first demonstration in Cairo.

Hunting Down the Muslim Brothers

In the 1970s the Muslim Brotherhood wanted to set up an Islamic state. But that project couldn't take place in the political context of the time even though a multiparty system under state control did exist in Egypt. The project went beyond Egypt and in Syria Hafez al-Assad understood the danger it represented.

In February 1982 the Syrian regime had faced its first dangerous emergency. At Hama, Baath party members and regime officials had been assassinated. The victims were mostly Alawites, the Shia minority (12 to 15 percent of the population) from which the Adasa clan comes from. That action had been attributed to the Muslim Brotherhood. The prospect of a Brotherhood seizure of power was not impossible and Damascus reacted vigorously. Rifaat, the bother of President Hafez al-Assad, and the head of his Praetorian guard nicknamed the "Pink Panthers" was in charge of the battle of Hama where 15 to 20,000 Muslim Brothers were killed.

In Bashar al-Assad's Syria, exploiting the religious factor is a way of hiding human rights abuses. Faced with mass protest the regime is using every possible angle but even though they are weakened, the Muslim Brotherhood and Islamist groups remain very influential. One of the first reforms adopted during the Damascus spring in a meeting with Sunni leaders was the return to work of one thousand teachers that had been fired because they were wearing the niqab. The government also decided to close the only casino in the country.

The other face of the regime are the repressive measures against the population and the way they were carried out is highly significant. Damascus tried to justify the repression by saying that the Sunni wanted to "liquidate" the Christian minorities that represent 10 percent of the population along with the Alawites. The army surrounded Sunni neighborhoods with tanks and opened fire before attacking the population itself.

Under Sadat's presidency in Egypt the Muslim Brotherhood was tolerated but then, three years after the Camp David Accords, he was to be assassinated at a military parade in Cairo. In September 1981 one month before the assassination, Sadat had ordered a wave of arrests. Over 1,600 people including communists, Nasserites, Islamist militants and intellectuals were thrown in jail. The president also took on the Copts even though the foreign minister of his government, the Francophile future UN Secretary General, Butros Butros-Ghali was part of that religious group. Sadat ordered that Copt Orthodox Patriarch Pope Shenouda III be placed under house arrest at the Saint-Bishoy monastery and numerous Copt priests and religious leaders were also the victims of repression.

The army men who murdered the president were part of the Egyptian Islamic Jihad a movement that was opposed to any opening to Israel, a stance that was widely shared by Arab public opinion and their leaders. Yet despite the group's name it is impossible to ascribe any religious motivations to that action, perhaps there was a belated acknowledgement in the fatwa approving the murder by a previously unknown imam living in the United States, Omar Abdel Rahman. He was to gain attention later by organizing the first attack on the World Trade Center on February 26, 1993, in New York. When Mubarak took over the Muslim Brotherhood remained as under Sadat, outlawed but tolerated.

What was the nature of the brotherhood created in 1928 by Hassan el-Banna, an Egyptian school teacher whose grandson is Tariq Ramadan? The main objective is the creation of a great Islamic state founded on Sharia law. Nasser had outlawed the brotherhood in 1954 by forcing it to become a charitable organization. Most of its leaders were part of the Special Organization, the brotherhood's paramilitary branch before the 1952 revolution against King Farouk. By the end of the 1970s the brotherhood had become the most important religious movement in Egypt. It had successfully infiltrated the institutions and the state administration except for the army, the police and the higher echelons such as the presidency, the prime minister and the ministry of foreign affairs.

The main strength of the movement comes from its structure: each Brother is part of a 'usar,' the basic cell of the group. When Hosni Mubarak took power in 1981 he received all the representatives of the opposition except the Muslim Brotherhood. But since it is not a political party it must be viewed as a borderline legal movement. The fact that the older Brothers were not received by the president was proof that Mubarak had no intention of recognizing them. The younger generation reacted by wanting to break the isolation and become part of the legal political process. During the elections of 1984 the Muslim Brotherhood formed an alliance with the al-Wafd party to get some of their candidates elected to parliament. That strategy was repeated in 1987 when they ran for parliament with two legal political parties: al-Amal and al-Ahrar. The Guidance Bureau that is the supreme leadership of the brotherhood refuses to create a political party, a strategy that the younger generation has trouble accepting.

The Mubarak regime while gaining control over politics in Egypt was also liberalizing the economy by the emerging middle class far more interested in economic improvement than political power or religious issues. Yet the government still feared the power of the Muslim Brotherhood that had become a "parallel state" through its educational and social efforts and the fact that it stood apart from the political and official class of the regime. The most active Brothers are young and have not fallen prey to the temptations of corruption that have plagued the nomenklatura and the business class that developed around Mubarak.

During the 1990s the Muslim Brotherhood had 100 to 150,000 active militants not including many sympathizers. The parliamentary elections of 2005 were a turning point: politics had been frozen for ten years and without changing their strategy the Brotherhood managed to get 88 deputies out of 454 elected. Five years before that they only had 11 deputies in their camp. Barring the irregularities that took place the brotherhood should have garnered more deputies and even the majority in parliament. That success increased the membership and the influence they have in Egyptian society more than ever before.

Even if Obama invited some brotherhood members to his speech to the Muslims at al-Azhar University, not as members of the brotherhood but as personalities this didn't inhibit the government from its continued persecution. In 2010, Hosni Mubarak decided to attack the Muslim Brotherhood once again. Mahmoud Ezzat, deputy to the Guide of the Egyptian Muslim Brotherhood, was questioned along with other officials. The reason was simple according to the Brotherhood: "It is part of a state-sponsored campaign against the movement. The movement is preparing for parliamentary elections and the campaign aims at stopping such activity."

In mid-January a conservative Mohamed Badie, was elected head of the Brotherhood. His wish was to take part in the elections of 2010 even though he would be unable to repeat the results of 2005 given the government's determination against the movement. On November 28, 2010 Mubarak's party took 95 percent of the seats during the first round of voting. The Egyptian president had warned Washington, according to WikiLeaks published cables from diplomats of the danger the Muslim Brotherhood represented as an Islamist group that had the support of Iran. The main opposition group didn't win a single seat after the first round of voting. The legal opposition was also poorly represented and some like Mohamed el-Baradei had called for a boycott of the voting and were dreaming of a "parallel parliament." The main alternative candidate to Mubarak for the presidency was also legally barred from running because he had resided for many years outside Egypt as head of the AIEA. He was in fact an Egyptian citizen without any rights.

While the man called "the Sphinx of the Nile" appears mummified at his trial, there remains the question of what Egypt will be like in the future. While Mohamed el-Baradei has the support of the West for the presidential elections and perhaps of the Egyptians, a new political landscape will come out of the parliamentary elections. The Brotherhood represents the best organized political force today with deep roots in Egyptian society. The question remains as to the attitude of the army that has been in power for five decades and controls over 35 percent of the national economy.

The Coexistence of Religious Beliefs

The attack on the Copts on December 31 and January 1 in front of the Church of Two Saints in Alexandria—21 Christians killed and 71 wounded—wasn't simply in response to the call to Jihad by an Iraqi group affiliated with Al Qaeda in November 2009 against the Egyptian Coptic community. The Mubarak regime was playing on religious antagonisms particularly just before elections when tensions would escalate. When the revolt began Copts and Muslims were marching together in Tahrir Square and during the attacks the Muslim Brotherhood gave its support to the Christians. The period after Mubarak was not devoid of religious tensions and in March 2011, a few weeks after the fall of the regime, anti-Coptic violence began again and attacks in an eastern neighborhood of Cairo resulted in 13 killed and 140 wounded.

According to the Coptic clergy the attacks were the work of young delinquents—former Mubarak supporters—and Salafists. The Supreme military council, aware of the volatility of the situation, announced harsh penalties for anyone attacking places of worship.

Given the increasing Islamization of Egyptian society the Copts have withdrawn and are taking a community centered position. Many Muslims have the same attitude. The Copts are asking for a change in the law that restricts the construction of churches and the creation of a special rights statute since they consider themselves as second class citizens. They feel that the authorities have failed to take adequate security measures to protect them while they are the target of specific threats. The synod of Copitc bishops in Alexandria was critical of the lax attitude shown by the authorities in response to anti-Coptic statements that were made. Some Copt candidates in the elections didn't have the support of the parties in power since they were thought to be unable to defeat the Muslim Brotherhood. These facts create resentment. In the context of this religious violence if a Coptic woman is thinking of living with a Muslim man she will also be the target of her coreligionists.

The events in Alexandria were even more disturbing given the situation of Christians in the Near East who are, according to Pope Benedict XVI, the victims of a "strategy of violence." During his holiday address of 2011 and for the first time, Nicolas Sarkozy invited all 37 representatives of the eastern churches to France. They account for 300 to 500,000 people: Orthodox and Catholic including about 50,000 Copts. The French president recalled that they had been the object of "a particularly perverse plan of religious cleansing in the Middle East."

Who are the eastern Christians? Their total numbers are esti-mated at 11 million in 11 different churches with different rituals (Chaldean, Syrian-Catholic, Armenian, Syrian-Jacobite, Copt, Assyrian), without mentioning the Roman Catholics and the Protestants. The killings in Alexandria were unfortunately not the last violent incident; the day before, on December 30, about ten bombs were placed in front of the homes of Christians in Baghdad leaving a trail of death. Just before the Syriac cathedral in the Iraqi capital was the target of an al Qaeda commando assault leaving 53 dead. It would be mistaken however to view these incidents and something new. The Armenians were the strongest Christian community in the Muslim world and the Turkish authorities were behind the elimination of two thirds of the population: 1.5 million were killed.

In Iraq violence against Christians began during the 1920s. Thousands were being persecuted before they were given protection by Saddam Hussein's regime. The emblematic figure of the Baath Party was the Christian Foreign Minister Tariq Aziz. Al Qaeda's action against the Iraqi Christians is aimed at the Syriac Catholics: in November and December 2010, about 1,000 Christian families fled Baghdad and the exodus continues. In Egypt violence against the Copts also continues.

Besides the terrorist attacks the fact that most countries have signed an international pact on civilian and political rights in 1966 guaranteeing freedom of thought and of worship doesn't stop them from ignoring the fundamental principles. Many Muslim countries pass legislation—the law on blasphemy in Pakistan or regulations repressing proselytism in Algeria—that are as many attacks on those principles. The laws usually concern the Christian churches yet history and tradition show that Muslims have always tolerated and even protected those that the Koran calls the "People of the Book." Freedom of religion and its immediate corollary, freedom of conscience, are on the same level as freedom of expression and of opinion that are the very fabric of democracy. But how many Muslim countries can call themselves democratic?

Even if Christians were in the Near East long before the coming of the Prophet, the balance between religious communities has always been precarious. During the colonial period in contemporary history the authorities had ways of keeping the countries united and by doing so they protected certain groups. Today since they are a persecuted minority, Christians are the victims and a source of tension in the Middle East. Yet all responsibility should not be placed on the Muslims, Christians have also been guilty of horrible acts for example the Christian Phalanges in Lebanon and massacres such as those of Sabra and Shatila.

Returning to the Copts in Egypt, the Islamic threat against them came before and after the various elections. If Mubarak managed to eradicate the main radical Islamist groups he also encouraged the Salafist movements as a counterweight to the Muslim Brotherhood. But the Salafists are openly anti-Christian. On January 2, following the massacre of Christians in Alexandria, the Grand Imam of al-Azhar, Sheikh Ahmed al-Tayyeb, stated that "according to Koranic law and patriotic duty this heinous crime is forbidden and all Muslims condemn it." He also condemned the Pope's appeal to protect Christians as "an unacceptable intrusion."An appeal by the pontiff can only increase tensions in the future not only in Egypt but across the entire region. Many think that the pact between the Sunni and the Maronites of Lebanon cannot survive in such a context. On Sunday October 9, 2011 twenty-five Copts were again murdered in Cairo and the Egyptian army didn't remain neutral since the Copts were protesting quietly when they were attacked by the Salafists. The victims were shot by army troops or run down by military vehicles.

The Other Side of the Border

On November 7, 2009 the French daily *Le Monde* summed up the situation between Israel and the Palestinians in a cartoon. Mahmud Abbas had announced that he wouldn't seek a new mandate as president of the Palestinian Authority. He is drawn swallowed up with his hand holding a Palestinian flag saying: "Au revoir!" From behind the security wall an Israeli soldier calls out to him from the top of a minaret: "Are you talking to me?" a bearded Hamas militant answers: "No! There's only you and me!" Mahmud Abbas is still presiding over the Palestinian Authority and the situation has not changed

The "Egyptian spring" has brought about a change and what was unheard of yesterday is no longer impossible. In an interview on *Corriere della Sera*, one of the oldest Palestinian prisoners held in Israel, Marwan Barghouti, justified Hamas politically and otherwise: "The capture of Shalit allowed something no dialog would have obtained:

the liberation of 650 prisoners." Even though he didn't benefit from that decision he stated what his plans were: "My main objective is to unite the Palestinian factions. Once unity is achieved I will be ready to be a candidate to the presidency of Palestine." After the events in Egypt and the protest against the Jordanian monarchy by the Muslim Brotherhood the fact that Israel has not freed Barghouti only increases his prestige and the possibility of staking his claim some day.

Even before taking office many observers thought that Obama should make Israeli-Palestinian peace the main goal of his presidency. Even had he wished to do so priorities and events decided differently. Between the exit from Iraq the Iranian issue, the Pakistani-Afghan conundrum and the huge problems faced by the United States (recession, economic growth, and health care) the administration had trouble making progress with Israel doing nothing to help. The Arab revolts could represent an opportunity to reset American policy in the region yet the complexities of the problem make it difficult to solve.

Israel is well aware that there can be no military solution to the Israeli-Palestinian conflict and that its policy in the West Bank will only increase problems. The defeat against Hezbollah in Lebanon in the summer of 2009 was seen as an unexpected tragedy by the IDF and the Israeli population that was convinced of its invincibility. The only possible outcome is a political and economic solution. The official French-Israeli Chamber of Commerce had this to say about Gaza early in 2010: "Basic needs (energy, construction and so on) are not covered and this keeps one and a half million Palestinians in the Gaza Strip in a very precarious economic position. The Hamas government has voted its annual budget of 540 million dollars that will be used exclusively to help the population survive, without any room for development. Since Hamas took over in 2007 the Gaza economy has worsened. The World Bank estimates that 95 percent of the 4,000 companies in existence prior to 2007 had to shut down due to a lack of raw materials. From now on observers of the Palestinian economy estimate that unemployment affects 60 percent of the population in Gaza. Some 80 percent are living under the poverty line (under 2 dollars per person per day), making them entirely dependent on humanitarian aid."

Will Hamas gain the support of the Muslim Brotherhood in Egypt and Jordan? Egyptian public opinion, unlike under Mubarak, can now pressure and possibly impose a policy on its government toward the Palestinians. But ostentatious support of Hamas by Egypt wouldn't be acceptable to Washington and Jerusalem.

In order to understand the Gaza situation one must go back to the birth of Hamas. In 1987 six Muslim Brothers set up the organization at the beginning of the first intifada. The charter of Hamas adopted in August 1988 defined the movement as "a branch of the Muslim Brotherhood in Palestine." The co-founder and spiritual leader of Hamas was Sheikh Ahmed Yassin, a former teacher and preacher who later became a professor at various mosques in Gaza. Even though Hamas and its founder had the implicit approval of Israel they later became the number one enemy of the Jewish State.

A symbol in his lifetime, Sheikh Yassin was killed by the Israelis in 2004 and became a martyr for the Palestinians and part of Arab public opinion. Hamas is the heir to the Muslim Brotherhood that was founded in Palestine in 1945 and reached 10,000 members by 1947. The Palestinians, as opposed to the beginnings of the Brotherhood in Egypt, rejected violence and focused on indoctrination through cultural and social associations. From 1948 to 1967, the West bank and Gaza were under the control of Jordan and Egypt respectively but when Nasser banned the Brotherhood in Egypt it continued its work with religious, educational and social activities along with a covert political branch.

The Jewish State considered Hamas as an occasional ally early on, to be used as a counterweight to Yasser Arafat and the OLP. At the beginning Hamas described itself as a charitable religious movement and Ariel Sharon, who was then a military commander in Gaza even, financed the mosques of the Muslim Brotherhood of Hamas. The 1989 creation of the Ezzedeen al-Qassam Brigades, the military arm of Hamas was a turning point, a real break in the Muslim Brotherhood strategy.

From the standpoint of their doctrine the Muslim Brotherhood always called for the re-Islamization of society and avoided active resistance to Israel. With Hamas, they bridged the tradition of the Brotherhood (religious proselytism and social charities) to a political Islam, dedicated to struggle and resistance as with the Shia Hezbollah in Lebanon. The Muslim Brothers of Hamas adopted the logic of Jihad that they see as necessary for the liberation of Palestine. Even if the Ayatollah Khomeini didn't succeed in exporting his Islamic revolution the symbolism of Iran and its closeness to the "God Crazies" in Lebanon influenced his strategy. To those Islamists, historical Palestine is a Waqf, meaning a Muslim Arab possession. That position makes it imperative to recapture all the lands to secure the return of the refugees and to create a state with east Jerusalem as its capital. The objective of Hamas is clear and shared by most of Arab public opinion and to understand this movement it is necessary to differentiate Hamas and the Salafi Jihadists.

Hamas will fight with the Palestinians and the Jihadists closely related to al Qaeda and attempting to set up an Emirate because the Palestinian movement is a nationalist religious group that is based on the territorial issue (Waqf). When Iran throws its support to Hamas it is only due to specific circumstances: the Palestinians view the Iranians as Persians who are neither Arab nor Sunni but Shia. When Hamas accepts the support of Iran it is a way to confront Israel since Gaza cannot count on support from Fatah or on the Arab world in general except for the financial aid from Qatar.

The 1993 Oslo accords created the most serious split among Palestinians: the Islamists rejected the accords and the recognition of Israel. Hamas came under pressure from the Palestinian Authority that was to administer Gaza and its security services, and opted to join the armed struggle. While the Palestinian Authority was sinking into corruption and favoritism, Hamas and the Islamists increased their influence because of their efficient organization of the population beginning with the poorest areas in the camps. Through a network of female-run local help associations they would provide training, education, health services and the teaching of the Koran.

They are also inside professional groups, guilds, the universities and the intellectuals.

Following the failure of the Camp David summit attempted by Bill Clinton in 2000 and during the second intifada, the economic crisis became catastrophic due to the Israeli blockade. The Palestinians then flocked to Hamas even those in favor of Fatah since that division among Palestinians is not limited to ideology or strategy: on the West Bank the weakening of President Abbas created encouraged a lust for power in some quarters. In 2010 Mohamed Dahan, the former head of Palestinian counter-intelligence, and a foe of Hamas, was accused of subversion against Mahmud Abbas. He had previously led the struggle against Arafat and was eliminated from the Fatah central committee. Dahan's mistake was to have backed Nasser al-Kidwa, Yasser Arafat's nephew and former foreign minister and attempting to force Mahmud Abbas to retire.

Israeli tolerance of Fatah as it presses Hamas can only increase the popularity of the Islamists who are the only ones, thanks to their charitable networks, able to soften the effects of the blockade. When Israel decided to leave the Gaza strip in August 2005 the retreat was seen as a victory of Hamas and not the Palestinian Authority. But there is more at stake and while support for the Islamists is very real it also reflects the expectations of a very conservative society. There is a return to religion in a country where faith is the monopoly of the Muslim Brotherhood for whom the only salvation can come from the Islamization of society.

As opposed to other Palestinian territories such as Ramallah and the West Bank, other religions, especially the Christian ones (200 Roman Catholics, 3000 Greek Orthodox and about twenty Baptists) becomes increasingly precarious. In September 2006, the Greek Orthodox church in Gaza was attacked by hooded men following Pope Benedict XVI's speech at Regensberg.[1] This small community was subjected to the consequences of Hamas taking over the area: during the night of June 15 to 16, 2007, masked men from the Ezzedine al-Qassam Brigades attacked and ransacked the Roman Catholic Church and the school of the Sisters of the Rosary. In

---

1. *La Croix*, October 9, 2007.

October 2007, Rami Ayyad, the owner of the only Christian bookstore in Gaza was kidnapped and murdered, his body also showed signs of knife wounds and torture. A few months before his bookstore had already been set on fire by a group that called itself "The Virtuous Swords of Islam." Former Prime Minister Ismail Haniyeh, the head of Hamas in Gaza, condemned those incidents as "sabotaging Palestinian unity and the strong relations between Christians and Muslims that are part of the same nation." Even more so since the Vatican had favored the Palestinians up to that time.

While Washington had requested elections under international control, the 2006 vote brought about the victory of Hamas. Israel's response was not long in coming: Jerusalem, and the EU imposed economic sanctions on the Palestinians. Hamas took over Gaza in mid-June 2007 because al Fatah, with U.S. help, was preparing a putsch against it. The result was the de facto split of Palestine and the complete control of Gaza institutions by the Islamists. There are now two factions within Hamas: moderates and radicals. The moderates see a mistake in the forced expulsion of Fatah from Gaza in 2007; this group represents a small minority. The radicals became even stronger because of the inflexibility of Israel and the international community and Fatah's inability to renew itself.

The newly found closeness between Fatah and Hamas is also a consequence of the Arab Spring and the split between both Arab factions that cannot last while Israel is increasingly isolated.

The Palestinian problem doesn't concern Israel exclusively and both Washington and Jerusalem must take into account pro western Arab governments but also countries such as Turkey, Iran and Syria and political groups such as the Lebanese Hezbollah. Even though Europe was part of the Quartet[2] and the main financial backer of Palestine, it is completely absent from this picture.

The Muslim Brothers will not give up on their goal to Islamize Palestinian society and time is on their side because of Israeli policy, to the point that no reasonably close solution to East Jerusalem is in

---

2. The Quartet includes the United States, Russia, the European Union and the United Nations, and was set up in 2002 as a response to the escalation of the Middle East conflict Moyen-Orient to encourage mediation between Israel and the Palestinians. Former Prime Minister Tony Blair was appointed as the envoy.

sight. The far right's gains along with the ultra orthodox parties can only contribute to an increase of Islamic fervor in Palestine. To Islamize society doesn't mean an Islamic republic as Khomeini saw it since Hamas will have to deal with the Palestinians on the West Bank.

The Muslim Brotherhood remains tied to social programs and education through which the Islamize society even though they also control the mosques following the logic of a society based on the Koran and the teachings of the prophet. Actually a conservative Islamic government in Palestine with secular representatives is a credible alternative to the current situation and could work since Turkey, a regional power, has already made such a choice. With Ankara's support it could mean an expanded role for Turkey in the region. Even though Israeli-Turkish relations are at a low point since the Gaza flotilla incident, an isolated Jerusalem cannot ignore Turkey having no influence given the fact that the Arab Street is increasingly showing its support.

This represents a risk for Jordan, in the past its almost incestuous closeness with Washington and Egypt has left traces in Arab public opinion. The Jordanians cast an envious eye on the relations between Israel and the Palestinian prime minister whose reduced authority doesn't go beyond the West Bank with only a theoretical sovereignty and is amputated by various Jewish settlements. The only positive factor is the economic success of the West Bank that is largely due to the Israeli economy more than the prime minister's and the choice Jerusalem made to help the West Bank and asphyxiate Gaza.

King Abdullah II of Jordan heads a country where tribal power is eroding in favor of Jordanians of Palestinian origin that control the economy. Yet the alliance with the Bedouins was the foundation of the kingdom; between 2005 and 2008 over 86,000 West Bank Palestinians were given Jordanian nationality. The Muslim Brotherhood sees this situation as cooperating with Israel to undermine the Palestinian cause. For the first time Bedouin tribes showed displeasure with the royal family and in 2011 they criticized Queen Rania for her lavish spending while Jordanians are in crisis and for the most part live very precariously. It was a roundabout way of targeting the king.

In November 2010 the Islamists deprived the monarchy of its only credible opposition: the Islamic Action Front the political branch of the Muslim Brotherhood refused to take part in parliamentary elections. The party didn't want to be considered only as the "opposition to His majesty." That stance had show nits limitations and the brotherhood was facing a dilemma: to live or to disappear. On one hand circumstances and reason made it loyal to the monarchy and on the other hand it was losing its most active adherents who were going underground. The government missed an opportunity by changing the electoral law it could have institutionalized political Islam in an acceptable way thereby limiting the influence of the most extremist brothers.

Since that call Jordanians have also taken to the streets demanding reforms and expressing support for the Egyptian revolt. The first demonstration was organized the day after a meeting between King Abdullah II and the leaders of the Islamic Action Front who were asking for real reforms and a constitutional monarchy. The same position is taken by the left wing parties that were protesting against the high cost of living. What would happen if tomorrow parliament was to have an Islamist majority? In that case both the relationship with Israel and the Palestinian issue would be deeply affected.

The Sudan and the Two Blocs

Even though the United States is gambling on the head of the Egyptian security service to counter growing Islamist fundamentalism and ensure a transition to civilian rule without reducing the army's role, two more issues could destabilize Egypt: the consequences of the partition of Sudan and a Muslim alliance against the Christian countries in the area.

What will happen to the Sudan after the self determination vote of January 9, 2010, that approved the partition? In the capital of South Sudan, Juba, actor George Clooney and U.S. Senator John

Kerry mingled with the happy crowds the results of the vote according to the peace agreement that ended half a century of civil war in 2005. There was no doubt that Islamist President Omar Hassan al-Bashir had to accept that secession. Some crucial issues were delayed until after the vote however regarding citizenship, dividing oil revenues that are 70 percent located in the south and the pipelines to move the oil as well as the exact line of the border and the outcome of the deputed area of Abyei that both Sudans are claiming and where a separate referendum has been set.

In the short term the role of the international community will be essential while most donor countries concentrate their help to the South to avoid that the new state fail because of its poverty they must also avoid having the North turn to radical Islam. The first consequences of the partition are not at all promising and while the South's independence was set for July 9, 2011, the invasion of the town of Abyei on May 22 revived the ghost of civil war that caused the death of 2 million people between 1985 and 2005. Some 20 thousand citizens of Abyei had to flee the plunder and arson that were being perpetrated.

The creation of two states will change the geopolitics and the balance of power in the region. Egypt always favored a united Sudan and now it must deal with a new player in South Sudan. The partition is happening along religious lines the Islamist Muslim North and the Christian South facing one another. American evangelicals under the guise of humanitarian aid have long been interested in the South for proselytizing as much as for economic reasons since companies have set up shop in the wake of the religious movement. Christian solidarity is also at work with heavy weaponry and tanks purchased from Ukraine and delivered at Mombasa in Kenya that were officially destined to the Ugandan army. Two states are facing off with their respective supporters looking on as a Muslim axis extending from Egypt through Northern Sudan down to Somalia faces a coalition of Christian East and Central African countries. It is the return of the ancestral struggles of two regional powers: Muslim Egypt and Christian Ethiopia.

The indictment of President Bashir of North Sudan by the international court at The Hague on charges of genocide and war crimes in Darfur also hangs over the future of the country. The president has always given his support to movements such as Hamas, the regime in Eritrea and was condemned by the UN for his support of the Somali Shebabs: he is considered a danger to regional stability.

The antagonism between Egypt and Ethiopia is ancient history Alexandria was the seat of the Orthodox patriarch that the Ethiopians belonged to. In 1959, the Ethiopian church declared its independence and named its first patriarch Basilios. In the past when there were tensions between Egyptians and Ethiopians the patriarch would refuse to travel to the neighboring country which could cause institutional problems when a new emperor was to be anointed and could take place only in the presence of the patriarch. To some Egyptians Ethiopia is an anomaly in the region, an exception that stands out as a Christian Orthodox Coptic country. Historically it is the reason why Egypt wanted a strong Somalia that would be counterweight to Ethiopia. One seeks to embody Africa and the Arab world: Cairo is the seat of the Arab League; the other has the offices of the Organization of African Unity founded on religion and culture.

When the orthodox Christians were still dependent upon Alexandria legend had it that the Egyptians would blame the Ethiopians for drought and the latter would blame the Egyptians saying: "You have withheld the patriarch and we withhold rain. If you don't let the patriarch travel you will have no rainfall." The issue of the parting of the waters of the Nile is far from anecdotal: the river crosses Ethiopia in great gorges that are sometimes 3000 meters steep. The north and west of the country have six to nine months of rain per year and the Ethiopians have no need for irrigation of their land. More than the Egyptians the Ugandans, Kenyans, Tanzanians and Sudanese need that water. Egypt was dealt a blow in May 2010 when Ethiopia, Rwanda, Tanzania and Uganda all countries the Nile crosses signed a water sharing agreement that replaces the original 1959 treaty that gave the larger portion to Egypt and the Sudan. Ethiopia and the bordering states: Uganda, Burundi, Tanzania and

Kenya all wanted the change. About 80 percent of the population of Uganda is Christian and Kenya 78 percent and Burundi 67 percent, in these countries Muslims represent about 10 percent and Tanzania has only 40 percent Christians, 35 percent Muslims but also 25 percent Animists.

This being said it takes very little to cause a fragile situation to explode.

The fact that the Shebabs picked on Uganda as the location for their first terrorist action outside Somalia in July 2010 is no coincidence. They wanted to hit a Christian land and it was too risky for them to attack Ethiopia and opted for Kampala since Uganda contributes to the peacekeeping forces of the African Union in Somalia (Amisom.) The mission is to protect the provisional government in Mogadiscio something that caused the member countries of the force to be threatened since the Somali Islamists view Amisom as an occupying army.

What will happen to Egypt after Mubarak? Will the Muslim Brotherhood be recognized in the future? Does the partition of Sudan announce the creation of two antagonistic blocs in a fragile region and could it be a bad omen for ethically and religiously mixed populations as in Iraq, Yemen, or Saudi Arabia? Will Islamists take advantage of such situations? Many open questions for an uncertain future. A few rare voices like that of Prince Talal Ibn Adul Aziz, the brother of the king of Saudi Arabia, say that if the Christians leave the Middle East the modernity and democracy of the Arab world would be endangered. It was in fact the Christian elites apart from many other contributions that conceived of the possibility of the unity of the Arab world as was the case of the Michel Aflak, a Greek Orthodox Christian and the ideologue of Arab nationalism and founder of the Baath party.

Chapter 7

The Challenge of Modernity

The Saudi Turning Point and the Domino Effect

Is Saudi Arabia going to remain a Muslim country unlike any other? It is still viewed as the only true theocracy even though Mohamed VI of Morocco and Abdullah II of Jordan are descendants of the Prophet as the keeper of the Holy Places Saudi Arabia will always enjoy a special prestige in the Muslim world. The ruling dynasty has benefited from this location and was not indifferent to spreading of a rigorous Islam known as both in Muslim countries and in Europe where no Saudi Diaspora exists. The status it holds in the Arab Muslim world has made the Saudis suspicious of political Islam. When the Muslim Brotherhood was being pursued by Nasser's vengeance one of their leaders went to Riyadh to ask for the Saudis for help. The king was said to have answered: "We are all Muslims and therefore we are all brothers." A way of not responding.

In spite of the problems that have plagued the country that had supported Bin Laden and his group and provided the largest contingent of Arab mujahedeen in Afghanistan during the Soviet occupation the king would like his kingdom to become more modern. We are already far removed from 1995 when Alain Gresh could write in *Le Monde diplomatique*: "Will it take an Islamist revolution to sweep away this throne in the manner of the Shah of Iran in 1979?"[1] He was calling the kingdom and western ally an absolute and backward monarchy. While the kingdom is far from being a democracy and power had been concentrated in the hands of one man, the king and one family, the regime did attempt a timid form of evolution.

Few observers have shown much interest in the changes taking place in Saudi society. While traditional and conservative circles are the dominant part of public opinion, youth and women in particular, those that are the relatively well educated, want change. This movement is part of an international context where the Saudis felt their isolation within the international community. The states in the region and Saudi Arabia in particular want to turn the page of Bin Laden and 9/11 type terrorism that is identified with Muslims and Sunni Wahhabism.

There is also a sociological and economic change the oil producing countries benefited from the petrodollars while remaining "desert people" for the most part. Only recently has a "globalized" youth appeared with individual and collective attitudes that will modify traditional societies while the legal time required for reforms is far behind all these mutations.

There is finally the Shia influence of Iran over all the countries of the Persian Gulf. However Iran may evolve, the country is in the midst of a secularization that will affect all the states in the region. This goes beyond the issue of the transformation of the Tehran regime that is already a fact. The Saudis fear the proselytizing of the Iranians since they view this as a people the Persians and a branch of Isla, the Shia which they consider as heretics and enemies. The modernity of Iranian youth could also play a role because of its culture and educational level its openness to the world also implies a thirst for freedom. This model of society that the Iranians aspire to is seen as risky since more freedom in Iran invariably reverberates in all

---

1. "THE MOST OBSCURE DICTATORSHIP IN THE WORLD. END OF A REIGN IN SAUDI ARABIA." *Le Monde diplomatique*, August 1995.

the Persian Gulf countries and could lead to the questioning of the petro-monarchies.

Demographer Emmanuel Todd showed that the statistics of the Iranian population (fertility rate, marriage, literacy, number of graduates, equality between men and women) are now close to if not identical to those in the West. This all leads to a secularization of society and a change in mentality that affects the political scene as well as in the Tehran demonstrations with many young people and women participating.

Even if Saudi Arabia can be influenced by the changes in its Iranian neighbor it will remain the land of Islam's Holy Places. This affects the kingdom's internal policies but also the role of the House of Saud on the region where daily life revolves around the holy days of the calendar. The pilgrimage known as the Hadjj brings 5 billion Euro to Saudi Arabia per year. In five days businesses make 50 percent of their annual sales. If the pilgrimage brings 2 million visitors today what will it be in the future? Muslims are said to number 1.3 billion people and in 2050 they are expected to reach 2.5 billion. In the Holy City the square meter of construction space is the highest in the world at 120 to 150,000 and the Bin Laden family still owns the largest construction business in the country.

Saudi Arabia, the Thwarted Revolution

The role of the ruling dynasty as "Guardian of the Holy Places" and in the country toward the community of Muslim believers can only limit the reform minded ideas of the House of Saud.

As the 1968 campus demonstrations in Berlin, Paris, Berkeley or Tehran were taking place, the Saudi kingdom was just abolishing slavery. More recently when King Abdullah entered into an interreligious dialog with Jews and Christians the Jews are still not allowed to stay in the kingdom. Even a non-Jew with an Israeli visa in his passport is still barred from entering the country and the king still gives his visitors a copy of the *Protocols of the Elders of Zion*.

9/11, 2001 unveiled a crisis that was brewing in Saudi Arabia. That event pressured the political and religious authorities to rethink their mission. First of all the world discovered that terrorism was being financed by the Saudis. Second that Iran was not the root of all evil for the region. The regime was already weakened when the World Trade Center was struck by two planes which helps understand its position today: in 2001 Crown Prince Abdullah of Saudi Arabia was in charge since January 1, 1996, while King Fahd was ill but still the reigning monarch. Even though he was not seen he remained very much in charge. Fahd had succeeded Faisal in June 1982 and Abdullah ben Abdelaziz al-Saud will ascend the throne in August 2005 some four years after the terrorist attacks on the United States.

The regency witnessed a reform minded group advising Abdullah made up of young men who believe in liberalism, educated in English speaking countries and in favor of a more enlightened form of Islam. This placed the spotlight on the divisions and frictions that had already appeared in Saudi society. During this period the struggle for power was fierce: Abdullah is the half-brother of the Sudayri, a powerful faction of the royal family that then included Prince Sultan minister of defense, Prince Nayef minister of the interior and Prince Turki head of the secret services. As soon as he ascended the throne King Abdullah castigated those princes who are also his half-brothers for their lavish expenses that increased the people's displeasure. The situation also encouraged renewed religious fervor, especially among the youth.

Under King Fahd there had already been a crisis in the kingdom with long standing consequences: the decision made by the king to welcome American troops on Saudi Arabian soil to liberate Kuwait that Iraq had invaded on August 2, 1990, during the First Gulf War. This gave rise to a protest movement among Saudi clerics which was unheard of until then. King Fahd weighed the risks involved and agreed to the presence of the "impure" on the sacred lands of Islam because he understood the vulnerability of his kingdom like all the crowned heads of the Persian Gulf as he witnessed the quick invasion of Kuwait and the Emir's escape with his entire family.

The kingdom's support of the Americans during the First Gulf War against Iraq brought about the political weakening of the conservative and traditionalist groups. At the same time the Saudi regime had to agree to a number of concessions to the latter to maintain the unity of the kingdom that remained in power in a number of areas affecting the lives of Saudi citizens. This strengthened the more religious groups and a rise of fundamentalism in a country where Islam was already one of the most rigorously observant. This is the context where links and solidarity between those who were at first the "freedom fighters" and later the Islamist terrorists and certain fringes of Saudi society were forged. Those links and that experience are closely related to the Taliban and Pakistani movements that were to expel the Soviets from Afghanistan.

The kingdom had experienced a wakeup call in 1979 when on November 20 some 200 Islamic fundamentalists mainly from the Obeida tribe of conservative Bedouins from the southern part of the country invaded the Grand Mosque at Mecca. Over 50,000 were praying inside when the leader of the invaders Muhammad al-Utaibi, proclaimed himself the "Islamic messiah that had come to establish the kingdom of Allah on earth." He opposed the royal family seen as corrupt, rejected western influence and called for the rigorous enforcement of Islam in Saudi Arabia. But infidels were to end this hostage taking in this instance, French gendarmes of the GIGN, using gas in the cellar of the Holy Places that would kill a number of hostages and insurgents. 170 rebels were captured.

To legitimize Desert Storm[2] and the presence of American troops Saudi authorities had a fatwa issued in January 1991 by the highest religious authority Sheikh Abd al-Aziz Bin Baz, who was at the time the head of highest council of the Ulemas authorizing war on Saddam Hussein and using non-believers to fight him including the coalition. Some religious leaders were opposed to that fatwa in effect criticizing the kingdom's foreign policy (loss of sovereignty and dependence on the United States for the kingdom's security, internal and external). This criticism widely disseminated throughout the kingdom helped create a "Religious opposition movement" that sent a petition to King Fahd in May 1991 requesting that the role of the Ulemas and preachers be reinforced. One year later in September

---

2. Name of the operation against Iraq used by the Pentagon after January 17, 1991.

1992 the religious leaders without criticizing King Fahd and the Grand Mufti Sheikh Bin Baz, addressed a ten point memo to the authorities with reform proposals (judiciary, public administration, economy and finances, army information and even foreign policy.) The religious leaders had in a way proclaimed themselves as parliament and opposition that didn't exist.

The Saudi conservatives were not well defined and were divided in many different factions from the religious establishment and tribal representatives. It was only Wahhabism and the advantages they enjoyed that kept them together. What set them apart was the amount of "dependence" they had toward the regime: religious leaders had a "certain degree of independence" of the Saudi while those representing the system are associated to the regime through the Higher Council of the Ulemas.

Between 1990 and 1995 the Islamist opposition emerged because of the first Gulf War and the attack on Mecca was a warning shot. The decade represented a turning point for the kingdom with the very steep loss in oil revenues since 1997 that forced Prince Abdullah to announce the end of "great era" of royalties and imposed urgently needed social and economic reforms. The privatization of education, health and even housing were started while until the end of the 1990s these were part of the "providential state" since oil revenues made it possible to offer them free of charge. The conservatives had problems in seeing those areas slip away from their control; religious leaders were against privatization since through education and health they wielded their influence in society. King Faisal had given them those privileges in the 1960s. In the educational field the conservatives still have strong influence: the High Council of the Ulemas imposed religious education at every level including the most technical. The authorities and the reformers thought this policy would be very costly and conservative resistance slowed down the reforms that Prince Abdullah wanted to introduce.

The Reformers and the Prince Regent

Abdullah assembled a young foreign-educated elite group hoping to reconcile modernism and Islamic society that represents a break with the time Fahd was in power. This may have been viewed by some parts of Saudi society as questioning the religious fundamentalism that was the basis of the country's system. On the throne Abdullah had to work with both factions and keep the support of the oligarchs. He facilitated their access to business and decided to abandon the reform of the statute of women even though it had been called a priority as well as the privatization program. He had to give something to both sides.

The pact between the religious leaders and the monarchy was not revised after the 9/11 attacks where fifteen Saudi nationals were involved. The attack revealed to international public opinion the responsibility of the Saudis: from circles close to the government, Islamic NGOs or "families" that gave financial support to the terror networks. The feelings of suspicion toward the Saudis at the time would lead to their withdrawal of many of their assets from the United States. The king then moved to break the ties to the conservatives and the backers of those factions that contributed to the financing of the Jihadist movements. "Saudi Arabia is paying a ransom to be spared. She cares nothing about those who suffer and will reap the harvest." Said an Israeli diplomat.

In the context of regional crises American interventionism that speaks of reforms and then the slow application of the same that limited the king's actions as he must face the hostility of the religious conservative faction. The latter makes any change difficult and rejects what could be seen as a beginning of democratization or modernization of the system. Yet Abdullah cannot cut himself off from his roots and the religious conservative element that makes up Saudi society.

With advancing age, health problems and the grinding wear and tear of power, Abdullah can no longer enact reforms. The kingdom is being run by a gerontocracy and the horizontal form of succession from brother to brother that doesn't favor change. The next in line to replace Abdullah is Prince Sultan who is 85 and in poor health prompted the promotion of his brother Nayef who is 80 and whose son Mohamed, the right hand of the interior minister, almost got killed in an attack claimed by al Qaeda in the Arabian peninsula.

This hereditary system encourages conservatism; the first generation of descendants of Abdel Aziz, the founder of the dynasty is still in power sixty years after his death. Another aspect that inhibits change is that the royal family and its affiliated members form an opaque oligarchy of some 20,000 people over 25 million subjects and are more interested in protecting their position than in bringing about change. Yet in 2006 King Abdullah tried to limit the influence of the Sudayri, the original brotherhood of six princes that were particularly powerful including the oldest Fahd, who was king until 2005. He had instituted an "Allegiance Council" that was given to Talal Ben Abdel Aziz, known as the "red Prince" because he favored a constitutional monarchy. The king wanted to dilute the influence of the Sudayri within the "Family Council" an institution that extends to other influential members of the Saud family. Prince Nayef quickly blocked his half-brother Nayef's plans.

What Kind of Modernity?

Religion always controls society in one of the oldest theocracies in the world. In Saudi Arabia even today this means a regimented system from grammar school to the university in daily life and the workplace where everything is bent upon controlling society in media, religious police, the official religious institutions as well the justice and administrative systems. The Mutawa or religious police is the power that checks on the daily life of the Saudis made up of several thousand men to enforce the respect of the Sharia from prayer rituals, fasting, abstinence to the radical separation of the sexes.

In Riyadh, following his speech at the Lateran in Rome where he discussed the concept of "positive secularism" Nicolas Sarkozy defined the role of religion and religions. He quoted God thirteen times praising the moderation of Wahhabi Islam. President Sarkozy's advisor Henri Guaino explained the president' speech in Riyadh: "Should the pact between the Wahhabies and the Saud family failed tomorrow it would have catastrophic consequences. We must help all those seeking to transform Islam in the direction opposite to fanaticism." The choice of Riyadh remains surprising: Wahabism[3] is one of the most important strains of contemporary radical Islam. Long before 9/11 Yves Lacoste gave his analysis: "The Islamists owe a large part of their influence in the Muslim countries to the financial power represented by the Saudi dynasty since the time they opposed the Nasserite ideas of Arab unity with a more obscure and distant goal that was the unity of all Muslims. The consequence being Saudi Arabia's financing of fundamentalist movements since the 1970s with the agreement of the United States who viewed it as an antidote to communist subversion."[4]

The split is between those who would "keep the citadel of Salafism," the king's desire and the aspirations of most Saudis for an evolution of society. There is a growing distance between religious precepts and sociological reality the status of society and way of life and the expectations of new western educated generations. Religious rigor had an impact on the country's development. The Saudi regime compared to other Gulf countries has stifled change while neighboring countries must all get ready for the post-oil world. In a report to the French senate dated May 2000 but still very much on target by Xavier de Villepin: "Land of Islam and oil producing country."

"The country's stability will depend on the possibility and will of its leaders to enact, besides economic reforms the necessary political and social changes." If it's true that women represent 60 percent of college graduates, they remain only a minority in the workforce. The prohibition to mixed sexes in the workplace is one of the reasons: the kingdom loses about 50 percent of its human and intellectual potential. An anecdote will best illustrate this situation: on May 22, 2011, Manal al-Sharif, a female consultant in computer security was arrested for driving in Khobar in the eastern part of the kingdom. Saudi women have no right to drive according to a custom that would be codified in a religious decree in 1990. With American

---

3. Salafism is a Sunni movement seeking a return to the original tenets of Islam. Wahhabism is an Islamic doctrine founded around 1745 by Mohamed ibn Abd el-Wahhâb. It seeks to return to the pure origins of Islam, its followers reject any tradition that is outside the Koran and the Sunna. The Saud family was always associated with support and protection of that group.
4. *Dictionnaire géopolitique des États.*

troops were stationed in Saudi Arabia 47 women often having studied abroad had caused a scandal by driving in a convoy through Riyadh and eliciting the condemnation and a fatwa by the Grand Mufti. Since then in response to social networks scores of women defy the prohibition and get behind the wheel. These facts are not the first in a vast country with few means of public transportation with all that reflect a rigorist interpretation of Islam that forbids mixing the sexes, the right to drive and move around which is an old demand of Saudi women.

In February 2009 the king proceeded with a government shuffle and the most noted change was the nomination of Noura al-Fayez as deputy minister of education the first woman to become part of the kingdom's council of ministers. King Abdullah gave her the task of preparing young women for the workplace. That nomination was a signal but one should not be too optimistic: the number of women in public life is very small and if a few of them were appointed to the Majlis al-Choura, it is not a parliament but rather a consultative council appointed by the king since in Saudi Arabia no official assembly is elected and the only organized voting is for local municipal elections. In September 2011 the king announced that women could take part in the vote and run for office. That will be in 2015: a limited but brave concession made by the king at the end of his reign as he faces the rise of the conservatives.

The issue of single unwed women remains, from a sociological and demographic standpoint, one of the traits of Saudi society where 1.5 million women over 35 are single. Saudi women are leaving the country in growing numbers and since in the name of religion a woman lawyer cannot start a practice in Riyadh, Saudi women lawyers move to Bahrain or Kuwait. In the Emirates women can ride buses, drive their cars, have a drink in any coffee house and work with men. As an example of rigorist rule: before Saint Valentine's day the 'Commission for the Promotion of Virtue and the Prevention of Vice' forbids the sale of red roses and the display of anything red in shop windows since the color is thought to be the symbol of love.

Religious institutions dominate the country with society under their complete control and their power embodied in the Grand Mufti the imam of the Grand mosque at Mecca and the members of the Ulemas council that represent the structural foundations of the regime.

The Waqf (religious affairs) minister reminded the religious leaders on many occasions that to disobey those who are leading the country is a "serious sin." Still this doesn't prevent the appearance of friction between the clergy and the Saudi princes and a rebellion could begin again just as it had in the past. If Nayef became king the conservative and religious factions would return to power. After Fahd's long reign King Abdullah decided to introduce reforms quietly and rebuild the influence the monarchy once enjoyed. Some decisions were the result of international events and others probably the consequence of more personal decisions even though the results for the Saudi people are limited. The risk is that in the near future a conservative personality might take power with the princes now waiting since the sovereign is aging and often ill, having been away from the kingdom in recent times.

Saudi diplomacy appears to have lost the role it had in the region as a consequence of 9/11 and the Israeli-Palestinian dispute and the repeated failures—both Saudi and Egyptian—to successfully mediate the conflict. Saudi Arabia therefore consolidated its relations with other Arab countries and tried to lessen its differences with the states in the region including Syria. During the Kuwait summit of 2009 it restated its goal to hold a prominent position in the Arab nation and the Muslim world. This approach has the support of American diplomacy promoting a strategy of dialog in the region. President Obama picked the three most important Muslim countries for his first visit: Turkey, Egypt and Saudi Arabia. The impression gathered in Riyadh of the end of a reign and issues of succession and the help given to several brother states (Yemen, the exile offered to Ben Ali and sending troops into Bahrain) shouldn't obscure the competition with Qatar or Abu Dhabi, both close to France, and who hope to play a role both regionally and internationally. Both countries took part in the anti-Qaddafi coalition.

Before those events in the Arab Muslim world King Abdullah had gone through a major reshuffling of the power centers: the High

Committee of the Ulemas was enlarged to include all doctrinal tendencies and the king appointed some women to the Majlis al-Choura. These decisions may seem very cautious but they represented a step forward with respect to the past.

The king was just as prudent in his reform of the justice system as he obviously cannot radically change the foundations of society and has no intention of casting off the Sharia. He did reorganize the judiciary[5] and his decisions make sense in placing Saudi Arabia in a global economy. The kingdom must adapt to its international environment and is conforming with the requirements of the WTO. The creation of specialized commercial and labor courts is a step in that direction as the kingdom improves its legal system to safeguard companies and its foreign partners. While it is not a revolution the king makes no changes to the criminal code and family law he does open a crack in the system.

The Domino Effect

The Saudis like the other monarchies in the Gulf have viewed the revolts as a wakeup call. If relations between Iran and Saudi Arabia may not be called cordial, it should be noted that they are not openly hostile. Riyadh is very pragmatic and realistic even though the king's private statements as reported by WikiLeaks are revelatory of his deeper thinking: "Two countries should be wiped off the map: Israel and Iran." The Saudi leaders know the key role played by Tehran on the regional scene. In 2007 the president of Iran was King Abdullah's personal guest during the great pilgrimage which doesn't put an end to tensions between the two countries. The improvement in relations comes in response to an internal reality the area where Saudi oil fields are located is inhabited by a population of Saudis who are 80 percent of Shia persuasion. The Saudi kingdom knows that Iran doesn't intend to export its revolution into Saudi Arabia while Tehran is becoming more secularized as Secretary of State Hillary Clinton stated the danger that the Revolutionary Guards might set up a military dictatorship to prolong the regime.

---

5. Royal Ordinance, October 1, 2007.

In any case those in power have the country under control and the Shia minority did stage protests after appeals on Facebook for the "days of anger" even though these were limited to Awana near Al-Qatif in the eastern province where they are concentrated. The Shia had several dead and wounded when the police force opened fire but beyond these cases the Saudis are still confronting mostly Sunni fundamentalists. Attempts to reeducated former fanatics don't prevent some of them from joining up again in the neighboring countries: Yemen is now the rear base of the al Qaeda Saudis.

It took an attack on a U.S. airliner to remind everyone that Yemen is at war and is the hiding place of Al Qaeda and Saudi Jihadists. Americans and Saudis have stepped in to help local troops in Yemen. The country along with Somalia which is the land of piracy and Islamic fundamentalism controls the "Gate of Grief" the straits of Bab-el Mandeb where one third of maritime shipping passes through. Djibouti is a peaceful center of stability in the region even though it has a border dispute with Eritrea where troops from Qatar provide a buffer between the two armies.

The war in northern Yemen drags on and according to UN humanitarian agencies in four years it has claimed thousands of victims and 170,000 refugees. It is taking place in the mountainous areas that constitute the borders of Saudi Arabia and according to Yemeni and Saudi intelligence the Huthy and Shia rebellion has the support of Iran. According to Sana'a the rebels are seeking to grab the southern portion of Saudi Arabia to create an enclave where they could operate much like the Lebanese Hezbollah. The territory would have an opening on the Red Sea and Yemeni authorities see Iran increasing its influence in the strategic region of the Horn of Africa which was already part of the strategy envisioned by the Shah.

The official line doesn't hold up too well looking at the facts even though there were signs of Huthysts in the Hezbollah training camps during the war against Israel in the summer of 2006. The war in northern Yemen began because of religious tension between the Zaidi community (A Shia faction that includes about 45 percent of Yemenis even though they do not uniformly support the Huthys) and the Salafis, that are considered more aggressive and have the support of those in power. While a majority of Yemenis is Sunni and is linked to Shafeism, a legal school of thought of that branch of Islam, it remains open to the pressures of a fundamentalist Salafi drive.

If the Huthy conflict has faith as its backdrop it finds its origins in political conflict. The Shia Zaidi minority never accepted the regime of President Ali Abdullah Saleh. With the abolition of the monarchy in 1962 the country became the Arab Republic of Yemen or Northern Yemen. After British troops left in 1967 the Federation of South Arabia and the Protectorate of Southern Arabia merged on November 30, 1967 to create a new independent state the Popular Republic of Yemen or South Yemen. Three years later it took the name of Popular Democratic Republic of Yemen and a civil war began that lasted until 1970.

The conflict, while regional, must be seen in the context of the Cold War: the "republicans" had the support of Nasser's armed forces while the monarchists were backed by King Faisal of Saudi Arabia. On May 22, 1990, the Arab Republic of Yemen and Popular Democratic Republic of Yemen merged to form the Republic of Yemen and the president of North Yemen from 1978 to 1990) became president of united Yemen in 1990. He has remained in power ever since and today once again South Yemen is demanding its independence.

By starting the war in the north, the Shia and Huthy leader Hussein al-Huthy, an influential member of parliament who died fighting in 2005, his aim was the restoration of the Imam. This was a millennial political and spiritual power that ended in the 1960s with the founding of the Republic of North Yemen. The rebellion was a tribal conflict between two large groups, the Bakil and the Hashid that were close to power. The growth of the war economy had much to do with the failure to mediate between the Huthys and the authorities against the backdrop of a struggle for power and a fight for succession. President Saleh was seeking to provide a future for his son Ali Ahmad, head of the Special Forces and the presidential guard. To do this Saleh had to undermine the powerful head of military forces in the north Ali Mohsen al-Ahmar.

The president offered a stark choice against every threat: "It's either me or Somalia; me or al Qaeda; me or Iran." In a country with a troubled history where political assassinations and internal wars are common the line: "Either me or chaos" remained the strongest card in the president's hand. The Yemeni head of state used a political line and every conceivable argument to justify staying in power. The al Qaeda threat allows him to get support from the United States and Saudi Arabia and accordingly he chastised the rebellion's hostility to America and Israel. The announcement of a reorganization of Yemen at the start of 2009 by al Qaeda in the Arabian Peninsula proves that it is not so much Tehran's support for the rebels (which is yet to be proven) but the presence of this organization that constitutes the problem.

Almost half of the Guantanamo prisoners (97 out of 210) came from Yemen and returning six of them to their country of origin could lead to the return of other prisoners. As published in the *Washington Post*, the Obama administration is now far more reticent to do so.[6] In the recent past former Guantanamo prisoners whether Yemeni or from other countries went to Yemen to join Al Qaeda once again. According to western intelligence former Yemenis enjoy the tolerance of the government in Sanaa. Even before the revolts the authorities closed their eyes on their activities as long as these were not being planned in Yemen. With anarchy gripping the country it has become fertile ground for the Jihadists.[7]

Saudi Arabia in the north has gone to war on the side of the Yemeni government since more that the Huthy rebellion it is al Qaeda that frightens the Saudis. Riyadh must therefore support the regime in Sana'a. Saudi air forces for the first time since 1991 took off to bomb Huthy bases located within its territory. Besides fighting in the north, the Yemeni army must face the autonomists in the south. In that context the nightmare for both Arabs and westerners is that Yemen should become even more destabilized allowing Al Qaeda to have a new emirate facing Islamist Somalia and on the borders of Saudi Arabia and Oman controlling the straits and the

---

6. December 18, 2009.
7. *The Clash of Civilizations and the Remaking of World Order.*

Gulf of Aden the only passage between the Indian Ocean and the Red Sea.

The rebellion turned into a civil war and when the presidential palace itself was bombed the head of state was wounded. A tribal clan war is also taking place in Sanaa between the Sanhan tribe of Ali Abdullah Saleh, of the Hached confederation… and that of Abdallah al-Ahmar, head of the same confederation and of the opposition Islamist party: it is a family feud!

Within this complicated context the problem is that of Ali Abdullah Saleh the man who was refusing to cede power and has delayed that moment ever since he took over in Yemen. His departure for Saudi Arabia to seek treatment after the bombing of the palace hasn't allowed a change in the situation. His return after several months of convalescence bodes nothing positive: will there be once more two Yemens, one in the south and an Islamic emirate in the north? No one can predict what the country will be like in the near future while between north and south one third of its territory has been turned into an al Qaeda area of operations!

The Alarming Shadow of Iran

While western countries worry about the future of Somalia and Yemen that could both become rear bases for Islamism and fundamentalism the true danger to Tehran is in nearby Eritrea where according to numerous sources Israeli presence is also active. If Eritrea supports the Shebabs and Sunni fundamentalists, Shia Iran that opposes Bin Laden and his groups would not be inclined to have Yemen and Somalia become emirates. It would thwart its ambition of becoming a regional power and the policeman of the Persian Gulf and the Indian Ocean as it was under the Shah. Eritrea welcomes a base of Iranian Revolutionary Guards as well as the Israelis and has been condemned by the UN for its support of Somali Islamists. In the event of a conflict with the West over the nuclear issue Tehran could also undertake a Naval Jihad. Control of the straits seems to have become a priority of the Iranian regime that had already threatened to block the straits of Hormuz in 2008. While all the armies of the world (Americans, Europeans, Japanese and Russians) have turned Djibouti into a rear base for the hunt for the Somali pirates in the Gulf of Aden a few nautical miles from there Tehran is setting its positions in the region.[8]

It is therefore under the very noses of the great military powers stationed in Djibouti that the Revolutionary Guards have set up a base in the port of Assab. Missiles that could hit Saudi Arabia or Israel and the men to operate them have been said to be delivered by submarine. Tehran's presence in Eritrea must be placed in its proper context: the decision must be seen as a pressure tool in the debate between the Iranian regime and the West. It is less a matter of support than Tehran's way of expressing its offensive capabilities even though Iran has no interest in opening a new front. In exchange anything that will bother the West will be a victory for Iran there are no other explanations to be found.

The issue of Eritrea sums up the problems of the moment: the future of the Arab World is in the balance in part in the Horn of Africa. The Sudanese, Eritreans and Iranians are said to have formed a regional alliance to thwart the West. Since the indictment of Sudanese President Omar al-Bashir, Khartoum is desperately seeking new alliances.

Iran's presence has a psychological as well as political impact and its consequences could mean more than Tehran's support for the Shia in Yemen. This positioning of Iran in Eritrea creates a new pressure point for the United States and an answer to French military strategy that has set up a base in the United Arab Emirates redeploying the troops that were in Djibouti in Abu Dhabi. Since France is the last western country ready to attack the "axis of evil" it should regard Tehran's presence as something like the final word.

It is understandable that France should wish to sell weapons to that Emirate while Paris is indebted to the Emir of Qatar for his financial contribution toward the liberation of the Bulgarian nurses held captive in Libya and the participation of that country in the "crusade" that ended the Qaddafi regime. However to think that the United Arab Emirates and Qatar have the means to control the

8. The Countdown in Jerusalem: an alert for the world…Last chance for peace.

future of the region is both a misunderstanding of reality and a risky gamble.

The choice made by French diplomacy to set up Qatar as the spokesman of the Persian Gulf Emirates almost to the detriment of Saudi Arabia is symbolic of the decision to turn its back on the Arab policy that France had pursued. Like it not it is still Saudi Arabia even with diminished influence due to the turbulence in so many countries of the region that sets the tempo of the political situation. That President Sarkozy spent only a few hours in Riyadh on his first trip to region and three days in Qatar is not just seen as an affront to King Abdullah, it was a gaffe and a misunderstanding of the of the realities in the region. Obama made no such mistake.[9]

The French base at Abu Dhabi even if it can add security to shipping in the straits of Hormuz was not necessary. The presence of the U.S. Fifth Fleet as well as the troops stationed in Bahrain is enough. France wanted to demonstrate that it was still a great power on equal footing with the United States and even more: that she was the last country opposing the Ahmadinejad regime. Less than 100 kilometers separate the Emirate where the French are stationed from Iran.

The Fourteenth Province

When the Iranians discuss the small emirate of Bahrain, it is as though they were talking about Iran's fourteenth province. Historically they view the emirate as an integral part of ancient Persia.

The emirate is the base for the American Fifth Fleet and that is what makes it strategic. Long before the revolt of the Arab Street the Shia opposition, the Wefaq had been protesting against the monarchy: during the elections in October 2010, they obtained only 18 seats out of the 40 that constitute parliament. In order to limit the displeasure the monarchy distributed 3,000 dollars to every family in the emirate. In that tiny state the Shia majority is governed by a Sunni

---

9. Radio speech for the Iranian New Year. The American president has repeated this event every year since he reached the White House.

dynasty and the authorities neglect the Shia who are considered second class citizens in such matters as housing and employment.

The Shia see the effort to rebalance the population in favor of the Sunni as a political affront in order to obtain demographic balance to their advantage; the authorities encourage Sunni immigrants to whom they issue Bahraini nationality. The Shia are in the majority with 64 percent of the population but the electoral apportionment prevent them from being adequately represented in a powerless parliament. All the ingredients were assembled for the Emirate to witness demonstrations with Saudi Arabia and the United Arab Emirates giving their support to the Emir of Bahrain to limit the revolt in spite of President Obama's pressure.

With the Arab Spring Riyadh and the Gulf monarchies are worried and view the statements of the United States for democracy in the Arab World as encouraging protest. In many other capitals Arab leaders are asking whether the Americans are not abandoning the Sunni while the latter still have all power in their hands. Beyond the Shia community in Bahrain the Saudi decision was made in the name of solidarity between all the oligarchies in the region. They know that should one monarchy be overthrown it would endanger all the ruling families. It was a simple message to Tehran to avoid getting involved even in the name of religious solidarity, in the affairs of its neighbors.[10]

If in Bahrain concessions were made in part to the Shia, such as the end of the state of siege, the repression continued and no major change was made to the statute and the rights of the Shia. Reform was impossible: the prime minister is on the job since 1971 and he is the king's uncle. When the ruler wanted to have a dialog the Wifaq, first opposition party representing the Shia was under represented in the round tables set up by the regime and the leaders ended up walking out.

The issues remain in spite of the message addressed to Tehran by Saudi Arabia and the United Arab Emirates that protect Bahrain while Iran looks on.

---

10. Paris, April 2011, Colloquium *Institut du Monde Arabe.*

Chapter 8

The Maghreb and Sub-Saharan Africa

An Arab and Muslim land, the Maghreb bears the imprint of French colonization. While Algeria's fate was different from that of its neighbors the wounds of history, decolonization and immigration created a complex and passionate relationship between France and those countries. Algeria, Morocco and Tunisia are confronted with the rise of Islamist fundamentalism. Each one attempted a different response and even Libya that had been on the list of states sponsoring terrorism of the U.S. Department of State and had in effect backed many extremist movements, also had to face the Islamist threat. In April the authorities freed 90 members of the Islamic Group fighting in Libya and affiliated to al Qaeda. The announcement came from the Qaddafi Foundation run by his son Saïf al-Islam. "The number of prisoners that were liberated represent one third of the members that are in prison." Saleh Abdel Salam, the foundation's secretary general indicated. The group was set up in the 1990s in Afghanistan by Libyan militants having as its objective the overthrow of the colonel's regime and its replacement with an Islamic state. When the Libyan revolt opposed Qaddafi, the supreme guide of the revolution would accuse the movement of having the backing of al Qaeda! Today the regime has indeed fallen but the

Islamists are very much present. The constitutional statement drafted by the rebels states that the Sharia will be the main foundation of "the law." Many radical Islamists took part in the fighting.

The Muslim countries have had to confront Islamist terrorism. And while Algeria experienced the most dramatic events leading to the worse possible outcome of civil war, Morocco and Tunisia experienced some of their citizens take part in attacks at home and in Europe: Madrid, Paris and London. Beyond the purely security oriented measures, each country in the Maghreb tried to create a relationship between Islam and the state to respond to the challenge of mounting Islamism. The latter may have external causes such as international events (Israeli-Palestinian conflict, bombing of the headquarters of the OLP in Tunis, Lebanon, Iraq and Afghanistan.) But it can also be explained by the internal situation (human rights, extreme corruption, social crisis, failure of the educational systems.) The appearance of a movement demanding a "word for word" reading of the sacred texts has also gained ground. All these reasons contribute to a split between public opinion and those in power. The demographic reality only increases the break between youth, the victim of the social economic crisis when inequality is so blatant, and the ruling classes that are prospering flaunting the newly acquired wealth. Fundamentalism must be viewed through the prism of new technologies: the cell phone, the web, satellite television have all modified individual and collective behavior. Access to such means of communication is no longer the exclusive preserve of rich countries: cybercafés, even in developing countries underscore that reality.

While censorship exists governments are increasingly powerless facing these attitudes and the consequences of social media networks. If Twitter, Facebook or even more BlackBerry which is encrypted can disseminate information and encourage mobilization another parameter is required for a revolution to be successful. In Tunisia as in Egypt the army dropped Ben Ali and Mubarak and without NATO bombing and without weapons shipments to the rebels Qaddafi would still be in Tripoli. The internet and satellite television have also become the best weapons of the fundamentalists: in the Maghreb the homilies by "Islamist television evangelists" from Egypt or Saudi Arabia find a growing viewership that the authorities worry about.

In Tunisia, the West wanted to preserve the heritage of the secular Habib Bourguiba in spite of the repression of the 1980s as the re-Islamization of the country was taking place. Yet the Islamists were not instrumental in Ben Ali's departure and didn't even attempt to take over the protest movement. The revolt was by young people demanding jobs and freedom. When the leader of the Islamist party Ennahda returned from exile in London the supporters of Rashid al-Ghannushi were only a scattered few to welcome him at the airport in Tunis. If Tunisian society is becoming increasingly religious there is no political Islam in Tunisia even though the Ennahda's dream is to follow the Turkish AKP model and laments that "Islam has become a symbol of anti-democratic [politics]."

A Land of Every Religion

Beginning in the II century AD, Christianity was introduced to the ports of the Maghreb making very rapid converts. Pope Victor (181-191) was a Libyan. North Africa also produced some of the Fathers of the Church such as Saint Augustine (354-430), born in eastern Algeria, near Carthage. The Berbers, probably a deformation of the word "barbarians" were opposed to the Arab advance. As a bridgehead of the invaders Kairouan in Tunisia was founded in 670 forty years after the death of the Prophet at a time when the near east was under Islamic domination. Kairouan, "the city of the three hundred mosques," is the fourth holy city of Islam and the oldest Muslim city of the Maghreb in a strategic location to the passage of caravans.

Islam didn't bring peace to the region and is actually at the center of the conflicts between Muslims. The Kharijite state founded in 766 based on egalitarian prosperity in the area of Ouarsenis.[1] In the west the Idrissids seized power in Fez in 788 and the Aghlabids took over Kairouan in 800. One century later a Shia state was set up in Little Kabylie, and took Kairouan before moving on toward Egypt with the

---

1. Northwestern Algeria.

Fatimid dynasty. The Arab Berbers conquered the Iberian Peninsula in 720 and the Maghrebis landed in Sicily in 878. It was only in 902 with the conquest of Siracusa that they would control the island.

At the end of the ninth century a decree made it compulsory for the believers of both branches of the faith to wear a piece of cloth representing a pig and a monkey, respectively. For a time Berber territory was united politically and religiously but the Almohad Empire that believed in divine uniqueness was to give the Christians a choice of converting to Islam or death. In the sixteenth century the Iberian countries eliminated Islam from the peninsula and even established control over coastal areas of the Maghreb. Morocco had a Portuguese presence, the Spanish went to Algeria, Tunisia and Libya. Two Turks, the Barberousse brothers, whose epic would be recounted in the book *Leo Africanus*[2] by Amin Maalouf, extorted money from merchant ships and proceeded to back and overthrow rulers in the area while establishing an alliance against Turkey.

The events in the Near East and their consequences on the Muslim world calls for the examination of the state of the Jews in those countries. At the founding of the Jewish State in 1948 the Jewish community in the four North African countries (Morocco, Algeria, Tunisia, Libya), numbered about 505,000 equal to that of all the other Muslim countries taken together.[3] By 2000 the Jewish community was reduced to 5,500. Today the largest Jewish community in Muslim countries is in Shia Iran with over 40,000. In 1948 there were 130,000 Jews in Algeria and at independence in 1962,[4] there were only 25,000 left and none by 2002 with most of them going to France with the other "pieds noirs."[5] Only 10 percent would opt to go to Israel. In Tunisia, the first wave of immigration came after the incident at Bizerte: in July 1961, the breakdown in the relationship between Paris and Tunis pressured many Jews and Europeans to leave. In Tunisia, 100,000 to 120,000 Jews emigrated to France from 1948 to 1966. By 2000, they would only number 2,500. The Israeli victory of 1967 gave rise to anti-Semitism throughout the

---

2. LGF – Livre de Poche, 1987.
3. 550,000 of which 130,000 in Iraq, 90,000 in Iran and 80,000 in Turkey.
4. July 5, 1962.
5. Meaning refugees from North Africa: it identifies Sephardic Jews and Europeans.

Maghreb: rioters destroyed the grand synagogue in Tunis. King Hassan II and Bourguiba condemned the violence done to their Jewish citizens. The image of Hassan II in France is one of tolerance through one of his Jewish advisors André Azoulay.[6] In 1948, the Jewish community in Morocco numbered 250,000 but by 1966, many were to leave. In 1969 there were 50,000 Jews, 35,000 in 1972 and by 2000 only 3,000. While many Moroccans (70 percent) did decide to emigrate to Israel it is important to understand how this happened. From 1961 to 1964, 100,000 Jews left Morocco illegally going to Marseille and later Haifa in groups of 1,000 to 6,000 per month. The immigration was handled by HIAS (Hebrew Immigration Aid Society) an American group and an operation codenamed "Yakhin" was carried out with the approval of the Moroccan authorities. According to the terms of the agreement between the two countries, the sum of $5,000 in 2007 dollars was paid by Israel to Morocco for each Jew leaving the kingdom. Later on, from 1965 to 1971 45,000 Jews were to leave Morocco not bound for Israel but to France and Canada. The belief that a special connection between the Moroccan monarchy and the Jewish community existed has survived for a long time. Many Moroccans were convinced that Mohammed V, the father of King Hassan had been declared "Righteous among the nations" by the Jewish State when actually it was only a rumor that became a legend!

Emigration and the War of the Mosques

King Hassan II had a clear view of Moroccan emigration: he was adamantly opposed to an immigrant right to vote in local elections as candidate François Mitterrand had promised during the presidential campaign. The king who is a descendant of the prophet considered the link between himself and his subjects as being of a divine nature.[7]

---

6. Councilor to Kings Hassan II and Mohamed VI, he is a member of the Committee of Wisemen for the alliance of civilizations along with Archbishop Desmond Tutu of South Africa, former Iranian President Mohammad Khatami, former French Foreign Minister Hubert Védrine... he is the delegated president of Foundation of the Three Cultures and of the Shimon Peres center for Peace.

7. The Cherifian Dynasty is a specific branch of Islam the Malekites. The Malekite School was founded by Malik ibn Annas (711-795), known as the "Imam of Medina" the city where he lived and codified the Law as inspired by Muhamad and his followers. A rigorist on dogmatic matters the rite recommends taking into account the general interest, the maslaha, and trusts the consensus of knowledgeable

Therefore the issue of control of mosques located abroad is at the center of Moroccan concerns as it is for the Algerians. For these countries it represents a way of maintaining their influence over immigrants and limit the inroads made by the Islamists. Mohammed VI sends imams, including women, to Europe for the month of Ramadan while the Habous and religious affairs ministry states that the king's action is meant "to help the religious needs of the Moroccan community and protect it from any extremist or deviant kind of appeal and shield it from all fanaticism and extremism..." Moroccans abroad are to "maintain the link to their Moroccan roots and the Malakite rite that anchors them to the values of citizenship."

In broader terms it is the issue of Islam in Europe that is at the forefront and its ties to Muslims and their roots. Most first generation immigrants to France or Europe now have grand children. Morocco is advocating adapting to the European reality while Algeria is attempting to exercise control over the Algerians through construction of mosques and immigrant associations. According to Islamic scholar Mohamed Darif: "The contest between the two countries [Morocco and Algeria] at the religious level in France is only the reflection of their existing political differences with each one seeking to recapture a part of territory it sees as its own." A third country, Turkey has also entered the influence war.[8]

Morocco understood that its policy limited to sending the imams was ineffective and not to the liking of the European countries. It is now part of the official organizations such as the Conseil français du culte musulman (CFCM) [French Council for the Muslim Faith] whose president is a university professor Mohammed Moussaoui. When the institution was created, Dalil Boubakeur, rector of the Great Mosque in Paris, had been co-opted following the directives of the French government and not truly elected. The desire to adapt Islam to immigration corresponds to the creation in Rabat of the Ulemas Council, the religious structure for Moroccans on the

scientists, ijma'. It was completed by several works by the doctors at Kairouan, it also encourages commerce and custom. It therefore included in realistic fashion popular traditions and even age old superstition that were part of Berber life who specifically honor the cult of the saints. It also explains whay Malekism was adopted by part of sub-Saharan Africa. *Les particularités de l'islam au Maghreb*, Paul Balta, May 2002.
8. See chapter 5.

continent. The kingdom needed an organization to act as interlocutor with the European countries on all issues regarding the life of Muslims of Moroccan citizenship. Morocco also decided to promote persons that are part of the communities abroad and are better informed about local situations as imams.

Algeria decided to increase its hold on mosques and associations through greater funding. Moroccan newspapers have denounced the Algerian offensive on Islam in France: 490,000 Euros to build the mosque in Tours, 270,000 Euros for the one in Toulouse, one million Euros for the Grand Mosque in Marseille plus an equal amount for the yearly expenses of the Paris mosque. According to the daily *El Abdallah*, these numbers are just a small portion of the official Algerian aid to its religious community in France.

Changes in Morocco

Abraham Serfaty, who opposed Hassan II, was pardoned by Mohammed VI and recently deceased, stated: "Morocco is still a complicated and even composite society. Islamism is spreading with unusual strength benefiting from poverty and destitution." According to Professor Mohamed Tozy[9]: "The Islamists are a useful scarecrow. But they are not that numerous and politically they are on the defensive since Mohammed VI became king and given his popularity among the poor." Tozy feels that: "From the start the Islamists always hesitated between two possibilities: Islamize the state or Islamize the individual. During the 1970s it was the Islamization of the state and then imposing the Sharia…these days on the contrary it is more the Islamization of the individual. Osama Bin Laden has little traction among Moroccan Islamists while remaining a subject of some fascination."

Nevertheless the authorities always point to the arrests of terrorists with networks developing in the poorest shantytowns of Casablanca where the attack in Marrakech in April 2011 was

---

9. Professor of political science at Hassan II University in Casablanca, interview given before legislative elections in 2002, *L'Express*, December 16, 2003.

conceived and several European tourists were killed. There is an Islamist terror center in Morocco.

The divine character of the monarchy helps contain its development. On March 9, 2011, as Tunisia and Egypt were going through their revolutions the king addressed the nation. He had to react decidedly to preempt any confrontations. At the end of 2010 facing potential social breakdowns the palace decided to double the 2011 budget to compensate for the increase of staple products. The March 9 speech was a response to the Movement of February 20 when in response to a Facebook group with support from the labor unions and other associations, some 370,000 people took to the streets in the large towns and the 53 prefectures of the kingdom. The king promised reforms and recalled the "sacred nature" of his person and his title as "Commander of the faithful," a red line that must not be crossed.

Mohammed VI wants change and modernity while protecting tradition. Does that amount to a difficult or even an impossible wager? In July 2005, the head of the American NGO "Global Rights" took stock of the reforms made to family law. The changes in the Mudawana, the civil code, were adopted in 2004 in spite of a demonstration organized in March 2003 in Casablanca by 100,000 people who opposed the reforms. It included mostly younger men who were not all members of Al-Adl wa al-Ihssan, the unauthorized group of Sheikh Yassin.[10] The judges in any case do not apply the Mudawana, and use and abuse exceptions to the law.

Another obstacle to change remains the high rate of illiteracy among 42 percent of Moroccan women in urban centers and 82 percent in rural areas. The promotion of women's rights and efforts to thwart religious extremism do not come easily to King Mohammed VI. Morocco is searching its path. For example a corps of women preachers has been created: the Murchidates. Having been given the same education as the imams their "missions go from prisons to factories the internet and television." The ministry of Islamic affairs assigned them a "role of leadership, orientation, information and

---

10. Considered to be the most important ideologue of the Moroccan Islamist movement and a backer of the Iranian Islamist revolution he was imprisoned several times by King Hassan II.

religious awareness." They must "contribute to faith, social and cultural activities in the mosques" and "take part in the preservation of religious unity of society and its cohesion."

Through women the authorities have created a way of controlling the religious sphere. Yet Islamism is making inroads in the universities as well as among the lower social classes. By recruiting the Murchidates from higher education, the authorities demonstrate their will to eradicate Islamic deviances at every layer of society. The candidates must have a bachelor's degree or similar diploma; fifty are trained every year and those who are successful receive a certificate from the ministry of Habous and Islamic affairs. Moroccan leaders see these concurring measures of a new civil code and women's contribution to the religious renewal as a response to Islamism.

Political Islam in Morocco is part of the institutional system: the king reigns and governs in practical terms: ministers are appointed accordingly within this institutional logic. There are ministries of sovereignty that depend directly from the palace (interior, justice, foreign affairs, religious affairs and defense) and the management ministries that are appointed by the head of the government. At the same time the kingdom had encouraged Malekism and Sufism while calling on the people for another return to the origins with the concept of "Marocité" (Moroccanism.) In his speech to the nation the king promised a version of constitutional monarchy. The following day Samar Abdelmoula left the PAM (Parti de l'authenticité et de la modernité), also known as "the party of the king's friend" and joined the Islamists of the party for Justice and Development (PJD). Abdelmoula is a 36-year-old businessman who was mayor of Tangier for seventeen months. Observers wonder if that switch may not mean the end of PAM founded in 2008 by Fouad Ali al-Himma, a childhood friend of the king. The opposition, including the Islamists, see this as an attempt to create a single political party as Ben Ali had done in Tunisia. Fouad Ali al-Himma and the king's private secretary Mounir al-Majidi were thinking along those lines. They are two of the three names mentioned in WikiLeaks that American diplomats cited as responsible for widespread corruption.

With the new constitution adopted by referendum, the prime minister becomes the true head of the executive branch and parliament will have more power. The regionalization program will take place after elections and the transfer of power from the governors and the walis (prefects) to the regions. After the reforms the enactment of these policies will be in question. According to Ahmed Benchemsi, founder of *Tel Quel*, and a researcher at Stanford University, "the sacred nature of the monarchy slows down democratization." He also states that "the Pandora's Box of democracy is open and nothing will close it again."[11]

If the constitution no longer stipulates that the king is "sacred" the people must show "respect and tawqir" an Arab term that describes "an attitude half-way between reverence and adoration." In closing his speech of June 17 calling for the referendum and basic constitutional changes, the king quoted the Koran (12: 108): "This is my path! I call to the way of Allah myself and those who follow me." Mohammed VI identifies his reforms as the path of Allah. One week prior to the referendum, the ministry of Islamic affairs distributed a homily to the imams that they were to read calling for a "yes" vote.

Algeria Under Control

Algeria experienced a different fate from that of its neighbors. Independence was achieved at the end of a heavy struggle that came at a high cost in human lives. In that fight the Ulemas, representing Islam had discredited themselves in the eyes of the FLN and the new men in charge because they had remained close to the colonial authorities. Since 1962 the army is the institution serving as the guardian of sovereignty with a decision making role in everything concerning the country. This is a key point in understanding Algeria: Ahmed Ben Bella[12] kept religion as part of private life even though Islam was then identified as the "religion of the people." His Arabization policy forced him to import thousands of Arabic speaking school teachers from Egypt most of whom were close to

---

11. *Le Monde*, March 16, 2011.
12. 1962-1965, first president of the Algerian Republic.

the Muslim Brotherhood that was being persecuted by Nasser's nationalist regime.

At the same time the desire to secularize Algerian society led the regime to adopt the Charter of Algiers in 1964 that declared the separation of the state and Islam. Houari Boumediene (1965-1978), gave the socialist regime a new impetus by creating the Superior Islamic Council, a ministry of fundamental education and religious affairs and reintroduced Islamic courts as a source of subsidiary law. The 1976 constitution stipulated that any constitutional revision may not affect Islam as the state religion and identifies the Algerian people as being only Muslim (Umma[13]). The head of state in his swearing in ceremony undertakes to "glorify Islam."[14]

In February 1979 the regime attempted to adopt the themes used by the Islamists for two reasons: the Shah was forced out of power and replaced by the Islamic Republic of Iran and the Ayatollah Khomeini was dreaming of exporting his revolution to the Muslim world. Algerian Islamists were encouraged by those events and the long wear and tear of the exercise of power, the ubiquitous presence of the one-party system drove them to use the mosques for the free expression of ideas. These were the only locations that had a degree of autonomy and were tolerated by the regime while official preachers that were paid by the state were discredited. The protest movement was to develop in those locations and the Islamists took advantage of the loopholes created by the government itself.

The state controlled only 1,000 mosques out of a total of 7,000 in the entire country. The imams, most of them younger and rising in popularity were criticizing the government. They would pave the way for the Islamists to become the main political force in the country by the end of the 1980s. The Islamists had been fighting any measures seeking to secularize Algeria since the 1970s. Many "actions" against women thought to be wearing inappropriate clothing in the streets were taking place as religious elements were persecuting those shopkeepers selling alcoholic beverages. The regime, in an attempt to limit their influence, tried to increase its popularity by making

---

13. A term used in the Koran that describes the community of believers.
14. Article 120 of the Constitution.

religious education compulsory, building 160 mosques and Koranic schools, financing 5,000 religious teaching jobs and 26 Islamic centers, it also Islamized audiovisual programs.

In November 1982, the Islamists adopted a charter to "create an Islamist state and abolish the constitution." The increasing strength of the movement coincided with an economic crisis since 1985 and 1986 were years of falling oil revenues. Algeria had to deal with increased unemployment and inflation as the diminishing purchasing power affected the least fortunate members of society. By contrast the Islamists engaged in social action and filled the space left open by the state as did the Hezbollah in southern Lebanon and the Taliban today in Pakistan. The social activism of the Islamist groups comes in contrast to the corrupt FLN that had ruled the country. The appeal of the religious fundamentalists was all the more widely accepted by a largely poor population, undereducated and illiterate. In 1988 President Chadli Bendjedid met with a delegation of Islamists including Abassi Madani and Ali Belhaj, giving them the prestige and legitimacy of being considered as major spokesmen. Both men were to create the FIS (Front islamique du salut) [Islamic Salvation Front].[15] The FIS described itself as an Islamist alternative that could contain the radical Jihadists and the army was intent on using the movement in seeking to preserve its privileges and limit the influence of Islamists returning from Afghanistan.

The FIS victory during municipal elections in 1990,[16] and in the first round of parliamentary elections in 1991[17] in spite of a modified electoral law just before the ballot (April 2, 1991) to favor the FLN, still drove the army, with France's approval, to cancel the run off thereby thwarting the Islamist victory. A compromise had been attempted to avoid such an outcome and the army had offered the FIS a "deal" to share power: the military would hold the most important (defense, interior, foreign affairs, economy, finance and

---

15. March 21, 1989.

16. The Fis with 54.25 percent of the vote won in 856 communes out of 1540. The FLN in power only received 28 percent of the vote.

17. Out of 430 seats in play, FIS won 188 and 47.2 percent of the vote. With the exception of Kabylie where a Berber secular party (FFS : Front des Forces Socialistes) won (15 seats) and in the South where the FLN was the winner (15 seats), Fis had won in the rest of the country. Voter participation was 59 percent.

energy) and the FIS would have the ideological ministries (education and religious affairs). The Islamists rejected the compromise, their leaders were arrested and the FIS was outlawed signaling the start of a civil war.

According to the 'Perspective center' at the University of Sherbooke in Canada, there were 60,000 killed among the Islamists from 1991 to 2004.[18] Algerian President Abdelaziz Bouteflika then began the era of pardons and national reconciliation. In September 2005 he proposed a referendum on a 'Charter for Peace and National Reconciliation' that was to garner 97 percent Yes votes with 80 percent voter participation.[19] The charter allowed the freeing of 2,200 prisoners accused of terrorist acts when it became law in February 2006.[20] Three hundred members of Islamist groups lay down their weapons and their exiled leaders have returned home. The national consultative commission for the promotion and protection of human rights (CNCPPDH) estimated that there had been "6,141 true disappearances"[21] and according to Algerian authorities 41,000 requests for assistance were on file by the victims of terrorism.[22]

Yet the attacks continued and the climate of insecurity remained to the point that no one can tell what will happen after Bouteflika. The Salafi Group for Preaching and Combat (GSPC) rejected any amnesty offers made by the government.[23] An article in *Le Monde*[24] reported that armed groups of the GSPC were operating "in the Kabylie, east, west and south." In September 2006, the GSPC repeated its allegiance to Al Qaeda. Today following pressure from the Algerian authorities those groups have preferred to "migrate" toward Sub Saharan Africa using a new label: AQMI [Al Qaeda in the Islamic Maghreb].

---

18. 100,000 dead, 1 million casualties, *Le terrorisme en Algérie: dix années de génocide au quotidien*, Monographie N° 74, July 2002, M Boudjemaa. According to Amnesty International, Report 2007, during the internal conflict from 1990, 200,000 persons were killed by armed groups and the security forces. To that human count one must add the destruction of 916 school and university buildings, some 5,000 businesses and the exile aboard of 400,000 managers, intellectuals, and artists.
19. Reuters, September 30, 2005.
20. Associated Press, September 19, 2006.
21. Declaration by the president of CNCPPDH on September 30, 2006.
22. *La Tribune*, September 16, 2006.
23. AFP, September 14, 2006.
24. August 27, 2006.

Starting in early 2011 the Algerian government distributed the oil dividend freely to preempt social protest. The state of emergency was lifted but the army and security forces control the country. Actually neither the government nor the Salafists want a revolution and it will take years for real change in Algiers.

A New Religious Clash

In Algeria since 2006, a law was introduced to regulate the conditions of non-Muslim religious practice: prison sentences of two to five years and fines of 5,000 to 10,000 Euros for anyone who "incites, forces or uses means of seduction to convert a Muslim to another religion." The historic presence of Christian churches is not being called into question even though they are under governmental pressure, it is rather the forcefulness and proselytism of the evangelical movements that is viewed as an "aggression" against Islam

In the past the Diocese of Algiers was considered the key venue in the dialog between the Catholic Church and Islam. Léon-Étienne Cardinal Duval was bishop until 1988. Favorable to Algerian independence he had been the butt of many insulting nicknames by those backing "Algerie française" who used to call him 'Mohamed Ben Duval.' His successor Monsignor Henri Teissier, a Frenchman born in Lyon, became an Algerian citizen in 1966 and held the position for thirty-five years, when he would experience the terrorist wave of the 1990s. Over the course of that decade 19 priests, monks and nuns were murdered including the seven monks at Tibhirine and Monsignor Pierre Claverie, the bishop of Oran.[25] Henri Teissier was a dedicated partisan of Christian-Islamic dialog and opposed the intolerance of the Islamists while he maintained the trust of the authorities and above all of the Algerian public. As an "historic" church in Algeria the Catholic Church has a limited number of members, a few thousand worshipers, expatriates and a small number of Algerians of European descent.

---

25. On August 1, 1996, Pierre Claverie who had taken Algerian nationality was murdered by a group of armed men.

The evangelical movements take a very different path since they view the country as a land to be conquered and the objective is to convert Muslims. Due to their aggressive methods they make large numbers of conversions. Under the presidency of George W. Bush they were identified with an imperial America and Algerians feared that those movements might be used politically by Washington. The government as well as the Islamists saw this as a strategy to create a Christian minority that could one day be used as an excuse for military intervention. Minister of Religious Affairs Buabdallah Ghlamallah, said so very clearly: the goal of the evangelicals is to build up "a minority to facilitate foreign influence on internal policies." The "historical" churches pay the price of this state of affairs. The former president of the Protestant Church of Algeria Hugh Johnson, was told to leave the country where he had been living for forty-five years. After a complaint to the Council of State the measure was suspended but he was expelled in the end.

In January 2008 a Catholic Priest Pierre Wallez, was given a suspended prison sentence because he had conducted a service for clandestine migrants from Cameroon. Four Algerian converts were given suspended prison sentences and two were pardoned by the Tiaret criminal court that was placing them on trial "for the illegal practice of a non-Muslim faith." They were accused of saying mass at the home of one of those accused while the location was not appropriate for such a ceremony. According to the law of February 2006 places of worship must be approved by the ministry of religious affairs.

Behind the struggle against proselytizing there is the fight by the government and the army against the Kabylie that remains opposed to the government in Algiers. The first measures were aimed at the two Protestant Churches, that had been active in the area for the past ten years and had about one thousand members.[26] Yet both in Morocco and Algeria, the Berber based movements represent a mass of resistance to Islamist ideology and do not identify with the Arab-Islamic identity that is proclaimed by the states of the Maghreb after independence. For them to promote a pluralist, Mediterranean and

---

26. Nouvelle vie and Ta Fath – the light.

African Berber identity is tantamount to rejecting religious mono-
theism.

Sufism: the Other Response

In the summer of 2009 both in Morocco and Algeria the Sufi
brotherhoods came to forefront: Sufism shows the tolerant face of
Islam based on ancestral roots linked to society. It is a far cry from
when President Boumediene was campaigning against the Sufi
brotherhood Alawiya as being a state within the state. Today
President Bouteflika got closer to them and when the brotherhood
celebrated its centennial the festivities had the patronage of the
president and his support.

Two Muslim factions were adamantly opposed to Sufism in the
course of the twentieth century. The westernized and secular
Muslims represented by Ataturk on one end and the Islamists that
embraced Wahhabism who consider themselves as the only true
models of Islam on the other. Post-Kemalist Turkey refused to allow
the Sufi brotherhoods to operate thereby creating a new religious
issue. The Algerian Islamists more recently were able to thrive in the
vacuum that had been occupied by the Sufi brotherhoods that for
centuries have been one of the more important manifestations of
Islam in art, culture, spirituality and society.

Sufism developed from one end of the Muslim world to the
other: from Rumi the Persian to Nusrat Fateh Ali Khan in Pakistan
or the Alhambra in Grenada and the Taj Mahal in India. The
Brotherhoods established their influence in the Islamic world
(Turkey, Iran, Indonesia, Senegal or Africa) and beyond in the west.
Why the renewed interest in Sufism? The concept of the pathway, the
initiation into a cult, which are both implicit in the Brotherhood and
are the expression of the same idea in Sufism. Beyond the religious
dimension: the Sufia or "he who has been purified"; and Silsila, the
chain of faith and initiation linking the masters to the Prophet
Muhammad; the Baraka, or divine inspiration that the master can
impart and by his presence contribute to the development of the
Brotherhood that is also a social link. Sufism places the individual

ahead of his group and as a community engages in individual or collective worship such as the Khalwa (a spiritual and solitary retreat that used to take place in a cave), the Dhikr (a meditation where the name of God is invoked endlessly) or Sama (a collective gathering to sing mystic poetry).

Due to its initiation side filled with spirituality and culture Sufism is tolerant. The Emir Abd el-Kader, a Sufi remembered for his resistance against the French army was also a poet and some of his verse has been put to music. In "Me" are the expectations of humanity / He who wants a mosque / To pray his Lord with fervor / He who wants a synagogue, a steeple and a crucifix / Or the Kaaba to kiss the stone / Or idols and fetishes / He who seeks a retreat to be alone / Or a tavern to sing the praise of beauties … An ode to tolerance, a solution against intransigence and elusive happiness.

The opposition of Sufism and Islamism reveals another dimension: the Brotherhoods can create a social link while Islamism carries with it division and the rejection of the other. This is why Sufism can create a state-based Islam, which is the hope of the Algerian authorities when they call on the country's Sufi tradition as a way to refashion a social identity with Islam as a symbol of national unity. In Algeria as in Morocco the political power centers are attempting to fray a middle ground between secularization and Islamism in seeking its links in the brotherhoods since the intermediate bodies such as political parties and trade unions have less and less credibility.

In this Sunni country the training and appointment of Sufi masters are guarantees against many deviations because the Sunnis have no clergy even though in a country like Morocco the monarchy trains and supervises the imams. The royal state-sponsored imams do not exclude the influence of self-appointed imams and the development of Salfism with as mentors young men trained in Pakistan or Saudi Arabia have a definite impact upon societies that are economically, socially and morally in crisis and where education is failing. In that context the idea is not to make Sufism a state religion but to use it as an alternative to fundamentalism.

King Mohammed VI explained the importance of the Sufi brotherhoods in Malekite Islam: the monarch concludes that "Sufism can meet the challenge of the criminal heresies of religious fundamentalism." The king reiterated the links between Moroccan history and Sufism: "The brotherhoods were spiritual and educational schools the way they organized society through the Zaouias that were in the cities and the countryside. Sufism influences both the elite and the larger population and in Morocco Sufis are known for their social, moral and educational involvement. They built schools and libraries and were careful to disseminate the values of solidarity and reconciliation as they put an end to racial and tribal differences." The king is convinced that Sufism is the right way to respond to today's challenges: "Today, humanity needs to privilege the values of tolerance, solidarity, altruism and reject the most destructive forms of selfishness."

With the caution commensurate with his status the king takes a position on a point of theology that caused friction in the Muslim world. As he recalled the great Sufi leaders and their contribution to Islamic civilization, he feels that those masters: "Allow us, who are attached to the values of the Sunna, to turn to those pure sources of creation keeping in mind the prime importance of what come from the Book and the Sunna that cannot be viewed as a fixed heritage or an old fashioned attitude." The monarch would then move closer to what makes the Shia such an original part of Islam meaning its modernity. In a Sunni world it is through Sufism that Islam can claim its place in contemporary society from a heritage that cannot be fixed: it is a response to Salafism and its deviations.

Islam in West Africa: Tolerance and the Risks of Islamism

According to AFRICOM (U.S. Africa Command), after Somalia the second area at risk is in Sub-Saharan West Africa: Mauritania, Niger, Mali, Senegal. The organization responsible is AQMI (Al-Qaeda in the Islamic Maghreb). Jean-Christophe Ruffin considers "the area has political violence equal to Central Asia or the Pakistani-Afghan zone." Long before 9/11, Africa was the continent where the

United States was the victim of Islamic terrorism when the embassies in Kenya and Tanzania were attacked. The terrorists included Somalis, Kenyans and Comorians. Somalia is under the control of pro-Bin Laden forces, the Shebabs, and the warlords. For the first time in the summer of 2010, the Shebabs had organized and claimed attacks in Uganda, a Christian country. With famine in the Horn of Africa the Islamists take advantage in pursuit of a political objective: to attempt to destabilize the region. The influx of refugees from countries that are socially or politically fragile (Christian Ethiopia, Djibouti the rear base used by the West in the struggle against piracy and fundamentalist Islam, Kenya in ethnic conflict) is magnified by the risk of Al Qaeda infiltration.

From east to west, Africa is under the Islamist threat. The struggle against the terrorists in Morocco and Algeria pushed the Islamo-terrorists toward the south, to Mauritania, Mali, and southern Algeria that are considered a no man's land. Since 1976, the authorities in Nouakchott had neglected surveillance of their northern border due to the Western Sahara conflict between Morocco and the Polisario Front that had Algerian support. Mauritania is a desert country, twice the size of France with borders drawn in long lines on the official maps.

As Jean-Christophe Ruffin points out that the desert is filled with traffic where nomads, caravans, terrorists and highwaymen come together, no one really knows where the borders are, and in Mauritania until recently and in spite of the outlawing of slavery, slave markets were still thriving.[27] The Touareg caravan drivers are also involved in contraband and in the desert they smuggle drugs from Latin America to Europe, weapons and illegal immigrants. The strip of the Sahara Sahel is at the same time a necessary pathway and a crossroads for trade and trafficking just as Somalia is today the hub where drugs from Colombia transit through Kenya. Smuggling and terrorism are often excellent bedfellows! In this context kidnapping has become a lucrative trade that usually entails the payment of a ransom. The funds are used to purchase increasingly sophisticated weapons in the region, a trade that may also involve the countries

27. *Katiba*, Flammarion, Paris, 2010.

themselves. Contrary to all its commitments, France did pay ransom money to groups tied to Al Qaeda to free several of its citizens.

The activities of the AQMI reflect upon government policy: in Mauritania, an emergency planning system "Vigie pirate" has been set up. Border posts have been created (over 45 in 2009) and a filing system of foreigners has been instituted. Such regulations are not acceptable to most nomadic populations that cannot conceive of borders. In Mali, Niger, Mauritania, the cost of security and the anti-terrorist struggle is very high in spite of western help as the help given to developing countries usually has a different set of priorities.

Both Islam in Sub-Saharan Africa and the mentality of those populations are far removed from fundamentalism. Islam was known for its tolerance and the question is why fundamentalist Islam took hold there. After fifty years of independence, it must be said that the results are extremely disappointing: corruption, unemployment, lack of democracy with youth having no prospects either professionally or individually. Besides, the changes in the traditional structures encourage young people to keep their distance or to avoid them altogether. The support offered by European countries or the Americans to African regimes led to the increasing rejection of the western political model. Debates such as the one concerning the veil in France, and the minaret referendum in Switzerland, are part of the rejection of the West as fundamentalist Islam grows among the jobless youth and the intellectuals.

In Nigeria, Africa's most populous country, the Federal government is secular while 12 out of 19 states of the federation have adopted the Sharia. This is in response to part of the population wanting to live under Islamic law and the proselytizing of certain sects taking their inspiration from Afghan Talibans such as Boko Haram. The latter uses the name "haoussa" that translates roughly "western education is sinful." The risks of a break between the Muslim north and Christian south are not just based on religious considerations. The north is poor while the south has mining and oil riches. During the Christmas celebrations in 2010, a wave of violence and attacks killed 500 people in the Jos area. This not only because of the north-south rivalry or the Christian-Muslim split: there is also tradition land ownership. For some ethnic groups land belongs to the individual while others consider it a collective asset. Many other considerations are part of this dispute that includes many other issues (religion, ethnic, legal), creating an explosive situation while in the past the various groups lived in harmony and at peace. Religion is not the sole source of all problems.

In Senegal Islam's traditional structures are part of the regime in power. The country is 90 percent Muslim and the religion is organized in two large Sufi Brotherhoods: mourides and tidjanes. Their leaders exercise political influence and they take part in elections. Under the presidencies of Leopold Senghor and Abdou Diouf, the tolerant Islam of the brotherhoods found that democracy, the links to France, the efforts in education and development aide were all policies that they accepted. President Abdoulaye Wade managed to obtain the support of the brotherhoods but later on, his policies (nepotism, lavish spending in an economic crisis and his new alliances: getting closer to Iran and other states upset the balance and the organization of society.[28]

To break its isolation Tehran is interested in Africa and in Senegal: in 2009 the African continent saw at least twenty official visits by Iranian dignitaries. President Wade decided to support Iran as a way of finding new partners beyond the traditional players which he calls the "new independence." Karim the president's son and president of the national agency of the organization of the Islamic conference organized a summit in Dakar in March 2008. He took part in negotiations to free Clotilde Reiss, who had been sentenced in Teheran. A photograph showed him next to President Ahmadinejad, along with the French emissaries he was introducing.

In 2009, he was on the list during the elections for mayor of Dakar and the presidency of the Senate. But Karim was defeated after seeing himself as the first judge in the capital city where he wanted to replace his father as head of state in 2012. Despite this defeat he entered the government on May 1, 2009, as minister of State minister of international cooperation, of land reorganization, air

---

28. President Wade designed the 52 meter high statue with an elevator to reach the top. Using copyright privileges President Wade collects a tax on the ticket sales and reproductions of his creation. The statue was built by North Koreans for a total cost of 25 million Euros.

transport and infrastructure. Karim speaks only French but he started to learn Wolof, the local language. The man who portrays himself as the head of the "concert generation" also declared himself to be Muslim something that no one aspiring to lead Senegal would have declared publicly while his father managed to draw the ire of both Christians and Muslims. It is a dangerous gamble.

Chapter 9

Islam and the West: Marriage or Divorce?

Integration or Communitarism

Jean-Paul Roux, who specializes in Islamic civilization, wrote:

> Muslims hope and believe that they will make the Sharia rule the old western lands of Christ... It may well be that Islam will overwhelm Christianity in the future that it may plant seeds in the great faithless and lawless masses and that conversions that are still rare will grow in numbers. It may also be that through immigration and fertility its followers will make it the most observed religion in the West so that it will submerge Christianity and finally win the long war.[1]

---

1. *Un choc des civilisations*, Fayard, 2007.

One ghost that is swept away—the Arabs were stopped at Poitiers by Charles Martel[2]—is usually held up by the European far right: the issue of compatibility among religious practices and way of life, the values and the laws of the West. Actually there is no confrontation to speak of and a "clash of civilizations" or of cultures is tantamount to using scare tactics and ignorance. However, the struggle against immigration has always been one of the main themes of the far right but there is a double evolution both in semantics and politics. Immigration is no longer the target but rather the risk of Islamization of European societies, a reality felt in most countries that are part of the EU.

The 2004 murder by an Islamist of moviemaker Theo Van Gogh, because of his provocations against Islam, unveiled another side of the Netherlands known for its tolerance. Since then and with the government of Mark Rutte, a coalition of Christians and liberal democrats, the country is under the influence of Geert Wilders, head of the Freedom Party (PVV). While the Islam phobic right wing leader is not part of the government coalition, he holds its fate in his hands. In exchange for support without participation, the government had to make concessions to the far right on many points. The coalition promised to check the construction of Muslim schools and mosques, to punish blasphemy, increase speed limits on superhighways, create a police for the protection of animals—some of the demands also made by the populists. One point of disagreement between the three political parties: two of them consider Islam as a religion while the far right refuses to grant it such a status and Wilders describes it as an "ideology." Yet prior to parliamentary elections liberals were criticizing Geert Wilders' "provocations" and his "racism" while the Christian Democrats accused him of fanning "hatred and fear at the risk of a religious war." Indicted in 2009 for inciting to racial hatred of the Muslims, he was acquitted on June 13, 2011. The prosecutor felt he had not been guilty of that crime for the words he said in his film *Fitna* (Discord). The populist leader mentioned the "backward" nature of Islam, and

---

2. In 732, Charles Martel came to rescue of the Duke of Aquitania to stop the march of the Saracens. They had come from Pamplona, and invaded the Basque country in a few months when they ransacked Bordeaux.

called the Prophet Mohammed a "sick pedophile" he also demanded that the Koran be banned in the Netherlands calling it an "Islamic *Mein Kampf*." At the end of the trial he said he would continue to say what he thought as he had done before.

A study undertaken in France and Germany shows that 40 percent of the people think Islam is a threat; 31 percent of French people associate "Islam and the rejection of western values."[3] Another poll in November 2010 by the University of Munster, concluded that among Europeans the Germans had a negative opinion of Muslims (about 66 percent) vs. 56 percent of Frenchmen and 62 percent of the Dutch.[4]

Politicians are fearful of discussing and condemning Islamphobia while anti-Semitic acts get a very different kind of treatment. When a veiled woman who had filed a complaint was called "an Islamist terrorist and a whore" was murdered by her aggressor in the courtyard of the Dresden Court of Appeals in Germany,[5] the Central Council of Muslims (ZMD) had to demand that the "political class including the Chancellor issue a clear and unequivocal statement." For many observers that murder demonstrates a growing fact that politicians underestimate: a climate of hatred for Islam incited by many publications, internet sites and local initiatives.

The work of Thilo Sarrazin was enormously successful in Germany leading up to a scandal. The suggestive title is, *Germany is Abolishing Itself*,[6] where he restated the multiculturalism issue in national culture. The same issue was mentioned by the usually cautious chancellor forcing then President Christian Wulff, to state that like Christianity and Judaism "Islam is also part of Germany." Thilo Sarrazin is not just anybody: as a prominent member of the Social Democratic Party (SPD), he was on the board of the German central bank. In his book he attacks "bad" immigration from Muslim countries that is making his country "more and more stupid." His entire argument is based on so-called "genetic reasons," that recall the darkest moments of German history. National culture according

---

3. Poll by IFOP/*Le Monde*, January 2011.
4. *Le Monde*, January 5, 2011.
5. July 2009.
6. Deutschland schafft sich ab.

to him is the "culture of reference" (Leitkultur). In spite of two legal actions against him he will not be expelled from the SPD. The ideas expressed by Thilo Sarrazin are not isolated. They are part of a mood that is spreading throughout Europe in Germany, Austria, The Netherlands and Switzerland and also in France.

The Birthplace of Human Rights

In 2007, those who elected Nicolas Sarkozy also came from the supporters of the Front national (FN), an older generation of practicing Catholics. The main issues at the time were about security. In his first government Sarkozy created the ministry of national identity, then with mounting losses in various by-elections—regional, European, local—and negative polls, the French government tried to adopt the vocabulary of the far right. The debate that Nicolas Sarkozy began and was carried out by Éric Besson on national identity created a sour feeling until it was stopped. The government had understood that by using that kind of rhetoric it was playing with fire and without obtaining the far right votes it was giving comfort to that position. The same happened when former interior minister Brice Hortefeux, tried to enforce loss of citizenship for criminals who had obtained French nationality through naturalization. The provision was aimed at only a handful of persons, about one per year according to Claude Guéant the interior minister, and one group originally from the Maghreb. When the former interior minister is guilty of racial insults in statements targeting persons from the Maghreb he legitimizes Islamophobia. Those facts and that context contributes to the revival of xenophobia and fears of a possible Islamization of society.

The lesson was apparently lost and when those responsible for Sarkozy's majority stated that "Frenchmen want France to remain France"[7] it is a rejection of the other and castigates the immigrant. When Claude Guéant invoked a "crusade" in Libya, the word is replete with meaning and recalls the Christian expedition to free the Holy Places that were occupied by the Muslims. Finally when an

---

7. Claude Guéant, *Le Monde*, March 16, 2011.

unknown member of parliament, was proposing: "In order to reassure the French people on the migration of populations coming from the Mediterranean… Let's put them back on the ships," she was flirting with hateful thoughts belonging to the past.[8] In the semantics of exclusion it belongs to Marine Le Pen's point of view on prayers: "Fifteen years ago there was the veil, then more and more veils. Then we had the burqa and more and more burqas. Then praying in public places… Of course there are no tanks and no soldiers but it's still a form of occupation and it bothers the population." Coming from Marine Le Pen or the leaders of the far right it is unacceptable and inexcusable. How then can we characterize those statements when they are made by public officials? The idea of a debate on "Islam and the values of the Republic" assumed a far less obvious conclusion on the part of the initiators. The great national debate started by the political party of the president, the UMP on the theme: "Secularism and Republican values." Three hours of internal discussions to close a polemic! Forty eight hours prior to the runoff elections,[9] Pope Benedict XVI addressed the crowd in front of the cathedral of Notre-Dame in Paris. His message came in response to the fears expressed by France's religious leaders about what they called "the stigmatization of Muslims" especially but not exclusively by the far right. The pope called upon his listeners: "To do away with the barriers of fear of strangers and foreigners." He also said that he was in favor of "a just secularism, a secularism that is open allowing everyone to live with their beliefs in accordance with each one's conscience […] The object is to build a world that is free with equality and fraternity of believers and non-believers who must feel "free" to be what there are, "equal" in their right to live their private lives in the community true to their convictions and as "brothers."

Can "positive secularism" thrive in a peaceful republic?

The law should be enforced excluding other issues. The dialog between the state and the churches should take place within the insti-

---

8. Chantal Brunel, a deputy from Seine et Marne.
9. March 27, 2011.

tutional framework.[10] Finally politicians should avoid approximations or passionate appeals.

In Europe, Islam is an integrated faith. It would be a mistake to lump the thousands of Muslims who practice their faith like Catholics, Protestants or Jews with the Salafist minority that are to Islam what fundamentalists are to the Catholics, some evangelists to the Protestants or the orthodox to the Jews. Due to their recent arrival in Europe the Muslim community faces some problems. Other monotheistic religions that are anchored in history had centuries to build their places of worship, their schools and gain through the institutions access to the political power. Since Islam appeared in France after the laws of separation of church and state of 1905 the problems Muslims have in their religious practice are magnified.

The issue of changing the law of 1905 in France obfuscates the problem. The Debré laws on Catholic, Jewish and also Muslim teaching today… with association contracts up to Mitterrand's presidency who would end the secular dream of a broad public education service. No one objects today to a pluralistic France. The laws of the republic allow Muslims to create schools, secondary schools and high schools. Mosques are being built in Marseille, Strasbourg and many cities in France: the issue is no longer one of approval by the authorities. Rental contracts and construction also benefit from state help and Jack Lang had the government finance the cathedral and the mosque at Évry with two museums, two cultural centers and two places of worship. The Council of State has also made some landmark decisions: out of the 1,800 churches built in the Île-de-France area after 1905, 405 benefited from the symbolic rental of one franc without any complaints.

Administrative courts have been busy with complaints filed for mosque construction projects and their financing mostly by persons associated with the far right. The Council of State has adopted a liberal approach to secularism and religious freedom while recalling that local government may not "offer help in the practice of a religious faith" Jean-Marc Sauvé, vice president of the Council of

---

10. CRIF, Consistoire, Conférence des Évêques de France, CFCM.

State considers that "with new religions needing new buildings it reconciles the 1905 law to other existing regulations." By contradicting the decisions of the administrative courts the Council of State has advanced "local public interest" authorizing local groups to finance facilities to be sued as religious buildings intended for worship.

Actually the problem is to be found in the transparency of foreign financing and the training of imams working in France. Laws and regulations exist and former Prime Minister Jean-Pierre Raffarin provided a framework to ensure financial transparency through foundations. Upon request from the Grand Mosque in Paris, the Catholic Institute has provided training in the values of the French Republic with financing from the ministry of the interior. French speaking Muslims work as preachers or to fill other functions within the institutions (chaplains in hospitals, prisons etc.)

The issue of the veil was seen as revelatory and a commission created by former President Chirac allowed to go beyond the narrow question of the veil and forbid all overt signs in school and within the public services. The case of wearing a burqa in public is different and that prohibition may well be removed by the European Court for human rights as contrary to free expression. Dominique de Villepin, then prime minister, created a charter of secularism in the public services.[11] The personnel involved received specific directives: every public servant has a duty to observe strict neutrality and must treat all persons equally by respecting their freedom of conscience. "A public servant who expresses his or her religious beliefs while at work commits a serious breach of his or her obligations."

The administrative court of appeals in Lyon[12] ruled that wearing a veil by a government official during work is contrary to the principle of secularism. It also concluded that for a public servant to announce his religious beliefs through an external sign is a breach of professional conduct and would therefore be at fault. This legal decision was reiterated in court after the firing of an educator in a private kindergarten.

---

11. Memorandum dated April 13, 2007.
12. CAA in Lyon, November 27, 2003, Miss. Nadjet Ben Abdallah.

But for those using public facilities things are entirely different since they may express their beliefs such as a scarf or a kippah, within limits for the proper functioning of the service and on condition that it doesn't disturb the peace.[13] When Claude Guéant stated that public servants… "may not express any religious preference" he is stating what the law says. But when he says "those using a public service should not" he is injecting a dangerous interpretation. A monk, a nun, a Jew wearing a yarmulke, could no longer ride a bus or enter a town hall.

There is also the reality of daily life: in September 2006 at the Robert-Debré hospital, Professor Jean-François Oury, the head of the gynecological section was on duty in the maternity ward. He had to examine a woman about to give birth as he was about to do so the husband became angry and attacked the doctor slapping him because in his view no man even a doctor should touch his wife! The husband was a young bearded man wearing a gown and was sentenced in Paris criminal court to six months in jail and a fine to be paid to the doctor, the Public Assistance office in Paris and the order of medical doctors as part of the civil complaint. The court reiterated: "This is a Republic and a secular venue a public hospital is a place where everyone can be born with the same opportunities, the first location where there is social mixing. It is not the place where religion may be invoked to secure a different treatment and this behavior is not acceptable."

Even though such events are very rare and the civil plaintiffs ensured that this kind of violence by patients using religious beliefs as their excuse in public hospitals does raise the issue of religion in a public hospital. The experts of the Stasi commission discovered some examples of problems at public hospitals (women giving birth wearing the burqa, refusing to be examined by a man, corridors being used for prayer, interns wearing the veil, a psychiatrist seeing patients with the Koran.) Dalil Boubakeur, a doctor and the head of Great Mosque in Paris said: "Let's stop the nonsense: Islam doesn't forbid physical examinations. We have examples of examination tables dating back to the time of Avicenna and there is no reason for a man

---

13. Conseil d'État, opinion of May 3, 2000, Miss. Julie Marteaux.

to refuse to examine a woman. A doctor examines a woman according to science."[14]

There is nothing to stop Muslims in France as in Rotterdam, from opening a hospital reserved for their coreligionists. This is a private initiative where Halal food is served and an imam is constantly on duty. Men and women are separated with men nurses and doctors and women for female patients. The personnel numbering 45 doctors and 275 nurses and doesn't necessarily have to be Muslim.

On April 11, 2011, the law of October 22, 2010, forbidding the full body veil went into effect. The law stipulates that "No one in any public space may wear a garment that seeks to cover the face." The legislation covered a very small number of women that didn't go beyond one thousand throughout the country including a majority of French women recently converted to Islam. Beyond a law of circumstance other laws already covered the underlying problem.

The Sarkozy law of November 2003 made the issuing of a resident card conditional to the "republican integration" of the person requesting it. In November 2005 a Moroccan woman was refused a resident card because "she was wearing a veil entirely covering her neck and the roots of her hair." The administration considered that garb "similar to the hijab of fundamentalist Islam" that wouldn't allow it to justify "a republican integration into French society according to current legislation." A ruling by the Council of State dated June 27, 2008, refused French nationality to a woman from the Maghreb due to a lack of assimilation. The ruling stated: "This person has a good knowledge of the French language but has adopted a radical practice of her religion that is not compatible with the basic values of the French community and in particular the principle of equality between the sexes." The judges noted that their decision didn't intend to limit the religious freedom of the person involved. The Council of State considered that the decree that she was objecting to that refused her French nationality didn't ignore the constitutional principle of freedom of expression nor the stipulations

---

14. Interview at Anticancer.fr, September 2008.

in article 9 of the European convention for the safeguard of human rights and basic freedoms.[15]

What was the motivation behind the judge's decision? The government commissioner explained: "The mere fact of wearing the Islamic veil is not a sign of lack of assimilation," adding that the ruling by the Council stated that if the Islamic veil is worn: "as a demonstration of strict religious practice it cannot in and of itself serve to justify a lack of assimilation." The Council of State considers that the husband in the couple in question had acquired French nationality and, "He describes himself as a Salafist and states that they belong to that movement… that had enlisted most of the young people in the neighborhood they were living in after the visit of a particularly aggressive imam." His wife stated that when she was living in Morocco she didn't wear the veil and only adopted it after coming to France upon her husband's request. While she was visiting the prefecture she was "covered head to foot with the type of cloth used by women in the Arabian peninsula: a long single color gown either dark or tan that falls to the feet, a veil that hides the hair, chin and forehead with another cloth that allows you to see the eyes only through a slit and is called the niqab in that part of the world." The Council of State considers that this person in practice was living "the life of a recluse cut off from French society." Since she had stated that she had "no idea regarding secularism or the right to vote the government commissioner came to the conclusion that this person "had not adopted the values of the Republic particularly about the equality of the sexes. She lives a life of submission toward men in her family which she finds normal and the very idea of protesting that submission doesn't even dawn on her."[16]

Danièle Lochak, a professor of public law at the University of Paris X: "Since judges cannot use religion because of the principle of freedom of conscience they are basing their ruling on the woman's

---

15. Anyone has the right to freedom of thought, of conscience and religion, that right implies the freedom to change religion or belief and demonstrate one's religion or belief individually and collectively in public or in private through ceremonies, teaching, and the practices and gestures of rituals. The freedom to show one's religion or belief cannot have any restrictions other than those provided for by law and are deemed necessary in any democratic society to the safeguard of public safety, the protection of order, health or public morality or the protection of the rights and freedoms of others.

16. Mrs. Prada Bordenace, Commissaire du gouvernement. Affaires N° 286798. Séance of June 27, 2008.

submissiveness which they deduce not just from her clothing but also from the description she volunteered of her social attitude."[17] According to the ruling issued by the highest administrative court, the criteria for French nationality are changing. And those changes appear against a backdrop of increasing denunciation of "communitarism" and the "condemnation of Islam."

The naturalization issue, and therefore the choice of acquiring the nationality of the welcoming country is how European society defines itself toward Islam. According to the constitution or the European convention, the rights of women belong to a set of fundamental rights. At the same time with the law of October 2010 on the full body veil, France is running the risk of being condemned for infringing upon freedom of conscience and of religion.

Integration, Community or Cohabitation

The basic issue is one of integration. As a visiting scholar at prestigious St. Antony's College Oxford in 2005-2006, and Senior Research Fellow in Japan and at the Lokahi Foundation, Tariq Ramadan was advising Tony Blair and the British government.[18] Ramadan is the son of Said, the son-in-law of Hassan al-Banna, founder of the Muslim Brotherhood in 1945. In 1961, Said Ramadan founded the Islamic center of Geneva in Switzerland. For some thirty years the center was the only voice of the Brotherhood in Europe. With a PhD in literature and a professor of Islamology, he was actively involved in the debate on the renewal of Muslim thought in the world and the place of Islam in the West and in secular societies. According to Gilles Kepel,[19] while a professor at the University of Rotterdam Tariq Ramadan was "the semi official spokesman to the Dutch political establishment." What the authorities in The Hague had in mind was to create an "Islamic center with a modern touch" inspired by the professor's advice to create a structure under the Sharia and Islamic dogma that would develop within society.

---

17. Interview, *Le Monde*, July 12, 2008.
18. Called as an advisor to the British government in 2005 to be part of a task force to examine ways of combating Islamic extremism in Great Britain after the July 7, 2005 attacks that resulted in 36 deaths in London.
19. Professor at Sciences Politiques (Paris), director of the chair of the Middle East and Mediterranean.

In such a context even before anything is set up it will inevitably bring about deviations. Polygamy goes against the principle of gender equality and it is illegal in the European Union. In August 2008 the daily *NRC Handelsblad* revealed that the Rotterdam municipality, along with three other large cities, was giving polygamy de facto recognition. Municipal workers were recording polygamous persons who had married in countries where such practices were permitted. The government in The Hague decided that men married to more than one woman would not be eligible for Dutch citizenship. Nebahat Albayrak, a young woman of Turkish origin who was secretary of state for justice, even wanted to forbid immigration into the Netherlands of polygamous persons asking whether polygamy could be a "disturbance of the peace."

In February 2008 Dr. Rowan Williams, Archbishop of Canterbury, the highest ranking member of the Church of England, issued a statement that upset the entire political elite. Gordon Brown, as prime minister at the time, had to reiterate that "British law in this country is based on British values." The archbishop said that the application of certain aspects of Sharia law appeared to be inevitable in Great Britain with a large Muslim population. While rejecting certain violent applications of Sharia (flagellations, decapitations or discrimination of women) for criminal cases he recommended British law and Islamic law for financial and family matters (divorce, child custody, inheritance.) The British clergy had to go on record in favor of a judicial system that would recognize the religious character of a minority.

The 104th Archbishop of Canterbury heads the Anglican Church that is a state religion of which Queen Elizabeth II is the "Supreme Governor." Rev. Williams is also a member of the House of Lords which would be the equivalent of having the president of the Conference of French bishops also sitting in the second chamber in France namely the Senate. The position of the Archbishop is in the minority even within his church. Trevor Phillips, who heads the commission for equality and human rights summed up the majority opinion:

It is out of the question for us to set up a parallel judiciary system. The statement is more of a retreat into one's identity than an encouragement for modern multiculturalism.

Identity and communitarian feeling is growing Great Britain. In 2006 some 40 percent of Muslims wanted the application of Sharia. There are ghettos in the northern part of the country where Christians are not welcome, a situation that was criticized by another clergyman Mon. John Sentamu, Archbishop of York. The Bishop of Rochester, Rev. Michael Nazir-Ali, born in Karachi, Pakistan of foreign parents, was sent death threats, after he had denounced in the *Sunday Times* the fact that some neighborhoods were no longer accessible to non-Muslims due to radical Islam.

The statements by the British archbishop, like the Dutch projects, follow the lead of Tariq Ramadan whose critics chastise as a two faced man with double messages, a description he doesn't deny. While the republican model may successfully integrate Muslims there is an incompatibility between secularism and an Islam steeped in tradition: republican values cannot be compatible with a system based on Sharia or that is dogmatic. In March 2005, Tariq Ramadan issued an appeal calling for "an immediate moratorium on corporal punishment, lapidation and the death penalty." He was requesting ways "to answer the question of what is applicable (and in which circumstances) according to the law and what no longer is."

France never issued him a resident card even though he is often invited by the media or give lectures. The United States also declared Tariq Ramadan persona non grata on U.S. soil for many years[20] and only recently has Secretary of State Hillary Clinton lifted the measure. When a petition was circulated by a number of Muslim cultural figures to put an end to the "debate and critical assessment of Islam" imitated important persons such as Martine Aubry and Laurent Fabius requested that their names be taken off the list once they found out that Tariq Ramadan was one of those signing the petition. The closeness of the UOIF leadership and the Muslim Brotherhood was never denied in France.[21]

---

20. Decsision to withdraw the visa of July 28, 2004.
21. Union des Organisations Islamistes de France.

Sharia in the West

The question asked by the Rev. Williams as well as the Dutch projects takes on a different dimension in a Europe attempting to harmonize its laws and regulations. Tariq Ramadan can only elicit reactions such as those mentioned by Jean-Paul Roux to the European far right struggle against the Islamization of society. When discussing the place of Muslims in Europe it becomes essential to examine the issue of Sharia and shed certain myths. While public opinion has a media enhanced view of the issue it is necessary to restate the sources and attempt to provide a definition. Sharia literally means "The path to follow." It is Muslim law taken from the Koran and the Sunna which is the Prophet's tradition composed of hadiths—a statement or a tradition attributed to the Prophet. For the uninitiated understanding the Koran is a complex and rather difficult matter since it is the dictation taken by the Prophet (Muhammad) of the words of Allah (God) through the Archangel Gabriel.

The language of the Koran is Arabic and Muhammad had his disciples transcribe what Gabriel had told him. The book was written in two periods the first called the Mecca period (610 to 622) that discusses the relationship of man to the creator and the second called the Medina (622 to 632), relates to man's relations with other men. In the final version (652) the surahs written in Medina appeared in the first part of the work. The hadiths discuss the entire life of the believer, whether dealing with religious practice or issues regarding social life, public and private law. There are several versions of the sacred texts. Interestingly the Prophet himself mentions his doubts about the way his companions transcribe his words and he doesn't encourage them to take notes when he gives advice on any one subject because he feared that they could get confused with a written revelation. In the Holy Book the Prophet explains: "May he who has written down something I said outside the Koran erase it." The debate is vivid throughout the Muslim world especially when involving the infallibility of the prophesy.

The lawyers (fuqaha) use a different approach from the theologians (mutakallimûn): the former view the issue as one of distinguishing what belongs to prophetic infallibility versus a commitment. There are actions taken by the Prophet that come directly from his mission as God's messenger (sunna al-hua, meaning the sunna of guidance) and actions as an ordinary mortal (sunna al-adiya, meaning the customary sunna). This analysis of Islamic jurists opens the pathway to interpretation giving Islam a measure of modernity. Some aspects belong to dogma and others to the temporal order of things. To the vast majority of theologians the prophet was free of any errors in matters of guidance. On all other subjects (those considered customary) the prophets were exempted from major sins but remain prone to human error and capable even of minor sins. Such an approach allows room for interpretation. For the fundamentalist the issue is a simple one, since there cannot be a divine error and a fatwa (a religious edict) can always provide a (divine) solution to a problem.

The fundamentalists demand a strict application of the Sharia. In Europe the law is the reference that allows us to live together through the rules the legislators have enacted. In France justice is rendered in the name of the French people and religion as such must not enter the court system. In the city of Lille upon a request of the minister of justice the district attorney appealed a ruling in a case of annulment of a marriage motivated by religion. The plaintiff could have started divorce proceedings and in a secular republic the complaint would lead to finding a legal reason allowing the error made by the original court judgment to be corrected. The prosecutor asked the judges to issue the annulment without mentioning the disputed reason known as a dol (a misrepresentation of the lack of virginity of the bride) to seek a motive that takes into account: the interest of society". The interest of society was to avoid rendering a decision on a motive based on values that derive from religion.

Islam may enter the French legal system. A criminal court trial in the city of Rennes that was to be held on September 16 was delayed to January 19, 2009. The defense lawyer[22] explained his request as the defendant would be unable to defend himself during Ramadan: "The requirements of Ramadan from a physiological point of view have the effect of debilitating the persons fasting." The attorney for the

---

22. Me (Attorney) Yann Choucq.

plaintiffs[23] stated: "This is an aberration, it's the first time anything like this has happened in France…" and he concluded: "We no longer are in a secular republic."

Islam and the Legal System

In the West the concept of human rights, references to humanistic values, and the Enlightenment often going against public opinion, led to measures such as the abolition of the death penalty. The modern outlook for society and justice has put an end to the use of torture and ensured the humane treatment of prisoners…even though a grey area between legal texts and their application remains. References to human rights have become the rule in the French legal system as in the EU.

After the revolts across the Arab Muslim world there are greater expectations for more freedom and respect for such rights. It is not just a request by some intellectuals it comes from an educated youth where women play a greater role. Even though the leadership's motivations are not always seeking to emancipate those countries must change. Some measures try to limit the influence of radical Islam, others are only motivated by security reasons (fear of terrorists or thieves hiding under a niqab.) Since September 2010 while many Syrian women have been wearing the full body veil a form of dress now forbidden in the universities where only the scarf is still allowed. The same is happening in the administrative offices in Abu Dhabi, hospitals in Egypt or Bangladesh. In Kuwait it is forbidden while driving a car.

In other areas the law and what is practiced are regressive. The Jordanian penal code still provides amnesty for rapist if the victim is nubile and accepts to marry him. In Saudi Arabia a woman who had been raped filed a complaint in court: the plaintiff was sentenced to 100 lashes! On an appeal the court didn't just confirm the sentence but doubled the punishment. In western societies beliefs belong to the individual and may be expressed in a democracy. What is considered intangible such as the fundamental rights as written in our

---

23. Me (Attorney) Pierre Abegg.

constitutions and laws: equality of the sexes or the right to abortion in certain circumstances. The conflict arises with the refusal to accept those rules in the name of customs, traditions or religious belief.

For some Muslims living in Christian lands religion and religious practice are often pretexts to keep women in a subservient position in the name of tradition to preserve a patriarchal society. Many incidents having to do with Islam known to the general public concern the position and status of women in welcoming societies. At a certain time institutions could have an ambiguous attitude and the courts tried to find attenuating circumstances to explain the crimes by looking at the customs of the country of origin of the accused that become a form of immunity?

In August 2007 the highest court of appeals in Italy justified the use of violence in the name of religion and tradition. The parents and brothers of a young adolescent Muslim woman were accused of having beaten her several times and sequestering her as punishment for her "western" attitudes. Found guilty by the lower court for "sequestration and bad treatment" the parents were acquitted on appeal. On August 2 the Supreme Court rejected the appeal filed by the district attorney against decision for acquittal issued by the court of appeals. The constitutional judges admit that the blows were "proven" but didn't find that were dictated by "vexing measures or contempt." The punishment was "for the good" of the victim, her family of the Muslim faith would not tolerate "her seeing an Italian friend," they wanted to punish her "for her lifestyle that didn't conform to their culture." The judges thought that this kind of violence was justifiable for some purported religious reasons seeking to justify a respect for multiculturalism that has no bearing in such circumstances. This was indeed an exceptional case but it took place in 2007 and today public opinion and the political class would rise up against such a verdict.

The Hidden Face or Another Side to Reality

There exist little known situations where women living in Europe of the immigrant population are subject to conflicting legal rules between the countries where they are living and their lands of origin.

French women of North African origin who are the daughters of immigrants often don't know that they have dual citizenship. If their father is Moroccan, Algerian or Tunisian he has given his nationality to his children according to the laws of those three countries. When they travel to Morocco, Tunisia or Algeria they are considered nationals of those countries and subject to local laws. The preamble to the French constitution of October 27, 1946 "guarantees that women shall have equal rights to men in every area." This principle of equality is also recognized in many international treaties including the European convention for the defense of human rights. Article 14 stipulates that "the extension of the rights and freedoms recognized in the present Convention shall be ensured without any exceptions namely those based on sex."

Marriage and therefore the condition of women is central to the problem of Islam in Europe. Some fathers have used this power to impose forced marriages as well as many cases of young women sent back to the home country by their parents before the end of compulsory schooling (age 16) or prevented from returning to Europe after vacations spent in their countries of origin. The website of the UOIF (Union des organisations islamiques de France) shows that the issue is central to the debates of the Salafist movement. The federation organized a national colloquium for its imams—some 80 participants—to discuss "Marriage, traditional procedures and French law."[24] Among its conclusions those dealing with marriage and one deserve particular attention. In order to prevent Hallal marriages, an expression that describes a religious marriage often celebrated by a self proclaimed imam and without a civil ceremony the final statement concludes: "the main orientation agreed to by most participants is to forbid any marriage before it is celebrated in front of the competent authorities." This statement was to be published and posted on the UOIF website but this hasn't yet happened. France forbids any religious ceremony that has not been preceded by a civil marriage. This is due to preeminence of the law in France over the private sphere and a way to protect individuals and women in particular. Repudiation, excision, crimes of honor…are as many ills

---

24. Union des Organisations Islamistes de France.

that young women and adult women suffer from. Repudiation for instance is not the equivalent of divorce. In a divorce there is a formal judgment with rules to protect the rights of both parties. Repudiation is contrary to the European convention and yet some bilateral conventions wind up recognizing it. These should have been declared unconstitutional since they do not respect the equality principle between men and women in the French constitution. For example the new Moroccan civil code makes repudiation almost impossible and makes the bilateral convention conform to the French constitution. The prior rulings of the High court of appeals reflected that ambiguity and were therefore in violation of the European convention.

These problems are often tied to generational differences and the country of origin. In 2007 in Brescia, Italy a young Pakistani woman Hina Saleen, had her throat slit by her father a fundamentalist Muslim. He could tolerate the fact that "she would become like the others." In western countries[25] honor crimes have been recorded in Germany, Belgium, the United States, France, Italy, Norway, The Netherlands, the United Kingdom, Sweden and Turkey that without being western is a candidate to EU membership. The convention against all forms of discrimination against women (CEDAW) was ratified by many countries that don't follow its requirements. According to *The Times* of June 12, 2007, each year in Great Britain a dozen young women are victims of such honor crimes within Muslim communities while official statistics indicate that the suicide rate among Asian women ages 16 to 24 is three times higher than the national average. In Belgium federal police records one honor crime every quarter and estimates the number at 17 for the last five years.[26]

Given its EU candidacy, Turkey has adopted a new criminal code without any references to the traditional customs. Mitigating circumstances are no longer awarded automatically to murderers accused of having committed an honor crime. In Germany these incidents take place mostly within the Turkish community and the legal system treats them as crimes without seeking any mitigating

---

25. March 15 and 16, 2008.
26. 2006, UN sources, Amnesty International, Women's News.

circumstances in tradition or religion. The Berlin association called Papatya—a welfare group helping young Turkish women—has tabulated over sixty court cases for honor crimes between 1996 and 2006 including 12 in 2008. One third took place in Berlin the city with the largest Turkish community in Germany and proves the retreat of identity or returning back into the community. In eastern France which is closer to Germany there are a few honor crimes within the recent Turkish immigrant community.

In 2004 for the first time, the Council of Europe looked into the issue of forced marriages. In France, the High Council for integration estimated at over 70,000 the number of adolescent victims of those practices. It is the main form of violence perpetrated on young women of Muslim cultures (African, Maghrebi, Turkish and also Asian, Pakistani and Sri Lankan). The forced marriage is a custom decided by the family at puberty or even earlier at the ages of 10 or 12. The groom is usually older and picked by the parents and of the same religion, ethnic background or even the same family.

The woman is never consulted on the choice of a husband and she may not refuse the one that was picked. The pressures to which young women are subjected are just as important. Traditions are obstacles to their using the legal system to defend their rights and benefits of legal protection in the countries they are living in. These young and adult women are subjected to the arbitrary demands of their husbands. Yet the laws enacted in the Maghreb, sub-Saharan Africa, Asia or Turkey require the consent of the couple as a condition to the validation of a marriage and are expected to prevent any forced marriages. The practice is difficult to quantify: a recent study by both INED and INSEE sheds some light on the issue in France.[27] Non-consensual marriages, the preferred term rather than forced marriages, are said to be receding. The study shows various elements: immigrant women parried against their will are 53 percent as not identifiable. Within the sample 34 percent were the daughters of immigrants, which is high given that they grew up in France and 30 percent of immigrant women and 25 percent of immigrant daughters not having given their full consent had parents with a high

---

27. *Gazet van Antwerpen*, February 21, 2008.

school diploma or a degree in higher education. As a sign of autonomy due to the French environment 68 percent of women married against their will end in divorce.

Practices such as excision still take place in our societies, they do not have any religious origin and are not even mentioned in the Koran. Such practices are "justified" by tradition and customs in certain Muslim countries. They represent inhuman and degrading treatment according to Article 3 of the European convention on human rights. In France, according to child protection associations, 10,000 to 20,000 small girls are at risk for such practices. In February 1999 a trial became the first case of this kind. An excision victim filed a complaint against those responsible for her mutilation meaning her parents and the person performing the operation that were all sentenced to long prison sentences (the Mariatou Koita case).

It is important to avoid lumping together and excoriating the members of a religious community as if they were all the same. Dalil Boubakeur understands the problem: "The most dangerous mirage that is threatening Muslims without a doubt is religious fundamentalism. But Catholics have experienced this throughout the history of the Church." French secular republican tradition that wishes to integrate and not assimilate has a universal dimension inherited from Rousseau allowing for multiculturalism. Using that vision the acceptance of different cultures has been a source of enrichment and the opportunity for boarder horizons.

Secularism

The French Republic recognizes blasphemy and doesn't punish it contrary to racism and xenophobia which are illegal: anti-Semitism is associated to racism as is Islam phobia. Those are the criteria used by French courts. The publication in *Charlie-Hebdo* (a satirical weekly) of the caricatures of the Prophet Muhammad is considered legal according to freedom of expression and of the press. A court is not qualified to pass judgment on blasphemy which is a religious matter and this kind of war of another age creates some unusual situations. In December 2005, the play by Voltaire *Le Fanatisme ou Mahomet le prophète* was to be performed at Saint-Genis-Pouilly in the Ain department. The Geneva mosque and local associations attempted to have the play banned because: "The play is an explicit attack on the values of Islam. It is an insult against the entire Muslim community of the Gex country and could cause a disturbance of the peace." It would take the common sense of the Deputy Prefect and the French administration to remind everyone that: "Voltaire wanted to criticize all fanaticism and that in 1741 when the play was written he was really targeting Catholic fanaticism." In an irony of history the town of Saint-Genis-Pouilly in the Gex area is across the border from Geneva. In the fall of 1758 Voltaire owned two estates in Switzerland. He was being criticized for breaking the law by having theatrical productions at his home that were open to the public and could bring the germs of immorality and contempt for religion into Geneva. Voltaire acquired two other homes one at Fernay and the other at Tournay in the Gex area which is in French territory. The "Patriarch" of Fernay then proceeded to build a theater where he could produce his plays and welcome the public from Geneva, Lausanne and other places nearby.

Chapter 10

The Vatican, Faith, and Diplomacy

Villa Medici, the Farnèse Palace, villa Bonaparte, the Church of Saint-Louis-des-Français, the cathedral of St. John Lateran... France owns and occupies a wealth of prestigious historical monuments in Rome. Most of the real estate that had been purchased by France in 1911 later became the property of the Italian state. The Italian government according to a clause in the agreement could repurchase the property at the same price it had been sold after paying for maintenance costs. The clause became effective in 1936 and the palace was rented to the French government for 99 years at a yearly rent of one lire but Paris was to ensure the maintenance of the interior and exterior of the building. The other French ambassador residing in Rome is to the Holy See as the Vatican is also called. That embassy was acquired in 1950 and is known as the Villa Bonaparte after Napoleon's sister Princess Pauline Borghese had purchased the property known as Villa Valentin. It was to remain in the Bonaparte family until 1906 located near the Quirinal Palace the residence of the president of the republic. Without going back even further the religious ties between France known as the Church's Eldest daughter and the Vatican easily account for such an important diplomatic presence.

The Vatican City State (the Holy See) exists only to guarantee the independence of the seat of the church among other international countries. This guarantee was formally agreed upon by the Lateran Agreements of 1929 signed by Secretary of State Cardinal Gasparri representing Pope Pius XI and Mussolini. The treaty was based on a double recognition giving Vatican City all the rights of a sovereign state while it recognized Rome as the capital of the Kingdom of Italy. The Pope's domain is the smallest state on earth (about 9 acres). Italy was also to pay 750 million lire in compensation for the loss of the States of the Church in 1859 (18,000 square kilometers.) The Catholic religion became the religion of the Italian State: divorce was banned, religious education was compulsory. The Pope took on a dual function: as a chief of state and at the same time as bishop of Rome which gives him precedence over all other bishops. This double status implies that he must deal with foreign countries on two levels: as any country the Vatican has diplomatic relations with other countries and the Pope can rely on a government known as the Roman Curia. Pope Sixtus V shaped the Curia as it is today.[1] The Curia is divided into "dicasteri" or ministries where the secretariat of state has two missions; general matters and relations with other states. The secretary of state is at once prime minister and foreign minister and the second most important person in the Vatican State. The Pope as religious leader has authority over local churches and relations with the national churches through the various representatives in each diocese. The Vatican is the only religious authority to have such an international legal status. The first permanent nuncio was created in 1500 to the Republic of Venice then came Madrid, Vienna, Paris, and Warsaw. In the sixteenth century there were also court nuncios: Gratz, Brussels, Munich in Bavaria. Prussia was the first protestant country to send an ambassador to Rome in 1805 and Japan was the first non Christian country to have diplomatic relations with the Holy See in 1942. Vatican diplomacy appears in the fourth century when the popes were sending their envoys to various kingdoms in the Christian world.

---

1. Apostolic Constitution January 22, 1588 "Immensa aeterni Dei."

Today the Vatican has relations with 177 countries along with "special diplomatic relations" with Palestine and Russia.[2] In Brussels there a special representation to the European Union where the nuncio is the dean of the diplomatic corps as he is in Paris.[3] The Vatican is present in 16 international organizations (permanent mission or observer status to the African union, the Organization of American States, Unesco, OMC, OMS OIT...) In July the UN general assembly approved a resolution to reinforce the Holy See's presence within the organization. The Vatican is part of the UN since April 6, 1964, with the status of "Permanent observer state." It doesn't vote in the general assembly but may speak and respond. It is a member of various subsidiary organizations of the United Nations such as the UN High Committee on Refugees (UNHCR). Within regional organizations such as the Arab League or the African Union, the Vatican has an observer seat. Like other countries the Vatican has signed international treaties and conventions, is part of the euro zone and has ratified the treaty of Schengen on opening borders and the common European space and has recently adopted the convention opposing money laundering. The American ambassador to the Holy See remarked: "The Vatican is one of the rare sovereign entities that has a presence in every country in the world."[4]

The last exchanges of ambassadors were with two Muslim countries: on March 31, 2007, the Holy See established relations with the United Arab Emirates and on July 18 with Malaysia, a country with a Muslim majority where Islam is a state religion.[5] The head of the Malaysian government explained his decision: "The world is at a crossroads. Irrational forces and discord threaten the dearly acquired prosperity and stability." Only 16 states do not entrain bilateral relations with the Vatican: eight are Muslim: Afghanistan, Saudi

2. When John-Paul II was elected pope, the Vatican had diplomatic relations with 84 countries.

3. Some states give the Apostolic Nuncio special status as to his importance. He is often recognized as the dean of the diplomatic corps who is the spokes person for the diplomatic corps at official ceremonies (offering wishes ...) He also generally after consulting with the diplomatic corps presents protest notes to the hosting country. That privilege of protocol was established by the Congress of Vienna in 1815 through the Convention on "The diplomatic law concerning diplomatic representations" that was confirmed by "The Vienna Convention on Diplomatic Relations." 1961 (article 16).

4. The quotes about the United States in this chapter are from the diplomatic reports revealed by WikiLeaks.

5. A country of 28 millions where Christians are 8 percent of the population or 3.5 million of which 900,000 are Roman Catholics.

Arabia, Brunei, Comoros, Maldives, Mauritania, Oman, Somalia; four have communist regimes: China,[6] North Korea, Laos, Vietnam; the other four are small countries: Bhutan, Botswana, Myanmar and Tuvalu. The fact that there are no diplomatic relations between the Vatican and those 16 states doesn't mean that there is no contact. The pope is the spiritual leader of over one billion people and while Catholicism has been receding in its historical territories its members are growing along with the world population on new continents like Africa and Asia.[7]

The Oldest Daughter of the Catholic Church

France has a special relationship with the Holy See through its representative the Papal Nuncio who is automatically the dean of the diplomatic corps. Due to the status of the Holy See the nuncios have a different kind of diplomatic activity from that of other countries but it would be a mistake to underestimate the Vatican's diplomatic influence. It relies on a vast and efficient information network and connections through the clergy, the associations and many links in society (scientific, intellectual, as well as political.) The importance of the nuncios becomes clear in an anecdote indicating the key role played by the institution. The Holy See like any country has a national holiday on the day the Pontiff accedes to the throne of Saint Peter. In France the reception is held in a townhouse offered by the Grimaldi family (of Monaco) and includes the top Paris intellectual and political elites, both on the right and the left, believers and agnostics, an assemblage that many an ambassador would dream of having.

The position of "Apostolic Nuncio" is also very much a political activity. In 1944 when General de Gaulle took over the provisional government at the liberation of France he was worried about the fact that the nuncio was the same person who had represented the

---

6. On April 9, 2006, the Archbishop of Taipei, Mon. Joseph Cheng Tsai-fa had to reassure Taiwan Catholics that an eventual normalization of diplomatic relations between the Holy See and Beijing wouldn't mean the end of relations between the Holy See and Taiwan.
7. In 2009, there were 1 billion 181 million Roman Catholics in the world with increases in the Pacific (+19 percent), Asia (+16 percent) compared to 2.3 percent in Europe and 2.6 percent in America.

Vatican during the occupation. The problem was not the prelate but the fact that he had interacted with Marshal Pétain at Vichy.

General de Gaulle informed Rome and the Vatican picked an atypical lower level diplomat that the leadership didn't hold in high regard. Monsignor Angelo Roncalli, a substitute at the legation at Ankara had played a role in saving the Jews in Turkey a fact that was known to General de Gaulle. He also was the future Pope John XXIII. When before Christmas he received a cable from Rome asking him to stop there before starting as nuncio in France he thought this was practical joke from a friend in the Curia. He sent his best wishes to the leadership saying that he could wait one or two years for such a gift since it was the season just before Christmas. A second cable informed him how urgent it really was: in France, the Vatican nuncio usually offers his best wishes to the head of state in the name of the entire diplomatic corps. In the absence of the nuncio the ambassador of the USSR was next in line to address General de Gaulle who didn't relish that alternative. Monsignor Roncalli made it to the ceremony and right after presenting his credentials he went over to the Soviet ambassador's residence who handed him the speech he had already prepared. The future pope admitted later on that besides a few changes he did use the Soviet ambassador's speech.

During his visit to France in 2008, Pope Benedict XVI was received at the Élysée Palace. The French president spoke of 'positive secularism' using the expression some twelve times in the course of his speech. The Vatican had a clear position on that subject and described the French position as being too "rigid" recalling that legislation had turned "France under the Third Republic into a model of antireligious behavior."[8] He called for "a modification" and "fruitful collaboration" between Church and State. Yet since 2002, Church leaders can only applaud the initiative taken by Lionel Jospin, who was then prime minister: the yearly meeting of government and clergy became a permanent event. It encourages a broad debate on all issues between the prime minister and the Catholic hierarchy. On December 20, 2007 President Nicolas Sarkozy, honorary canon of the Papal Basilica of St. John Lateran stated : "Secular morality runs

---

8. July 2008. Cardinal Tarcisio Bertone, Secretary of State.

the risk of failing when it is not backed up by a hope that fulfills the aspiration to the infinite... in the transmission of values and the learning of the difference between good and evil, the school teacher will never be able to replace the priest and the pastor because he will never have the radical sacrifice of his life and the charisma of a commitment carried through by hope." By designating secularism in symbolic terms he reopened an issue that was difficult to put to rest.[9]

From Old Europe to the New World

If there is one issue that magnifies the importance of the papacy in the twentieth century it is the contentious history of the relationship between the Holy See and the Third Reich. Was Pope Pius XII "Hitler's Pope" or the "silent Pope"? In examining this area the sensitive nature of the Holocaust becomes paramount: the polemic was relaunched by the film by Costa-Gavras *Amen* that is inspired by the play by Rolf Hochhuth, *The Vicar* that explores the relationship between Pope Pius XII and Nazi Germany. Costa-Gavras simply states that there would have been no genocide if Pius XII had forcefully denounced Nazism! In Bernard-Henri Lévy's magazine *La Règle du jeu* Laurent Dispot comments on Pius XII and the Vatican as they faced Nazi Germany: "Germany where the Nazi cancer grew and spread was not under the control of Catholicism and the Vatican. On the contrary, it was two thirds protestant with Catholicism under constant negative propaganda within a general anti-Papist Lutheran outlook which the Nazis constantly referred to and exploited to the hilt." This being said as Secretary of State Cardinal Pacelli, who would become Pope Pius XII had been Papal Nuncio in Germany and was considered pro-German at the time. Later on he was to be in the number two position within the Church under Pope Pius XI and was responsible for Vatican diplomacy. What could Pius XII do as pope to oppose the Nazis?

---

9. Since the seventeenth century, French Kings and Heads of State receive the title of Canon of the Basilica of Saint John Lateran. The tradition goes back to 1604 when King Henri IV decided to donate to the Lateran the Benedictine monastery of Clairac (Lot-et-Garonne). In thanks the Lateran chapter decided to erect a statue which is in the basilica and give the king the title of honorary canon.

The Vatican's position was influenced by Pope Benedict XV's failure as mediator to prevent and then put an end to the First World War. Just before the outbreak of the Second World War Pius XI then Pius XII felt that "Christianity is threatened to die forever." For the papacy the struggle against Communism was the main problem while Nazism was an entirely different issue.

In *La Règle du Jeu,* Laurent Dispot analyzed Pius XII:

> During the war the Vatican had no military forces and had to continue its resistance to Nazism with the means at its disposal, waiting for it to pass by engaging in an active form of silence. It would undertake salvage actions rather than issue irreparable statements. The Nazis were waiting for an excuse to move in and take over the convents, monasteries and churches and destroy the Catholic communications and intervention system that they were unable to control. And that would elude their grasp to the end. Pius XII decided that giving the Nazis a pretext to start a repression against the Catholics wouldn't end the massacre of the Jews. He was constantly informing the Americans who were flying over the death camps in their bombers. In wartime you do not exist without military power.[10]

When the play *The Vicar* was performed in 1963, Pope John XXIII, who had called the Council of Vatican II (1962-1963) and the Church's renewal, was on the throne of St. Peter since Pius XII's death in 1958. Pius XII had faced two totalitarian regimes Communism and Nazism and had a grand vision after the war to build a united Europe that would be reconciled with Germany. The plan came to pass with three Catholic politicians: Konrad Adenauer, Robert Schuman, and Alcide De Gasperi. The Kremlin didn't want such an outcome while it controlled part of Eastern Europe. This view of the Cold War was held by Bernard-Henri Lévy during a debate with Jean-Marie Colombani on the television program Public-Sénat. He referred to the attack on John Paul II, which was planned by the soviets and undertaken by the Bulgarians, a thesis which is rejected by Bulgarian university professor Romania Ougartchinska who offers the scenario of a possible manipulation of the Turkish

---

10. December 2010.

far-right by the CIA.[11] If one follows the official version it would tend to prove that the last communist leaders hadn't adopted Stalin's famous question: "How many divisions does the Vatican have?"

In 1964, three years before the Six Day War Pope Paul VI decided to go on a pilgrimage to the Holy Land where he visited Jordan, the Holy places, Jerusalem and Bethlehem. It was the first time a Pontiff traveled outside Italy. That same year he agreed to the publication of documents on the Second World War. These were the archives of the secretariat of state with the complete records of the daily and often hourly activity of the pope and his cabinet. Father Pierre Blet, a Jesuit directed the work leading to the publication from 1965 to 1982 of 12 volumes of the Acts and Documents of the Holy See Relating to the Second World War.[12] Huber Wolf, professor of history at the University of Münster, published a work in 2009 that completes and critiques the ideological orientations that were used over several decades.[13] Many other Catholic leaders were far more outspoken than the Vatican, for example Cardinal Gerlier, the bishop of Lyon, and Primate of the Gauls wrote on January 21, 1942, to the Grand rabbi of France that "If Christ were to return today he would to be taken to Drancy." As well as Cardinals Saliège in Toulouse or Liénart in Lille who as early as 1938, were condemning the racial ideology of Nazi Germany. Obviously some religious congregations were to help Nazis escape such as Adolf Eichmann, Josef Mengele, Klaus Barbie could only cause bewilderment. British American historian Tony Judt explained that after the war a new political animal made its appearance and was known as Christian Democracy that would leave its imprint on several European countries. The MRP didn't advertise its Catholic affiliation given the secularism of French society with leaders such as Robert Schuman and Georges Bidault, the Christian Democratic Union (CDU) led by Adenauer in Germany or Italy's Christian Democratic Party under Alcide De Gasperi. These Christian political parties were to lose much of their influence after the fall of communism in an increasingly social democratic Europe.

---

11. *La vérité sur l'attentat de Jean-Paul II*, Presses de la Renaissance, Paris 2007.
12. Pierre Blet summarized the work in his book *Pie XII et la Seconde Guerre mondiale d'après les archives du Vatican*, Perrin, Paris 1997.
13. *Le pape et le diable*, Éditions du CNRS, Paris, 2009.

The Church is present in public life in episcopal conferences and various movements in Italy and Spain. The social encyclicals add their weight to the debates as in Pope Benedict XVI's letter "Caritas in veritate." Published just prior to the G8 Conference in L'Aquila, that document was calling for thoughtful meditation in the midst of the crisis: the Pope was advocating placing ethics and faith at the core of globalization.

The influence of the Church can give rise to many theories as with the group known as the Opus Dei. In Dan Brown's *Da Vinci Code*, and the subsequent film the organization is described as "Roman Freemasonry." With its special legal statute as a "personal legacy" the Opus Dei reports directly to the pope and doesn't come under the authority of the bishops in the countries where it operates. The history of the group is an interesting one: founded by Monsignor Balaguer, who saw the Spanish Civil War as a struggle between Catholics and Communists. Catholicism in Spain was saved by General Francisco Franco's coup. In due course the Opus Dei became an economic, financial and political organization by investing in areas like education, creating schools, high schools and universities, the media and the Spanish political right wing.

For centuries until recent times Spanish society was characterized by the presence of the clergy in many institutions (schools, universities, associations, hospitals). The Constitution of 1862 began with the Holy Trinity: in the name of the father, the son and the Holy Spirit. At that time bishops were members of the Cortes, as senators or deputies and the changes in the Spanish church since then have seen its influence limited in a democratic regime while it remains powerful. Demonstrations in the defense of the family (against abortion, and homosexual marriage) mobilize hundreds of thousands of Spaniards responding to the associations that have the support of the church. The courts must often remind citizens of the provisions of the law such as the judgment of the High Court that condemned a Catholic school that had fired a catechism teacher who was being paid by the government because she was living with a person who had been divorced.

Within the Catholic Church some groups are included in the movement called "liberation theology." The "preferred option for the poor" had been reiterated by various popes including John Paul II. Very quickly, however, the leadership turned against it since the clergy could not become involved in politics even more so since those inspiring it were close to Marxism or the far left. The movement was also a response to the leadership of the Church in Latin America that had given its support to military dictatorships, business interests and large land owners. The former Archbishop of Recife in Brazil Dom Hélder Câmara, was among the various symbolic figures of the preference for the very poor. His action was not only to correct injustice but also to replace a failing government administration in social areas. In El Salvador, Bishop Oscar Romero would pay dearly for his commitment as he had dedicated his life to the defense of the poor and the oppressed. He was assassinated on March 12, 1977, by death commandos in his cathedral in San Salvador where he denounced the excesses of the military junta in power.

This thinking began in the early 1960s when in Brazil the JUC (Christian university youth)—filled with French progressive Catholic culture (Emmanuel Mounier, the journal *Esprit*, Father Lebret and the Économie et Humanisme group, Father Jean-Yves Calvez, SJ the author of *La pensée de Karl Marx*[14])—expressed a radical proposal for social transformation in the name of Christianity. The liberation theologian Leonardo Boff was active on the World Social Forum attracting other social activists—labor unions, the Landless Workers Movement or MST, women's movements—often coming from church communities that had embraced liberation theology.

Beginning in the 1990s, Leonardo Boff focused increasingly on ecological issues with a mystical Franciscan love for the earth and a critical approach to the capitalist system. The movement still has broad influence and inspired former Brazilian President Lula da Silva, as well as part of the alternate world movement going beyond Latin America.

---

14. Paris, 1956.

A True Diplomacy

Europe is not the whole world. For the United States of all the major problems the pope's political statements and his geopolitical influence have considerable consequences. The State Department gives them the most careful scrutiny as it quotes issues as diverse as Turkey's request to join the EU, Iraq, the Near East or ethical and social problems such as the NGOs, stem cell research or climate change.

Vatican diplomacy's forceful presence was symbolized by its participation in the Helsinki Accords of 1975. Those agreements established non-intervention into the internal affairs of other states, self-determination of populations in choosing their political system, the inviolability of borders established after the Second World War and increased cooperation in guaranteeing the defense of human rights (free movement of individuals, freedom of the press.) On that last point the Vatican would display the greatest activity. Leonid Brezhnev signed for the USSR. It was seen as a turning point: in 1977, a group of intellectuals launched Charter 1977 in Czechoslovakia, the freedom movement that was to extend into Eastern Europe despite pro-Soviet repression in the satellite countries. Recent activity shows that the Vatican bases its actions on principles that are not purely religious or theological concepts. During the Iraqi crisis besides the mediation by Cardinal Étchegaray to Saddam Hussein before the invasion of Kuwait (in relation to France's demarche initiated by François Mitterrand), the Vatican always supported international mediation by the UN before reporting to the use of military force. This diplomatic activity may be extremely discreet. It was the Vatican's intercession that led Jean-Claude Duvalier to leave power in Haiti, before American troops landed. The departure was negotiated with France as the welcoming country for "Baby Doc" until his return to Port-au-Prince in January 2011. Countries with old Catholic traditions will often request the mediation of the Holy See to handle international problems. The Vatican was instrumental in ending the border conflict between Argentina and Chile.

John Paul II's involvement in the Polish question contributed significantly to the collapse of the Soviet empire. The Pope was in constant contact with Solidarnosc, and received Lech Walesa at the Vatican. This of course didn't prevent General Wojciech Jaruzelski from decreeing the state of siege but as he later revealed Rome's influence over the free labor union led to his decision to avoid a worse situation since he was in turn under pressure from the Kremlin. Throughout the Polish crisis John Paul II played a key role after an agreement with President Ronald Reagan of the kind that no other ally of the United States would have. Each week a CIA flight would convey an emissary of the president of the United States directly into the private apartment of Pope John Paul II. Vernon Walters would bring and analyze the confidential reports and satellite photographs from the president to the pope. It was through Rome and the networks of the religious congregations that funds from the U.S. Administration and American labor unions (AFL-CIO) would reach the Poles and Solidarnosc in particular.

Within traditional diplomacy and for many years the Vatican refused to recognize the State of Israel. It would only be in December 1993 that both parties signed an agreement to exchange ambassadors starting June 1, 1994. This normalization of relations ended tensions lingering since 1948. But reality was far more complex due to the positions taken by Israel later on. The Synod of the eastern bishops took place in October 2010 and on that occasion of the meeting of the Catholic hierarchy relations between Israel and the Holy See became tense once more as Jerusalem described the Vatican's positions as "political attacks." The heart of the matter was the recognition of the Palestinian State and the status of Jerusalem.

Since the Balfour Declaration of November 2, 1917 announcing "the establishment of a national home for the Jewish people in Palestine" the Holy See has supported the notion that "If the Jews in Palestine should have equal civil rights to those of other nationalities and faiths they cannot have a privileged and dominant position."[15] With the establishment of the State of Israel Vatican diplomacy supported the creation of a Palestinian State as well. The Vatican

---

15. Letter from Cardinal, Secretary of State, Gasparri of May 15, 1922.

never accepted the annexation of the holy city in agreement with the UN resolutions and it requests an international status for Jerusalem a city that is claimed by all three monotheistic religions. Symbolically, John Paul II appointed Monsignor Michel Sabbah, a Palestinian, to be the Patriarch of Jerusalem.

The issue of East Jerusalem is at the heart of several conflicts including that opposing France to the Israeli government. The main reason is that the French consulate is in East Jerusalem while the embassy is in Tel-Aviv. That diplomatic mission is not considered by Israel as a normal consular structure but rather as a political representation to the Palestinians.

French presence in the Levant is closely tied to religious and political issues. When in 1535 King Francis I made an alliance that would never be signed between a Most Christian King and a Muslim Monarch he was getting around his rivals grouped around the Emperor Charles V of Austria. He shocked the Western world by obtaining from Suleiman the Magnificent the right to protect the Christians in the Holy Land. The treaty of 1536 that would be extended allowed France to have a protectorate over the Empire that was once part of Rome. This right to protect the Christian communities of the Near East would become the preferred instrument of French influence throughout the area. In 1929, the current consulate general was built and its imposing structure recalled the preeminent role France played and intended to continue playing in the region. The division of Palestine was decided in 1947. The precinct of the consulate general included Jerusalem and the territories occupied by Israel in 1967 (Trans-Jordan and Gaza Strip). Its consular tasks are to serve the French community within the United Nations resolutions whereby diplomatic contact with the State of Israel is handled exclusively by the French embassy in Tel-Aviv.

The autonomous nature of the consulate allowed it to play an unusual political role with the Palestinians. Even prior to the establishment of the Palestinian Authority in 1994 the consulate was involved in an important policy of cooperation in the occupied territories in terms of medical, humanitarian, educational, cultural, economic and financial affairs. The establishment of a Palestinian administration reinforced this cooperation. The consulate also represented France to the UNRWA the UN agency set up for Palestinian refugees.

But the particular nature of the work of the French consulate general in Jerusalem does not sit well with the Israeli government.

French personnel complain of regular violations by Israeli policemen and soldiers of customary consular conventions.

On June 11, 2008, Catherine Hyver, deputy consul in Jerusalem, was held for seventeen hours without food or water by Israeli security at a border crossing at the Gaza Strip. In December 2009, France found it "excessive" to have Israeli police surround the French cultural center in east Jerusalem. The action was intended to prevent a cultural event recalling the Arab part of town annexed after the 1967 war and claimed by the Palestinians.

Other incidents have since opposed the French Consulate general in Jerusalem to Israeli authorities that have increased the harassment of that representation that acts in lieu of an embassy to the Palestinian Authority seeking to prevent it from its cooperation work in the occupied territories.

John Paul II: the Active Diplomacy of a Great Actor

The personality, origins and influence of a pope like John Paul II were of the utmost importance to the Vatican's diplomacy toward Eastern Europe.

Begun under Pope John XXIII and continued vigorously by Paul VI and his Secretary of State Cardinal Agostino Casaroli, the Vatican's Ostpolitik created a number of contacts in communist countries and a policy of opening to the east. The election of the bishop of Krakow was a turning point. The newly elected pontiff didn't change the political line taken by those that preceded him and the secretariat of state continued its state by state relations. At the same time John Paul II carefully tracked events taking place behind the Iron Curtain and in Poland in particular. The face to face struggle that for some ten years would pit him against the communist power center, his various travels back to his home country were to be the catalysts of the crisis and its evolution.

The break-up of Yugoslavia along the historical divide between Catholics and Orthodox in the Balkans created a difficult situation for the Vatican. On January 13, 1992, the Holy See recognized the independence of Croatia and Slovenia two traditionally Catholic lands within the former Yugoslavia. The destruction of the communist empire allowed John Paul to travel back to the other side of the "wall" into the old socialist republics. The first trip east was to Czechoslovakia in 1990, in 1994 John Paul II went Zagreb but not to Belgrade and he would have to wait until 1997 to visit Sarajevo. The diplomacy of the Holy See was very active: in Cuba in January 1998 the Pope clearly restated his opposition to the embargo that the United States had enforced for thirty-five years.

This Vatican position would be restated in Iraq and Serbia. The Holy See always opposes reprisals that affect the population that becomes the first victim; its diplomacy places people first. In Cuba, Iraq, or Iran the Vatican will always take a stand against sanctions. Such a policy can bring indirect results: in 2010 Raul Castro freed 52 political prisoners held since 2003 that were welcomed by Spain. The decision took place after a meeting between the Cuban president, Cardinal Jaime Ortega, archbishop of Havana mediating for political prisoners and Miguel Angel Moratinos, the Spanish foreign minister. The 52 opponents are the last ones incarcerated in the wave of repression that had rounded up 75 dissidents and intellectuals in March and April 2003. Some of them had been sentenced to up to twenty-eight years in prison: "They will be free and can leave the country." Said the press release issued by the archdiocese.

These releases are the largest since the freeing of 299 prisoners— both political and criminal—in February 1998 after Pope John Paul II's historic visit to the island run by the Castro brothers. A summary by the Archbishop of Havana Cardinal Ortega shows that during the summer of 2011 some one hundred political prisoners were freed thanks to his advocacy. The Catholic Church has become the only institution to enjoy real independence from political influence. It has managed to stay at the center of the political game through its message calling for dialogue and fostering a "theology of national reconciliation." For the liberated prisoners: "The Church today is the main agent of change in Cuba."

John Paul II used a diplomacy that advocated human rights. The pope denounced the armaments race and championed the right of humanitarian intervention. The African tragedies (Rwanda, Sudan) were painful to him.

The Philippines or the Influence of Power

In the Philippines, the only Asian country where Catholics form a majority of the population (85 percent), the Church has played a key role in politics. Cardinal Jaime Sin, Manila's influential bishop has been at the helm for over thirty years. He is known for his positions on most subjects such as poverty, politics, the Iraq War. He became internationally known in February 1986 when he encouraged thousands of Catholic priests, nuns and ordinary citizens in protests that would bring down the Marcos dictatorship. While Imelda and Ferdinand Marcos were emptying the state coffers the regime was filling up the jails with protesters. For nine years the country was under martial law and 10,000 Filipinos were to disappear. Marcos put an end to the state of siege in January 1981, and one month later John Paul II who had steadfastly refused to visit the country as long as the law was effective, traveled to the Philippines.

The 1983 murder of Benigno Aquino, the exiled top opposition who had been allowed to return home, triggered the mass demonstration that brought about the end of the Marcos regime in 1986. Ferdinand and Imelda Marcos were helped escape by the Americans who offered them protection in Honolulu. While he had been close to power when Marcos took over in December 1965, Cardinal Sin kept his distance from the dictatorship during the years of martial law. He practiced "critical collaboration" until the 1986 military insurrection headed by General Fidel Ramos. The cardinal broadcast a radio message to the population requesting that they assemble in front of the military barracks where the main Marcos opponents had taken refuge. That appeal became the tipping point that would ensure the success of the events that pushed the Marcos family to leave.

The cardinal also gave his support to Cory Aquino, the martyred senator's widow, allowing her to become president of the Republic of the Philippines. Cardinal Sin continued to offer his support while voicing criticism of the corruption gnawing at public institutions. In July 2003 the cardinal again called upon the public to remain vigilant a few hours prior to the coup attempt against President Gloria Arroyo. With a mother of Spanish origin and a Chinese father Cardinal Jaime Sin was well known for his sense of humor and straight talk with a marked taste for controversy. Until his death in 2005, he remained the "grey eminence" of the Philippines, taking part in every issue, which made him controversial.

Without a doubt even though the constitution calls for separation of Church and State the involvement of the Church in public affairs was possible for three main reasons: it is rich and powerful, it has true sway over a majority of the population and had a charismatic leader at the helm.

There is also the importance of the Philippines to the Holy See. The country is the vanguard of Catholicism facing China while the Vatican has no diplomatic relations with Beijing. The main issue is the nomination of bishops by Rome and the coexistence of a Church that is recognized by the regime while it also obeys the authority of the Pope. Even if there were a softening, the appointment of bishops by Rome remains a disputed issue. Beijing did make a show of goodwill when John Paul II went to the Philippines in 1981, the Chinese government issued exit visas to some priests so they could say mass with the pope during the World Youth Day in Manila. John Paul II held private discussions with the Chinese delegation numbering 800 representatives on the broadening of relations between the Holy See and China. While the Catholic Church remains powerful and influential it must face competition from various sects that have appeared recently.

The Vatican Networks

At some point some kind of reference to Sun Tzu's *The Art of War* is bound to appear. Among the Chinese scrolls of 1759, one of them was wrongly attributed to someone who would be called a double agent today. He was in fact Giuseppe Castiglione, an Italian Jesuit who was posted in the Middle Kingdom.[16] Was his work inspired by the need for a civilizing conversion or simply as an agent of influence? The Jesuits had understood many realities very early on but Rome wouldn't follow their advice which turned out to be a geopolitical mistake. The Vatican uses several levers to exert its influence on the international scene. Sant' Egidio is one of them but first the Vatican's diplomatic capabilities should be examined. As any state Rome can count on the mass of information that it receives from other countries but it also has access to sources that are the envy of most other intelligence services of nation-states. These come from the nuncios, the religious orders, and secular sources whether they are believers or not throughout the world. WikiLeaks has revealed the "excellent sources of information about Chinese dissidents or population control by the Beijing government." The same is true in North Korea where Catholic charities are active.

The initiatives by the Sant' Egidio groups are closely watched by the U.S. State Department that views the organization as an irreplaceable tool with particular influence in Africa. The media calls it the UN of Peace and Andrea Riccardi, the founder of the community of Sant' Egidio, is convinced that "peace is far too important to be left up to politicians and diplomats." Under John Paul II Sant' Egidio was considered a tool of the pope's diplomatic initiatives in that it could also take some risks that the secretariat of state could not.

What prompted Andrea Riccardi to follow that path? As he stated it was the opportunity of "making the old dream come true." For him "without a doubt after 1989 and the end of communism we were hoping for a long sustainable peace. The conditions did exist to resolve many conflicts and create the basis for a long season of peace. Negotiations for the Holy Land had yielded considerable results. In South Africa the apartheid regime had collapsed. In El Salvador, the land of the martyred Archbishop Romero, peace had returned after many hard years."[17]

---

16. A Jesuit and an artist, he was officially named "court painter". He served several emperors and remained in that post for 51 years.

17. Cathedral of Strasbourg, lecture byAndrea Riccardi, December 7, 2004.

In 1992, peace came to Mozambique after a war with one million dead. Sant' Egidio acted as mediator and brokered the agreement. Mozambique representatives faced a team that included Mario Raffaelli, representing the Italian government, the Bishop of Beira Monsignor Jaime Gonçalves, Andrea Riccardi and Matteo Zuppi of the Sant' Egidio community.

At the close of negotiations in Rome, the parties signed a peace agreement to establish a true democracy. All sensitive issues were included in the protocol: creation and recognition of political parties, an electoral law, the disarmament of the belligerents, a cease-fire, and guarantees until the convening of a conference of donors to establish the reconstruction of the country. With the successful outcome in Mozambique several requests for help reached the community. The most covered by the media was certainly the mediation for the resolution of the crisis in Algeria, a Muslim country. In the course of meetings set up by Sant' Egidio, in Rome, the leaders of the main Algerian political parties finally met after years of ignoring one another. The platform for Algeria was an "offer" of peace to stop the violence on shared values and in view of the necessary democratization process of society and political activity. The regime rejected the document. The limits of the attempt were reached once the main actor in a given crisis is absent from the proceedings.

The key to success is the method used to allow a dialogue to begin. This was the case in Burundi. The former president of the African country Colonel Jean-Baptiste Bagaza, president of PARENA (Parti pour le redressement national- Party of National Recovery), gave his reasons to accept Sant' Egidio's offer. A previous agreement signed at Arusha had led to a "dead-end and a new framework for negotiations had to be found." The Arusha accord hadn't ended in a cease-fire between belligerents nor the setting up of institutions of transition or even an agreement on an electoral system. Jean-Baptiste Bagaza couldn't negotiate in his own country Burundi. "We had no choice: we will be hunted down and imprisoned inside the country or else forced into exile."[18]

---

18. Kampala, May 28, 2001 (Net Press).

This diplomacy in the shadows is another example of the often more effective action of the Church which is also a facet of religion. That influence goes beyond the usual especially on morality and bioethics issues. Religious lobbying in countries in the Christian tradition is far more effective than the American Religious Right.

Chapter 11

The Pakistani Cauldron and Asia

Half of Pakistan was paralyzed by flooding in August 2010 affecting over 15 million people. One third of the crops in Sind and Punjab were destroyed. During those dramatic events President Asif Ali Zardari, Benazir Bhutto's widower, was traveling in Europe, a trip that included a very luxurious private vacation. Every observer including journalists, experts, diplomats and his most highly placed supporters in Washington know that the regime is corrupt. Once again they could under the circumstances take note of the government's indifference. The Islamists on the contrary acted promptly by filling the vacuum. Yet a few years before on October 8, 2005 when Kashmir was rocked by a massive earthquake leaving 88 000 killed and more than 5 billion U.S. dollars in damages the Pakistani army immediately stepped in. The difference was that the earthquake had hit Kashmir a politically and historically sensitive territory under Pakistan's control that is also claimed by India. The Islamist NGOs became major actors and stepped in when the government failed at its task. As they already had done in Kashmir they were the first to appear during the floods bringing support and food to the victims. The Islamists demonstrated their efficiency and obviously improved their image while increasing their influence among a majority of Pakistanis that already support them. They made no mystery of what they intend to do: turn Pakistan into an Islamist emirate and take over control of all of Kashmir which was historically a Muslim region. Among the Islamist NGOs some are religious as the Jamaat-ud-Dawa, the Pakistani Islamist group accused of having engineered the Mumbai attacks. The movement called on the government to reject American aid that was to gather 20 million dollars for the victims. At the same time the IHH (Insani Yardim Vakfi) a Turkish NGO and one of the organizations involved in the Gaza flotilla initiative was able to raise 15 million dollars in a few days for the Pakistani flood victims. Islamic solidarity or political calculation: no answer is possible at this time.

In such a context who is in charge in Pakistan? The issue keeps coming back and many governments would like to know. Is it the elected president or the prime minister, the army chiefs or the heads of the intelligence services the formidable ISI? The Americans discovered this at their own expense. Bin Laden was hiding near Islamabad in the same town where the prestigious Pakistani military academy is located and where many high ranking officers have retired. He must have benefited from support at the highest levels of the government, the army and the ISI. The *News* at the end of February 2011 gave its assessment: "The extremist mindset has deeply penetrated Pakistani society with support from some of the highest state institutions." Mostly a military regime with a few democratic intervals, Pakistan is more of an army than a true nation and remains the epicenter of many tension points. Its history with India was marked by several wars and the Kashmir issue was used as a pretext for becoming a nuclear power in 1998 as an answer to India that had tested its first nuclear bomb twenty years before in 1974.

Besides the Islamist threat, the attacks, the dreams of independence of regions such as Balutchistan, Pakistan is located geographically at the crossroads of every conflict: Afghanistan, Kashmir, India, China with the Xinyiang region where the Uyghur are located and the issue of Tibet. The government agencies and ISI in particular can give their support directly and discreetly to terrorist movements in Kashmir. This is the case in those areas of Kashmir under New Delhi's control or support for groups that intend to attack India. The ISI also supports the Taliban together with Pakistani fundamentalists and this situation could bring about an ethnic, religious or political explosion.

The Historical Background

Pakistan's history may be compared to series of wounds. The India-Pakistan border was drawn along religious lines by Sir Cyril Radcliffe, a London solicitor. The separation was required by Muhammad Ali Jinnah, the leader of the All-India Muslim League. At the end of the nineteenth century the idea that both communities should be viewed separately was making its way. They were represented individually in the colonial administration and were to form two different nations. Reacting to the founding of the Congress party in Bombay in 1885 a nationalist movement that was dominated by Hindus, the Muslims created the Muslim League in 1906. The British were to agree to their requests and set up separate electoral colleges for the election of representatives to the assemblies for India.

The main objective of the colonial power was to limit the influence of the Congress party and secure the support of the Muslim minority by acting as its protector against the majority Hindus. Partition would also mean ethnic transfers that would become violent. The departure of British forces from India and the independence of the two countries in 1947 brought about a double exodus. The Hindus left what was to become Pakistan and Muslims living in India moved to the new country. All of them didn't leave and it is estimated that one million died while 15 million crossed the borders in both directions: 9 million Hindus and Sikhs left Pakistan while 6 million Muslims went into exile in India. Gandhi who understood the risks had voiced his opposition to partition as a monstrous form of surgery.

Henri Tincq described that event:

> As soon as the border line became official on August 15 the houses were emptied out. In Delhi, rear the border between the two countries,

Hindu militia was emptying the neighborhoods of the Muslim population that had taken refuge in the mosques to make room for Hindus that were arriving by the truckloads. Karachi also was emptied of its Hindus as Delhi was of its Muslims. In mixed areas ordinary people were murdering their neighbors just because they were of a different religion. It was the first time that India witnessed physical elimination on such a scale of entire populations to create ethnic and religiously cleansed areas.[1]

For some the word Pakistan was created from two Urdu words meaning "land of the pure."[2] For others it was an acronym invented in 1933 by some Muslim students in Great Britain around Rehmat Ali, founder of the Pakistani national movement using the Urdu initials of the provinces that wished to separate from India: Punjab, Afgahni, Kashmir, Sind, Baluchistan. Whether it was a newly minted name or an acronym it didn't change the situation of the country since independence.

The proclamation of the double independence of India and Pakistan on August 15, 1947, didn't end the violence especially in Kashmir where there were hundreds of thousands of casualties. Following a period of instability the Islamic republic of Pakistan was proclaimed in 1956. In another anomaly the new state was composed of two parts separated from one another by India and a distance of 1,600 kilometers, the reason being the Muslim religious majority of the inhabitants. Bangladesh, the eastern province, wasn't considered a priority by the government in Islamabad.

In the early 1970s, the country was torn by the autonomous demands of eastern Pakistan. André Malraux asked his friend the Indian writer Raja Rao: "Given serious situation I would like to know your thoughts on Bengal. Is the cause is worth dying for, yes or no?"[3] That same August 9, 1971, India signed a friendship treaty with the USSR for cooperation and assistance to serve as counterweight to the United States and China that were supporting Pakistan. In September on the French radio station *Europe 1*, Malraux declared that he was

---

1. *Le Monde*, August 4, 2007.
2. Pâk means "pure" and stân means "country," the "i" in between is to tie the two words.
3. Letter quoted by Michaël de Saint Cheron, *Malraux, le ministre de la fraternité culturelle*, 2009, in site Malraux.org.

ready to head a legion of volunteers to fight for the independence of the country that was enduring the worse kind of atrocities. He wouldn't repeat the International Brigades adventure but as Raja Rao predicted, he was "the only man in the world who would be listened to by everyone about Bengal in the East as well as the West." The Bengalis declared their independence in 1971. Bangladesh, the "nation of Bengal," emerged after a war of independence with the support of India and the USSR. On December 16, 1971 independence was achieved once Pakistani forces surrendered to the combined armies of India and Bangladesh.

When in December 1971, General Yahya Khan handed over power to Ali Bhutto, the new Pakistani president was the only politician able to remedy a catastrophic situation. He was successful on the diplomatic front, establishing relations with Bangladesh, and reaching an understanding with India. He reestablished his country on the international scene and became one of the most trusted spokesmen for developing nations. He decided to withdraw Pakistan from the Commonwealth and established closer relations with the USSR. Following the vote by parliament to modify the constitution by transferring the most executive power from the president to the prime minister, Bhutto had himself elected to that position. In 1974 under pressure from Muslim fundamentalists he added a constitutional amendment declaring that the Ahmadis were not Muslims.[4]

In 1977, Pakistan was paralyzed by strikes and close to economic bankruptcy. Despite the repressive measures, order couldn't be reestablished and riots threatened to bring about civil war. The prime minister then had to face extensive opposition including the right that feared his Marxist proclivities, the regionalists and religious parties that represented 35,1 percent of the electorate (at elections in March 1977). The army was called upon to establish law and order and began to look more and more as the main national arbitrator. Even the opposition was asking the army to "save the country." Arrested on October 11, 1977, Ali Bhutto was officially charged with ordering the murder of a political adversary three years before.

---

4. A community founded by Mirza Ghulam Ahmad en 1889. An Indian religious leader who claimed to be a prophet sent to revive Islam. Even though they call themselves Muslim the majority Sunni consider them as heretics.

On February 6 he was sentenced to death and General Muhammad Zia-ul-Haq, army chief of staff who came to power in a coup refused to consider a pardon. General Zia became president of the republic eight years later in elections that every observer described as fraudulent. Zia-ul-Haq would create the Pakistan we have today. He turned his country into the back base of the struggle against Soviet occupation in Afghanistan. He opposed the secularism of Ali Bhutto and wanted a "socialist and Islamic state" with the support of the mullahs. Zia would forbid interest rates on bank loans, make charity compulsory, reintroduced public corporal punishment, forced women to wear the veil when appearing on television and in 1986 instituted the law on blasphemy. During his presidency the influence of the clergy and fundamentalist Islam would increase. Zia also based his power on other institutions such as the army and the intelligence services. Four months prior to his death in airplane crash Pakistan detonated its first atomic bomb in May 1998. It had been financed for the most part by the Saudis.

The rise of radical Islam in Pakistan divided the country. In 1999, a new coup allowed General Pervez Musharraf to take over. In 2001, Pakistan officially ended its support of the Afghan Taliban like the Saudis who stopped financing Osama Bin Laden. Relations between Pakistan and Saudi Arabia continued with Iran in their sights even though Islamabad and Dr. Khan, the father of the Pakistani bomb were helping the Iranian nuclear program.

Relations between Pakistan and Saudi Arabia require some background explanation. Abdul Qadeer Khan had traveled to Riyadh for the purpose of assisting the kingdom in nuclear technology in exchange for lower costs on oil. The agreement was signed during King Abdullah's visit to Islamabad in 2003. Following the Pakistani Sunni bomb, Riyadh has been increasingly planning as a reaction to the Shia Iranian nuclear project, to build a bomb of its own.

In northern Balutchistan, alongside Afghanistan, the Federally Administered Tribal Areas (FATA) is a territory 2,000 Kilometers long by 50 wide that is a dangerous powder keg. The poor and un-educated population has strong conservative leanings and is hostile to foreigners and drawn to Muslim fundamentalism. The area holds 5 million Pashtun—the ethnic group of the Taliban—divided into 1,200 tribes and clans and is used as a sanctuary and rear base of the Taliban and Al Qaeda. Weapons, hashish and heroin are freely exchanged and the area is practically independent even though it is administered by and part of Pakistan. Military operations are carried out from Balutchistan to the northwestern border (Khyber Pakhtunkhwa). Because of the Afghan conflict the "Talibanization" of the tribal areas is now an unavoidable reality.

Thirty years ago a dictator could still control Pakistan while today each group acts according to its own interests. The growing rivalry of opposing religious groups Shia and Sunni that have settled their differences by shedding blood increases the fear that Pakistan with a population of 165 million people could be seriously destabilized. Many Pakistanis are convinced that their country should be an Islamic republic governed by mullahs who would be the councilors of the elected representatives. Pakistan is today a mosaic of nationalist revolts (the province of Balutchistan), Islamist Emirates (the region of Waziristan in the North West with a Pashtun population,) military and economic fiefdoms (the cities of Rawalpindi, Islamabad and Karachi), and no one can predict what the future outcome will be.

The presence of the Taliban and other fundamentalist groups on both sides of the Pakistani-Afghan border ties the future of both countries to one another. In both Afghanistan and Pakistan, the two regimes each have their "good" and "bad" Taliban. President Karzai who says that corruption is of secondary importance even went so far as to ask for the latter's support to begin a dialogue with Mullah Omar.[5] Iran is also taking advantage of the situation since Teheran has traditionally been the ally of the Afghan Shia minority and today even the Sunni need Iran's support as the only stable power in the region.

It is a guarantee of future security meaning the day when the western powers will leave as the Afghan president recognized recently that he receives suitcases filled with dollars from Iran. Even though the Sunni Taliban are not exactly welcome in Shia Iran the

---

5. December 2009.

role it plays as a regional power compels Iran to increase its influence in Afghanistan. Teheran cannot abandon the Shia and Farsi-speaking under the hostile domination of the Taliban. Since Iran's objective is to contain western influence it helps Taliban factions as long as they are not affiliated to Mullah Omar. Iranian influence is all encompassing and today Afghanistan has some 7,000 graduates from Iranian universities and thousands of Afghan Shia clerics are receiving instruction in Teheran. These continue to have financial support after they return home in the form of a monthly salary. Iran can only hope for peace in Afghanistan since it would mean that over one million Afghan refugees could go back to their own country lessening the financial burden on Teheran.

The U.S. Army would also like to separate the wheat from the chaff and looks to the Neo-Taliban. But what makes the difference between one Taliban and another? During the 1990s the Taliban were raised in the Koranic schools: the Madrassas in Pakistan. The new generation experienced war and refugee camps making it far more radicalized. The former did benefit from American and Saudi financial support. Today the Neo-Taliban control the opium trade that finances their war effort. During Mullah Omar's time as head of the Taliban it was forbidden to grow poppies. In 2001, at the end of the Taliban period, Afghanistan only produced 5 percent of world opium. That number has increased dramatically to 90 percent. The Taliban movement is divided into "moderates" that are faithful to Mullah Omar and radicals that are closer to Al Qaeda. The moderates are ready to negotiate with President Karzai to share power. While the "Talibanization" of Afghanistan has the approval of the Pashtun it also frightens the Farsi-speaking populations.

In Waziristan, Pakistani troops began an offensive against neo-fundamentalists in October 2009, attacking the areas that provided shelter to the Taliban and Al Qaeda terrorists. The government was selective in targeting terrorist groups and focused on one of the most radical Islamist groups: the TTP (Tehrik-e-Taliban Pakistan). A member of the Mehsud clan, of Pashtun ethnicity, TTP was formed in 2007. The clan is thought to be a Taliban group responsible for the attack that killed former Prime Minister Benazir Bhutto, then a candidate for president, as well as other attacks on Pakistani cities.

The army decided to attack the TTP which had declared war on the Pakistani state. Such a strategy was greeted with skepticism by NATO and the West. Terror groups and good Taliban in the eyes of Islamabad, the ISI and Kabul were not on the target list for elimination and continue to operate with impunity against coalition forces in Afghanistan. The closeness of ISI to certain Islamist groups serves Pakistani geopolitical interests in both Afghanistan and Kashmir. In Afghanistan, the prospect of the Taliban controlling the country is seen favorably by Islamabad. As Olivier Roy indicated, Pakistani support for Afghan mujahidin must "end in legitimizing a quasi-protectorate over a liberated Afghanistan, in the name of Islam—but also more subtly thanks to ethnic Pashtun networks on both sides of the border." By consolidating its influence in Afghanistan, Pakistan can then concentrate on Kashmir.

Islamist fundamentalism in Pakistan managed to stifle the liberals. Salman Taseer, governor of Punjab the political core of the country was murdered by one of his bodyguards who cried out "Allah Akbar." His crime was to have opposed the blasphemy law an article of the penal code that provides capital punishment to whoever is found guilty of having offended the Prophet of Islam. The current rigorist application of the law proves the vigor of radical Islam. It dates back to the period when General Zia-ul-Haq had launched his campaign for the Islamization of the Pakistani state and contributed to the weakening of religious minorities whether they were Christian (1.6 percent), Hindu (1.6 percent) or Adhami (2.3 percent).

A few weeks after Salman Taseer's murder, Shahbaz Bhatti, a Christian minister of religious minorities, would also be assassinated. The crime committed by these two liberal political figures was to support the idea of a Pakistan with an enlightened form of Islam respectful of its minorities. In January 2010, when offering his wishes to religious leaders President Nicolas Sarkozy condemned the blasphemy law by using an example from a case he was interested in. A housewife and mother was recently condemned to death. "Asia Bibi is poor, Christian and a former untouchable. What crime had she committed? Having used the glass of her neighbor to drink who saw this as an impure action, a blasphemy. Asia Bibi was therefore sentenced. Some in her country have protested against this and paid a high price for speaking out. But Asia Bibi was on the wanted list of the extremists. If she is freed from jail she risks being killed." The president concluded: "France is concerned about this situation."

The Shia are also victims of Sunni violence. The struggle for local power, rivalries over the Holy Places, tension between Iran and Saudi Arabia, all serve as a pretext to create conflict... the Pakistani Shia are considered enemies... as much as the NATO soldiers are. On July 1, 2011, the Pakistani government announced the elimination of the ministry of religious affairs. That decision caused fear and worry among the various religious denominations other than Sunni Islam as a new sign of the radicalization of power and a new concession to Islamist radicals.

Kashmir Between Pakistan, India, and China

Kashmir was an old princely state and a vassal of the British Empire. After the British sold the land to a Hindu maharajah the state of Kashmir, that was mostly Muslim with a Hindu minority, it became after India's independence the object of claims and the reason for several local wars between India, Pakistan and China. "In Kashmir, with a majority Muslim population and a Hindu Maharajah [...] thought it best to hold on to the political autonomy and integrity of the state. However the revolt of the Poonch region favorable to Pakistan, and the support of the Pakistani army for the rebels led the maharajah to choose India in exchange for military help from New Delhi (October 28, 1947). Following that decision the armed intervention by both countries in Kashmir brought about the first India-Pakistan war that led to the partition of Kashmir between the two countries along the 'Line of Control' of the ceasefire that ended the conflict on January 1, 1949."[6]

India claims Kashmir that is occupied by Pakistan (Azad-Kashmir known as "Free Kashmir" in Pakistan, and called Pakistan

---

6. Report n° 336 Sénat, June 24, 2002, written after a mission to India and Pakistan.

Occupied Kashmir or POK in India), the Northern territories (Northern Areas of India) and the area under Chinese occupation (Aksai Chin). Pakistan claims Kashmir under Indian occupation (the State of Jammu- and- Kashmir). China on the other hand claims part of the Indian Ladakh which prolongs the Tibetan plateau. A very complicated situation indeed!

During the Cold War, India was allied to the USSR. A border dispute between New Delhi and Beijing led to war in 1962. The Chinese invaded Assam in north eastern India on October 20 and were threatening Calcutta. On November 21, China declared a unilateral ceasefire and Nehru's India experienced a humiliating defeat. Beyond that conflict there were two other disputes: Chinese Kashmir that is occupied by India and Tibet and the Tibetan government in exile that had been proclaimed in 1959. Initially located in northern India it was moved to Dharamsala in 1960 with India's agreement. The 14th Dalai Lama, decided to move there as well… creating a casus belli in Beijing's eyes.

Since 1989, seeing they couldn't defeat India in a conventional war and to modify the demographic balance in the valley of Kashmir to favor Muslims, the Pakistani leadership and the ISI infiltrated thousands of Islamists of all nationalities, trained in Pakistan and led by Pakistani and ISI officers. Those fighters brought Jihad to the Hindu infidels and began what amounted to ethnic cleansing against the Hindu population. Since then more than 50,000 Hindus were the victims of Jihadists and some 300,000 fled Kashmir to refugee camps in Jammu, near Delhi where they live in misery. Today less than 5 percent of Hindus are living in the Kashmir valley. The jihadists with the help of ISI are responsible for many attacks in India itself.

In Indian Kashmir that is claimed by both Pakistanis and Indians, New Delhi keeps a force of 500,000 men. The authorities make every effort to prevent protest: forbidding programs on local television and blocking SMS messages to prevent the assembly of possible protesters. Incursions by armed Pakistani militants have receded in twenty years.

But not the number of Kashmiri separatists. Indians fear a Muslim Kashmiri intifada imitating the one by the Palestinians that is starting in Kashmir.

The Mumbai Attacks

India and Pakistan had already fought four wars (1947, 1965, 1971, 1999)... and New Delhi always fears that Pakistan will seek a solution to its problems by resorting to a frontal clash: "The world epicenter and terrorist sanctuary," "terrorism as a government policy," "the troubling game of the army and the intelligence services," those are the conclusions Indian authorities faced with the Jihadist threats from Pakistan; and yet both countries attempted to relaunch the peace process.[7]

Pakistani terrorism often used India as a target. Yet some attacks attributed to Pakistanis were perpetrated by Hindus in the past. Response of a "bomb for a bomb" or quite simply the radicalization of Hindu religious or ultra nationalist groups, terrorism also exists in the world's largest democracy. An attack among many others on February 18, 2007, targeted the train Samjhauta Express, "the friendship train" between New Delhi and Lahore. There were 68 casualties including 42 Pakistanis at Panipat (India). According to the weekly *Tehelka*, published in New Delhi, those responsible were a Hindu extreme right-wing sect. It is a diverse kind of movement. According to *The Nation*, a Pakistani weekly close to the army "the scourge of terrorism" had come to India "under the guise of democracy and secularism." The driving force behind the attack was a Hindu religious leader from the State of Gujarat. Swami Aseemanand also admitted to being responsible along with his group for attacks on the mosque of Hyderabad and the Sufi center at Ajmer. In 2006 they opted for armed struggle specifically targeting the Muslim population.

Another group, the Abhinav Bharat, from the State of Maharastra, created a network that operates throughout the country. It is led by an army officer whose dream is to establish a theocratic

---

7. May 2011.

Hindu state based on violence. Two attacks at Malegaon have already been attributed to the group (September 8, 2006: 37 killed; September 29, 2008: 7 killed).

China After Communism: a Return to Faith

To the leaders of China, any ethnic or religious movement or issue that goes against national unity must be eradicated. If the events are in the media they can create sympathy in western public opinion and this becomes intolerable. The Chinese Communist party considers both the Dalai Lama and the Tibetans as well as the Uygurs and their leader Rebiya Kadeer, who fled to the United States as two communities that are enemies inside China. Xinjiang where the Uyghur live is on the border with Afghanistan and a strategic province with the largest oil reserves in China. The fact that the United States has placed Uyghur organizations on the terrorist list and that some are imprisoned at Guantanamo have given a kind of "legitimacy" to Beijing's repression. Even though the Uyghur always appeared suspect to Beijing because of their Muslim religion it is the competition with the Han—the majority of the Chinese population sent by Beijing into the provinces such as Xinjian to control the areas—that contributed to the clash between populations of different ethnic origin.

Gheynet Niyaz, Uyghur journalist and author at the *Economic Journal* of Xinjiang, was sentenced to fifteen years in prison for "endangering State security." He had written that inter-ethnic clashes had been the result of the forced linguistic assimilation policy and the program of sending young Uyghur workers into Chinese border areas. Religion played a uniting role within the Uyghur community but was not the main reason for the riots even though they were organized by "Hezb- ut-Tahir al-islami," an Islamic group created by an Afghan made up of poorly educated young men from the countryside. These are groups of one hundred were "moving unarmed in a very well organized and disciplined way" yelling "kill the Han, let us establish Islamic power where the Sharia will be law."[8]

---

8. *Libération*, Philippe Grangereau, July 26, 2010.

The Uyghur dissident leader, Rebiya Kadeer, living in exile in the United States offered Beijing an excuse: Chinese authorities can refer to it as "a separatist plot arranged by a foreign power." The main issue being Beijing's refusal to respect cultural, religious and ethnic differences among populations that do not belong to the ethnic Han majority even more so because those groups reside in strategic areas with natural resources such as water in Tibet and oil in the Uyghur territories.

In October 2010, students at Minzu University in Beijing, the largest university of ethnic studies in the country held a demonstration calling for "equality of nationalities, equality of languages." At the same time the high school students in Qinghai, a Tibetan province, were protesting against the "bilingual" educational policies that Tibetan teachers must follow. The new policy also encourages hiring teachers and professors who speak Mandarin and therefore are ethnic Han.

The Tibetans even more than the Uyghur, are the larger problem. The welcome extended to the Dalai Lama by western leaders and relations between states are often the object of commercial retribution against the countries involved. The Living God, a spiritual and secular leader fled from Tibet in 1959 ahead of the Chinese army. He went to Dharamsala, in the Indian State of Himashal and set up a Tibetan government in exile at Pradesh, a resort during the British Raj. Such a political decision was unacceptable to Mao and the post-communists. At the same time it was also true that the Dalai Lama's predecessors had behaved as despots and that Tibet was still in the Middle Ages at the time the religious leader left. That heritage made the secular and religious leader an enemy of the people. While the Dalai Lama no longer demands independence but supports autonomy for Tibet and has changed "government in exile" to "Tibetan administration" the issue will remain as long as the religious leader remains overseas and no one imagines him returning to China. Tibetan monasteries and the monks are an opposition force that has the sympathy of world public opinion.

Ugyen Trinley Dorje was a challenge for both Tibetans and the Beijing authorities, a casus belli even for the communist regime. In

1992, four Buddhist leaders identified a seven-year-old boy who was next to last of nine children, born under exceptional auspices: a rainbow, a bird under the tent, and strange noises in a barrel. They recognized in him the reincarnation of a lost master. The Dalai Lama at first approved of the choice and later withdrew his agreement. Beijing was convinced it had found with that child a way to counter the ambition of the "old separatist." He was recognized as the seventeenth Karmapa, the heir to a line of grand masters of wisdom, the oldest in Buddhism. The regime nurtured him and provided for his tutoring at the monastery of Tsurphu near Lhassa. On December 28, 1999 under the pretext of a spiritual retreat he left the monastery and after a colorful escape arrived on January 5, 2000, at Mac-Leod Ganj... not far from the Dalai Lama's monastery. His successor refused to be Beijing's puppet in Tibet.

The Dalai Lama placed himself in danger when he announced in March 2011 that he was retiring from politics. He wished to "freely transfer his power to a leader who would be freely elected by the Tibetan people." That same month of March he had parliament elect a new prime minister. Those decisions did not mollify Beijing toward the Tibetans. A theocratic democracy, with elections even by a small group of voters could only appear to Beijing as a form of provocation as well as a precedent where the political goes beyond the religious and opens up a door onto the unknown.

India faces a difficult situation: the exile of the Dalai Lama and Kashmir are two disputes it has with China. But both Beijing and New Delhi remain realistic in facing the issues. The development of Tibet requires breaking the isolation of that remote region. On July 7, 2006, after some forty years China and India decided to reopen the border crossing at Nathu located on the old Silk Road that had been closed since the 1962 war. With the new Indian-Chinese co-operation Beijing has a double objective: integrating Tibet into China through development and as much as possible modify the relationship between the Dalai Lama and India.

Today China is opening up to religion. The leadership is ready to tolerate this development while attempting at the same time to limit its influence by rehabilitating Confucius and his philosophy.

Catholicism faces a difficult situation because it is western and tied to an existing state. While there is more tolerance toward foreign faiths it must also be viewed as a way for the Chinese to control the changes of a country opening to the rest of the world. The Chinese Communist party remains ubiquitous and is the overarching structure holding the country together. Since 1951, the party has complete control over religious matters while the Vatican in the name of its fundamental rights cannot accept to have Catholicism under state and party tutelage. Relations between Beijing and the Holy See are difficult since the Vatican recognizes and maintains diplomatic relations with Taiwan. There are therefore two Catholic churches in China: one that remains underground and is faithful to Rome and the other called patriotic that is a creation of the regime.

Since 2006, the relations between the two states have had their ups and downs. The Chinese authorities can be accommodating in appointing bishops with the consent of the Holy See. In November 2010, the consecration of a bishop of patriotic church over Vatican objections was "a serious violation of religious freedom and freedom of conscience" according to the Holy See. In December 2010, Beijing appointed Ma Yingli who headed the diocese of Kunming since 2006 and had not been approved by Rome, as president of the Conference of bishops that assembles the official high clergy of China.

Since 2007 Fang Xingao, a bishop appointed by Beijing is president of the Association of Chinese Patriotic Catholics. Pope Benedict XVI reiterated the incompatibility that exists between Roman Catholic doctrine and the government sponsored association. This control of the religious by the political is even more serious than one might expect since it comes under the authority of the Bureau of religious authorities a rigid institution controlled by the party's most radical wing. The extreme left-wing policy has undermined the trust that had been built between China and the Vatican and slows the opening that part of the Chinese leadership wishes to see. In a further hardening in July 2011 Chinese police forces practically kidnapped four Catholic bishops loyal to the Vatican so that they would appear at the ordination of bishops by the official Church. The patriotic church in a further sign of coming tension announced a project to ordain 40 new bishops.

The Chinese regime cannot make the case that Protestants have an allegiance to a foreign country as it does with the Catholics. The angle is one of Christianization perceived as western by part of the regime. According to the official statistics, 23 million Chinese call themselves Protestants. As with Catholics the Protestants also have an "underground" Church that refuses to pay tribute to the Movement of the three autonomies which is the government structure set up to control the Protestant faith. The Protestant church of Showing, a neighborhood of Beijing, is very active and has several thousand parishioners.

There are three Sunday services and those in attendance include many young people, employees and middle managers in the capital city who would meet in a commercial building. These are the members of the new Chinese middle class attending before the authorities shut the meeting place down. Besides arrests and periods of detention some Protestants lost their jobs and were evicted from their homes and apartments.

Following the capitalist turn taken by a Chinese Communist party that has never officially denied its Marxist orientation it now favors a doctrine that it had earlier called decadent and reactionary. "If Confucianism has been rehabilitated today it is because the Maoist revolution has failed and the country is faced with an ideological and moral void." writes David Ownby, director of the Center of East Asia. The Chinese Communist party must "recast its authority on new foundations and is turning therefore toward Confucianism. The party wishes to extend its control in the Chinese manner." To achieve this goal, the Chinese leadership is focusing on a few basic points of Confucianism that can be favorable such as respect for authority and hierarchy to ensure social harmony. Since Confucianism is based on traditional morality and ethics (obedience due to one's superiors, importance of the family, nurturing of personal virtue, the possibility that all citizens can become moral), its rehabilitation may be viewed as a solution to fight corruption and cynicism which as David Ownby states, are ubiquitous in China.

The Arab movements were an inspiration to the Chinese opposition. In the Middle Empire, bloggers have called upon all those who wish to criticize the regime to walk around the most crowded parts of town at 2 pm on Sundays. It was a call against corruption and in favor of freedom. They were asking that the government accept "the people's supervision" and demanded that the Communist party "leave the scene of history." Human rights and Party dominance are issues that polarize the leadership. They know and the awakening of the Arab world tells them, that more freedom runs the risk of encouraging protests that would mean the end of the central role played by the communists. One event may serve as an illustration: the Nobel Peace Prize, to Beijing's great disappointment, went to the dissident Liu Xiaobo. Chinese diplomacy did what it could to have countries friendly to Beijing boycott the event calling Nobel panel members "anti-Chinese clowns" and their choice of the prize winner "obscene." Beyond China, only eighteen countries[9] refused the Nobel Committee's invitation to attend.

As a response Beijing created its own peace prize. A Chinese association announced that it would give a "Confucius peace prize" just before the Nobel Prize. The winner was Lien Chan, former Taiwanese vice president who had been favorable to a rapprochement between Beijing and Taiwan!

"Barry Comes Home"

The headline of the *Jakarta Post* was the Indonesian salute to the return of the man whose classmates used to call Barry when he was living in Jakarta with his mother and Indonesian stepfather. Barack Obama returned in November 2010 to that Asian country of 230 million that is more than 80 percent Muslim. The country whose motto is "Unity within diversity" is marked, as the president noted, by "its tolerance symbolized by its mosques, churches and temples." What was the leader of the first world power praising? A society that after the authoritarian regime of the Suharto years, managed to

---

9. Russia, Kazakhstan, Colombia, Tunisia, Saudi Arabia, Pakistan, Serbia, Iraq, Iran, Vietnam, Afghanistan, Venezuela, Philippines, Egypt, Sudan, Ukraine, Cuba and Morocco.

reconcile democracy and development. The Jakarta visit was also an opportunity for Obama to reflect on the Muslim world after his extended hand during his trip to Cairo in the early months of his term. He did concede that "no speech can erase years of suspicion (between the United States and the Muslim world)... and a lot of work is required to bring about renewed mutual confidence."

Leading Indonesia, the world's most populous Muslim country is President Susilo Bambang Yudhoyono, a Muslim in the Sufi tradition. Once a month he holds nights of invocation and meditation at the presidential palace. To his citizens he symbolizes democracy and reason. In spite of this opinion and while the country remains peaceful (the last terrorist attack was in 2004), his popular reelection was marked one week following the vote by two deadly attacks in the Marriott and Ritz-Carlton hotels in Jakarta. The terrorists belonged to dormant Islamist networks and were fighting democracy and tolerance.

Behind western images and ideas about Asian countries there are also overlooked realities. Some countries are deeply involved in inter-religious tensions that may even go so far as violent insurrections. In Malaysia, Islam is the state religion and the constitution guarantees religious freedom: some 57 percent of the population is Muslim. Two legal systems function side by side: one based on Sharia (Islamic law) the other on English common law. The government in fact gives precedence to Islam and tends to limit the freedom of other religions. Since 2007, the government forbids non-Muslims from using the term Allah because "it increases the risk of tensions and creates confusion in the minds of Malay Muslims." Murphy Pakiam, Archbishop of Kuala Lumpur, took the matter to court and explained that Christians have used the term Allah to name God for the past four centuries without it causing any problems. His complaint was given satisfaction.

Southern Thailand borders on Malaysia and 87 percent of Thais identify themselves as Buddhists. The kingdom is known to be one of the most tolerant countries in Asia from the point of view of religious practice. Buddhist monks and monasteries have both power and influence. Clashes and arrests of Buddhist monks have increased in recent years but are tied to political issues and have nothing to do with religion. This is not the case in the Muslim south: in the Thai area an insurrection caused over 4,400 deaths since January 2004. Since the early twentieth century on the other side of the border rebels have been fighting the rule of Bangkok. Every government had failed in the search for a political solution and the conflict intensified at the beginning of 2009. One of the goals of the insurrection is to create a Muslim state and therefore expel non-Muslims from the south.

The Philippines are a majority Christian country (over 87 percent of the population). Mindanao, an island south of the archipelago has a Muslim majority and for the past forty years has been the scene of a war between the army with American military advisors and the Islamic Moro Liberation Front (MILF), the main Muslim separatist movement. The Front is demanding control of the island and is fighting for an independent Islamic state. In 1987, the central government gave autonomy to a large portion of the island creating the "Autonomous Region in Muslim Mindanao" (ARMM).

Yet the government's initiative was not enough and clashes and attacks between the army and the MILF have never really ended. A second group is fighting the government in Manila: the organization led by Abu Sayyaf that the UN identifies as close to Al Qaeda. Some of its members have studied in Saudi Arabia and have spent time in Pakistan and Afghanistan, having established networks with other terrorist organizations. Abu Sayyaf extended his influence and his reach to countries close to the Philippines such as Malaysia and Indonesia. In August 2008 Philippine President Gloria Arroyo, seeking to defeat the rebellion, decided to launch a strong offensive using artillery. In less than nine months the conflict made many victims and over 750,000 Muslim and Christian refugees. In September 2009 in Kuala Lumpur (Malaysia), the MILF and the government of the Philippines reopened negotiations to end the conflict. In spite of the agreement of MILF leaders to cooperate with Manila, Abu Sayyaf's terrorists and other Moro representatives broke with their leadership and resumed the offensive.

Within the anarchy that plagues the region there is an unwritten agreement among the factions to make sure the rebellion keeps on going. The Moro Front, sees it as a way to increase its influence among terror groups. The army concentrates its efforts against the Abu Sayyaf group. The military also obtains better and more equipment; the Muslim clan leaders and politicians have created militias. Thanks to weapons smuggling they can extend their power over entire areas and make a lot of money.

Beyond the situation in each country, the main issue is one of compatibility between the ideas of democracy, peace, modernity and Islamism. Historian Richard W. Bulliet explains the Islam that has flourished in the Arab world is pluralist and progressive. He sees the current crisis and the rise of fundamentalism coming from a lack of democracy.[10] This has created a crisis of religious authority because of the repression of the Ulemas, and religion by the kings, emirs, and lifetime presidents of Arab Muslim nation states set up by Europe and America. To put an end to the "God Crazies" it is urgent to bring the Islamist movements into the political process and allow them to take part in free elections and not prevent their participation.

---

10. *La civilisation islamo-chrétienne. Son passé, son avenir,* Flammarion, 2006.

Chapter 12

Iran: from the Middle Ages to Rebirth and Beyond

The 2007 Iranian elections will stand as a historical watershed. The process did more than renew the mandate of Mahmoud Ahmadinejad: it revealed the divisions in Iranian society. It also represented institutional and political change, even a kind of revolution following the revolution that created the Islamic Republic in 1979.

The election demonstrated the Iranian people's interest in voting, with participation close to 85 percent. There certainly was fraud—no observer would deny it—but nothing indicated that the incumbent would not have been reelected. Mahmoud Ahmadinejad was supported by the street, by the poor, not to mention those indebted to him—Revolutionary Guards, the Basidji, government workers—and by the rural and conservative heartland. The election was by no means worse than Ali Bongo's in Gabon, Karzai's in Afghanistan, Ben Ali's in Tunisia or Mubarak's in Egypt. The last two presided over the destinies of their countries for, respectively, 24 years and 30 years with the West's full approval with repeated Soviet-style scores in fully democratic elections until their unexpected downfall.

Without seeking to rewrite History, had the international community not contested the results, a second round of elections giving the presidency to Mahmoud Ahmadinejad, even if by a small margin, would have allowed him to change the course of events. He could then have been free to pursue negotiations with the U.S. Instead, the climate and the incidents surrounding the elections and the international community's condemnation caused the hardening of the regime. The sanctions that hit the Iranian people the hardest made matters worse. The president then withdrew to safety, relying on his trusted Basijs and revolutionary guards and the support of the poor. At the same time, he was able to make a decision that no other Iranian Muslim or Arab leader could have made, proving how secure his power base was. In late 2010 and early 2011, he abolished state subsidies for oil and other energy products and for selected foods. Even though these subsidies had increased the living standards of the Iranian people, and especially the poorest, their heavy cost was a burden on economic growth. In 2007 oil subsidies had to be maintained: angry customers had destroyed several gas stations. This time the way Iranians accepted these measures confirmed the degree of trust in the president after the election and during the demonstrations that followed. At the same time, in the Republic of Oman, in Algeria and in Morocco, the authorities were busy handing out cash to households or increasing social budgets, in the hope of limiting the contagion of the Arab Spring.

There's another aspect to the election: the illusion, spread mainly by the Western media that the leaders of the opposition were democrats and defenders of freedom. It is important to differentiate, regarding the opposition, between the electoral candidates and the Greens, a largely leaderless and unstructured movement. The candidates who were running against the incumbent were all granted permission to run by the authorities.

Mousavi, for instance, with his good Islamic revolutionary credentials was a thoroughly acceptable candidate even if, during the campaign, he used his wife, presenting her as a 'liberal'. In 1981, he was the chief editor of the *Islamic Republic*, the new theocratic republic's main newspaper; he was also Minister of Foreign Affairs during the hostage taking at the American embassy and then head of government in 1981. Considered a hawk and also known for taming the universities, organizing the purges and the repression in the first hours of the Islamic Republic that resulted in thousands of deaths.

Mehdi Karoubi had been one of the strongest supporters of the revolution. He met Ayatollah Khomeini during his religious studies. He was a top leader of the regime, having become an advisor to the Ayatollah, and a member of one of the highest councils of the regime: the Expediency Discernment Council.

As for the third candidate, Mohsen Rezaï, he was, at the time of the election, Secretary of the Expediency Discernment Council, having been for 16 years the Commander in chief of the pasdarans!

The green demonstrators had no choice but to back these candidates. When they took to the streets it was not so much because they supported these men, but because they wanted to show they rejected the system represented by the incumbent and the Supreme Guide. Even if someone like Mousavi may have changed, it isn't easy to be a Gorbachev and after all, the father of perestroika brought in people such as Yeltsin, Putin and a return to the Romanovs. According to Abbas Milan, head of Iranian Studies at Stanford University, the greens are not an opposition in the political sense of the word. They are made up of people who believe their vote was not taken into account and who, first and foremost, were demonstrating for the right to a normal life. This was a large movement and it appeared organized although it was not: only the child of the Twitter and cell phone revolution. The demonstrations were very well attended and the world was able to see them while journalists, for their part, were held in hotels by the authorities. This was in large part thanks to Hillary Clinton's intervention with the social media executives.

The U.S. Secretary of State asked that the supplier delay a maintenance operation that would have cut Iran off from the rest of the world. It should be remembered that Iran boasts more internet users than the entire Middle East, from Egypt to Pakistan, with a percentage of people connected to the web comparable to Israel's. Since these events were made highly visible by the media it convinced the West, even more, of the ills of Iran under Ahmadinejad. But after the emotional responses and the new sanctions imposed, did nothing to find a way out of the dead end where Iranians and Westerners have found themselves for the past 30 years. Paradoxically, the events strengthened Ahmadinedjad's power. This in turn is the sign of truly revolutionary institutional change in the structure of power in Iranian theocracy, which is based on the judiciary.

Ahmadinedjad engineered a coup: placing the President of the Republic above the Supreme Guide of the Revolution. The word "coup" should not be taken literally. It must be understood in the spirit of François Mitterrand when he criticized the way Charles de Gaulle returned to power in 1958, or when he denied any democratic value to the election of the French president of the republic through direct popular vote in 1962.

The Art of Adapting

For the past forty years there isn't a day without a story featuring Iran in a major newspaper. And yet journalists have rarely been interested in the Iranian people, or the fate of that nation. Coverage of events by the international media is often partial, biased and inaccurate for the ordinary Iranian in Teheran or Tabriz because of its hasty analysis or lack of knowledge of the country. This contributes to many Iranians feeling misunderstood and isolated.

Iranian society is surprisingly young. Thirty something year olds make up the majority. It is educated and feminine. More than fifty percent of students are women and contrary to many other countries the quality of the universities is on a par with Western institutions. Women hold responsibilities in the public as well as the private sector. To understand this complex society, one must first accept one fact: yesterday's Persia as well as today's Iran successfully melded tradition and modernity. Iranian people have an acute sense of national pride, a character trait that has always been and remains today a determining factor in the regime's staying in power: it plays this card, as it has in the particular case of nuclear power. But this does not necessarily mean support for the regime. How then do Iranians cope in a society which is simultaneously open and modern (70 percent of Iranians live in cities) and under the influence of the clerics?

Some people in the West seem to have discovered a typically Iranian practice, Tarof:[1] an art of extreme politeness that Persians used to practice. Exercising Tarof means presenting oneself as more humble than one's interlocutor. To express good will, an Iranian will say "walk on my eyes" and to thank a person he will say "I am your slave." In this formal exchange both participants know that is not the case and that one of them will have the upper hand. The deepest recesses of Iranian psychology and soul surfaces in these expressions. This ancestral practice allows for some duplicity. It allows people to overcome difficult situations by avoiding head on confrontation. This typically Persian dialectic allows Iranians to not despair completely. The idea is: "We were the first to found an Islamic republic; we will be the first to abandon it and get out."[2] Meanwhile the Iranian people compromise and adapt to the situation.

In my book, *Iran, The Return of Persia*, I mentioned the multi-faceted character of the clergy.[3] To understand Iran today, an essential point must be taken into account: the Islamic revolution has altered the traditional social composition of Shiism with conse-quences for the status and position of the clerics, particularly for the higher clergy. Imam Khomeini was acknowledged as Grand Aya-tollah and Supreme leader of the revolution: history gave him that status. The present leader, Ayatollah Khamenei was designated by his predecessor in his will. In 1989, when Khomeini died, the Council named Khamenei Supreme leader for life. Before that he had been elevated to the rank of Ayatollah which represented a promotion normally granted only after a long career. This is regulated by custom and requires the express recognition of his peers. The membership of the Council was renewed in December 2006. At that time, the 'conservatives' eliminated reformist clerics on the pretense that their candidacies did not conform to Islam! The members of the Council are elected for a period of 8 years so they will be renewed in 2014. That date will have consequences for the future of the country since it will coincide with the year of the presidential election.

---

1. Catherine Millet, *Libération*, June 19, 2010: *l'Iran, les arts et la manière*.
2. Ardavan Amir-Aslani, *Iran, le retour de la Perse*, Jean Picollec, mars 2009.
3. Op. cit.

The exceptional circumstances and the way elections are conducted and the Supreme Leader is designated constitute a break with Shiite tradition. Not only did the position of Supreme Leader not exist before the Islamic revolution of 1979, but everything in the high clergy relied on the notion of consensus with a single objective: to maintain the unity of the Shiites. The consensus was focused on personality but even more so regarding the religious credentials of the candidates. That promotion process within the hierarchy did not entail a monolithic structure, for the contrary. Each ayatollah, each marjah or "source of imitation," each seminary, constituted its own network, collected religious taxes thereby possessing religious and secular influence. The play for influence among these groups, as long as it did not threaten the community's unity, encouraged consensus around a single person. In fact, it created emulation. Further, since Shiism relies on interpretation of confrontation with the contemporary world and contemporary problems, those choices were conducive to modernity, and tied to the evolution of society. Consensus was also the rule in the theological centers. The most respected ayatollahs designated the marjahs much as the cardinals choose the pope. Contrary to the Catholic Church, there is no preeminence of one particular ayatollah, or one marjah, which makes for the intellectual and spiritual richness of Shiism and its adaptive nature.

Iran's importance in the Shiite world increased because of Saddam Husseins's policy of systematically eliminating the Grand Ayatollahs of Nadjaf and eradicating the influence of Shiism and the Shiites in Iraq. The best known took refuge in Iran. The decline of Najaf gave more importance to Qom. The "dark years" of the Iraqi Shia were partly responsible for the increased influence of Iran and the Iranian high clergy in that community, which had in any case always been dominated by Iranians.

How then did the accession of Ayatollah Khomeini as head of the Islamic republic modify the social composition of Shiism and its clergy? The father of the Islamic republic did not assert himself as a religious expert, which he was not, but as a politician opposed to the imperial regime. After Grand Ayatollah Montazeri, Khomeini's dauphin, was shunted aside, Khamenei was chosen to succeed the founder of the republic not on the basis of religious criteria or because of his theological learning, but because he could sustain the regime. An unexpected consequence of Khomeinism, and a paradoxical one, was that a large part of the clergy no longer confined itself to tradition but became involved in the modern world. An instance of this is Rafsanjani who is as much a businessman as a politician and one of the richest men in the country. As a candidate against Ahmadinejad in 2004, he tried to make people forget his status as an ayatollah, at least for the duration of the campaign. He is not well respected in the country, but as an ex president, and standing president of the Council who had just recently given up the presidency of the Expert's assembly, he understands the country's aspirations for more freedom and its wish to westernize everyday life. Described as a wheeler and dealer by the national and international press, he represents a system that is enduring even as it is being criticized: the 'mullah connection.'

Much of the Iranian clergy has an experience that is unique in the Muslim world: being or having been in government. This is very different from heading a religious foundation under the empire or from owning a business.

The Iranian state is large and complex, especially since Iran is an energy producing country. The clerics who are active at every level of government possess for the most part relatively modest theological knowledge often acquired only to supplement a traditional secular university curriculum. An official like Hassan Rouhani, responsible for negotiations on nuclear power, is a good example of this new type of man. He first received a diploma in physics from Oxford University, only then did he pursue studies in political science and theology. The Iranian clergy is therefore well versed in world affairs and, even if it was not in 1979, the clergy has had time to learn over the last 30 years since it has been in power.

In Iran clerics have authority over, or directly manage key sectors of the government such as the judiciary and the secret services as well as big foundations or state enterprises, even if the revolutionary guards' hierarchy are its competitors, particularly in the economic sector: the guards—like the army in Turkey—head a military industrial complex. Created in 1990 Khatam al-Ambiya coordinates the activities of multiple businesses overseen by the pasdarans and now controls over 800 companies operating in multiple sectors: armaments (rocket and missile manufacturing); construction and development (roads, dams, mining, irrigation infrastructure, etc.; oil and gas (in June 2009 it was awarded a contract to build a 600 km pipeline to India, for $2.2 billion); communications (in the summer of 2009, the Tosseh Etemad Mobin Consortium, linked to the pasdarans, took control of more than 50 percent of the state owned telecommunications company Sherkat Mokhaberat Iran, without any bidding at a cost of $8 billion); finance (two welfare credit unions of the pasdarans and the basidji were turned into banks.)

Here again the Revolutionary Guards are far from being a monolithic group and have their differences. Part of their base comes from low income people and they do not approve of this repressive business oriented take over. The status of the Guards could be jeopardized in the event of a democratic transition. The state will have to integrate these two sectors inside its structures. This could also be a means of attracting the West in a policy of development of the country by opening up the companies' capital. Something Iranian youth aspires to.

Contrary to the French revolution where priests who did not pledge allegiance to the regime had to hide, in Iran two clergies exist side by side. One group is pursuing careers in the power structure and not in the mosque or the theological centers, whereas those who refuse to join remain in their purely religious positions: they are called 'quietists'. The move of part of the Shiite clergy toward business rather than religious activity contributed to the secularization of the country, even though obviously it was not the goal of the republic's founders. At the same time the clergy allows all clerics to maintain a moral authority in a country that is fundamentally attached to religion. One more important purely Iranian paradox! The clerics who refuse to join are increasing in number and influence. This position sometimes offers an easy way out for political clerics. The debate on transition is centered entirely on when the country will abandon theocracy, not on whether it should do so.

As for the Greens, it is important to remember that at no point did they overstep the limit. It was never a question of challenging the Islamic nature of the regime. Even if the demonstrators have a different vision of Iran, they know that secularization cannot be discussed in the same terms as in other Western countries. Calling for the boycott of Ramadan in a Muslim country is a crime. Islam isn't just a religion in the Muslim world: the Koran and the hadiths are the poles around which social and political structures are built. The ultimate expression of the symbiosis between religion and society is the strict application of Sharia law in some Sunni countries, even though this is not the case in Iran.

What the Green demonstrators aspire to is more individual and collective freedoms. They dream of a country that could westernize. They want to be able to listen to music openly or see films of their choice, go out and not be subjected to the dress militia. On this point also, there is a split between the educated urban population and the rural or urban poor living on government subsidies.

The greens, in the end, represent a rejection of the power structure and consequently of some of the clerics but not a rejection of religion. Religion remains an essential component of society, as Fernand Braudel has shown. The Greens are aiming, beyond Ahmadinejad, at the Supreme Leader and what he represents, that is to say the government of the Leader, the velayat-e faqih. Their positions could be summed up this way: they are for the moral primacy of the clergy, but against their prescriptions touching private life, and against the clergy handling the affairs of state. They are demanding a de facto separation of Mosque and state. When they speak of a moral dominion, they mean to return religion to the private sphere as opposed to the public sphere where it is still entrenched today in Iran. This is a movement toward the secularization of society. It should also be remembered that velayat-e faqih does not belong to Shiite tradition.

Montazeri: the Cleric Who Remains the Image of Iran

In Iran, people often judge the present situation by referring to the constitutional revolution of 1906, the first one in Asia. At that time Ayatollah Khorasani's actions had led to the departure of King Qadjar Mohammed Ali Shah, who was replaced by his son. Since that revolution, nationalism and Iranian patriotism are based on ideals of democracy, national independence and freedom. The man who best embodied those aspirations remains former Prime Minister Mossadegh.

Among clerics, Grand Ayatollah Montazeri also represents the dream of the 1906 revolution. He died in Qom on December 19, 2009, a few months after the election of the president. The former, discredited, dauphin of Imam Khomeini was buried in the holy city of Shiite Islam, a figure venerated by all Shiites. There were many demonstrations during the funeral and the period of mourning that followed. When he died, the government sponsored media omitted his religious titles of ayatollah and marjah.

Hossein Ali Montazeri was a paradoxical figure who became an embarrassing critic of the regime. He supported and created the ideological foundations of the Islamic revolution. Having been the regime's main ideologue, he became its most ferocious critic. He formalized the velayat-e faqih, the principle that established the predominance of the religious over the political which was inscribed in the preamble to the constitution. At the time he was the successor designate, the regime spokesman, its propagandist. He was the Imam who said Friday prayers at Teheran University, which was the center of the opposition to the Shah. Finally, he presided one of the key institutions, the Expediency Council of discernment that was to designate Ayatollah Khomeini's successor after his death, and was also empowered to dismiss him.

Strangely, one of the causes of the rift between this grand ayatollah and Imam Khomeini centered on the principle of velayat-e faqih. At the time, he was worried at the way the regime was drifting toward repression and totalitarianism: not that they were the product of the velayat-e faqih but of its application by the clerics.

After Mahmoud Ahmadinejad 's election, Ayatollah Montazeri called the way the country was being 'led', 'tyrannical'. He opposed both the president and the Supreme Leader and told the Iranian people not to 'be afraid'. Ayatollah Montazeri thought that 'every good Iranian had a duty to oppose the injustices being committed by those who would deny the people's rights.'

The Grand Ayatollah's stand had a considerable impact. His condemnation of the Leader was certainly the strongest criticism of a high ranking official, religious or political. To qualify Ali Khamenei, he used the word 'jaer', meaning 'usurping despot'. This word had only been used twice throughout history. The first time was when Ayatollah Khorasani used it against King Mohammed Ali Shah. The second one was when Ayatollah Khomeini used it against the last Shah, Mohammad Reza Pahlavi. When Montazeri took that position, he was no longer isolated among the higher clergy. He was expressing a growing sentiment, particularly in Qom.

Ahmadinejad tried in vain to get, if not a blessing, then at least a message of congratulations from the clergy in Qom: he received none. Even well known clerics such as Ayatollah Ostadi who is at the head of the religious schools of Qom, and had been favorable to the Leader until then, attacked the regime, not by targeting Khamenei but by attacking the president and the regime's tools for repression. He denounced the "illegal schemes of the Basidji militias". The government militias the president used against demonstrators, with the Leader's assent. He criticized Hodjatoleslam Ghassem Ravan Bakhch, their leader, for the repression he carried out. He also targeted Ayatollah Mesbah Yazdi, the president's fundamentalist mentor.

So, even though the government asked for their help, the religious leaders remained remarkably silent. Only one did respond... Ayatollah Abbas Vaez Tabasi, a high ranking conservative called the leaders of the opposition 'enemies of God' who deserved to be put to death. As for the other high ranking clerics, they chose their words: 'despot', 'usurper', 'injustice', 'illegality'. The rejection of Ahmadinejad signals a rift between part of the clergy and the executive. Never before had religious dignitaries condemned the political drift of the regime embodied by the Leader of the revolution. This situation contributed to a reshuffling of power toward the president and away from the Leader.

Which Way Iran?

Before we can answer this question another one must be asked: Who governs Iran? Up until now, under the Islamic republic, the president has been a kind of prime minister, as in France for instance, where the prime minister has powers granted to him by the constitution and the practice of the Fifth Republic. This hierarchy remained in place up to now. At the head of the country stood the Supreme Leader of the Revolution and numerous councils presided by clerics (Council for the Discernment, Council of Experts…) and below them the president of the republic. Parliament is in effect a kind of counter power to the president: It can refuse to confirm his ministers or can directly oppose his projects. This kind of action on the part of the parliament has sometimes been approved by the Leader. For instance, during the presidency of the reform-minded Khatami, the man who symbolized dialog between civilizations, no important decision was ever validated by the Supreme Leader. Not only did the president not enjoy the Leader's support, but parliament, even though the reformists were in the majority, did everything it could to block the president's policies. That episode shows how difficult it is to understand Iranian political life and the Iranian political class. How different is a conservative from a reformist inside this complex power play?

According to many observers, Iran could very well have drifted toward a conservative—Islamic regime like Turkey's. But the latest presidential election has made that doubtful. If Ahmadinejad had not taken such an extreme position, he might have been the man able to open a dialog with the West. If he had he would have entered History as Begin did with the Arabs when he signed the Camp David peace accords with Anwar Sadat. On the other hand, it cannot be said that Iran benefited from much goodwill on the part of the West, as the Israelis and the Egyptians did. Recall for instance Bernard Kouchner's (then France's Minister of Foreign Affairs) bellicose attitude: he called for war against Iran as did the neo-conservatives in the U.S. and the Republican administration. The West's attitude contributed to a consensus around the image of President

Ahmadinejad. It was one of the causes—although not the only one—of the events that followed the first round of the presidential elections.

Mahmoud Ahmadinejad's reelection had several consequences. First, the speech the Leader gave, validating his election, reduced his own legitimacy. Then, for the first time in the history of the Islamic Republic, the president imposed his own decisions on the Supreme Leader of the Revolution. Khamenei lost the upper hand against the president when having given him a straightforward, public and handwritten order to dismiss his vice president, Esfandiar Mashaei. Instead Ahmadinejad gave Mashaei more power than any other of his ministers. In the early days, Ayatollah Khomeini had dismissed Banisadr, the first president of the Islamic Republic, for a far smaller offense.

Esfandiar Mashaei

He is the father in law of Ahmadinejad's son. He first came to the public's attention for saying things that were deemed pro-Israeli! In 2005 he declared that Iranians were "friends of all the people on earth—even the Israelis." At the time, four marja-e taqlid (grand ayatollahs) and fifty of the eighty eight members of the Council of Experts expressly ordered the President to dismiss him. He refused to do so. When Ahmadinejad then designated Esfandiar Mashaei as vice president, this became a casus belli for the conservatives. But Ahmadinejad did not dismiss him. On July 26, 2009, Esfandiar Mashaei resigned. Institutionally the vice president has a purely formal position even if in the order of protocol he is considered first among the twelve vice presidents. In a rebuff of the Leader, Esfandiar Mashaei was made chief of staff, one of the most important functions in the wheels of government. The president refused to obey the Leader's verbal and then written injunctions to dismiss him. This is proof of the new importance of the president over the Leader, nothing less than a revolution in the institutions of theocratic Iran. Since the current president cannot run for a third term, he could designate Mashaei as a candidate in 2014, but, in Iran, nothing is certain.

Another consequence of the election that also represents a break with the clerics' Republic is the militarization of power since its main pillars are now the revolutionary Guards and the basidjis. Following the election, the Guards' secret service has taken over the Ministry of Information which was not until then within its purview. The Guards' leader dismissed the Minister and his appointees and purged the ministry. Thousands of people have joined the basidjis, not for ideological reasons or in a show of support for the regime but to enjoy the benefits and privileges of membership in the militia. There are many more such examples. Still it would be empty speculation to say that today's Iran is simply a country governed by a triumvirate headed by the Guards, the Supreme Leader, Ayatollah Khamenei and finally President Ahmadinejad. In fact all three groups sustain each other even if there are some open disagreements. This is the price to pay in order to maintain the regime.

A New Renaissance

Whether one finds it regrettable or not, there is no organized opposition, neither inside the country nor outside, that could be an alternative to the regime, however much the demonstrations may have created that impression. Iran feels isolated and different from other countries. It is a nation or a people that wish to claim allegiance both to the ancient heritage of Persia and to its identity as a Shiite state in the midst of a hostile Arab and Sunni environment. Iranians are also more open to the outside world than any other Muslim people: a large part of its population is westernized or aspires to the "American way of life." They are proud of their rich culture and find it painful to have experienced a Renaissance of its own only to fall back into the Middle Ages. Today, what Iran wants above all is to relive that glorious time, to return to Persia.

Change will also come from the clergy and in particular the high clergy. This is Iran's Kafkaesque dimension. A cleric created the

Islamic republic and clerics will lead the country to secularization. This change will have consequences for the entire Muslim world.

Shia Islam's strength comes both from its hierarchical organization and its doctrinal modernity. Like other great religions—Catholicism, Protestantism, Orthodox Christianity, Judaism—Shiites, in contrast to Sunnis, have a clergy. This clergy is hierarchical and clerics are trained in seminaries or theological centers. Shia Islam is modern because its most prestigious clerics, who become marjah, are models to be emulated. They have the authority to interpret the faith and thus allow Shiism not to be fixed in time but to evolve with Iranian society and the outside world. Shia Islam, as opposed to Wahhabi Islam goes beyond a literal reading of the Holy Book.

Shia Islam relies on the Prophet's Holy Book but its particular quality of emulation gives it its non dogmatic dimension. It should be said that this quality also exists among a minority of Sunni as well. It is represented for instance by thinkers from the Maghreb such as Malek Chebel, author of an Encyclopedic Dictionary of the Koran and many other books.[4]

In theory and according to the law, the institutions founded by Ayatollah Khomeini allow for the dismissal of the Supreme Leader of the Republic. But this is fictitious. On the other hand, the weakened status of the current leader together with the reinforcement of the high clergy's legitimacy are two factors which will play a role when the time comes for a successor. The renewal of the Assembly of Experts who elect the leader and whose members are elected by popular vote—therefore by the Iranian people—should result in increased influence for the higher clergy without questioning the principle of velayat-e faqih. The leader's duties should then be what they were originally meant to be, as advocated by Grand Ayatollah Montazeri. The leader would again lead in the real sense of the word, meaning show the country the right direction. This could contribute to the increased secularization of society. Religion would not be absent. Its role would be similar to the great Western democracies. This does not mean that Iran is ready for French style "secularism," but that the power enjoyed by the guards and the bassidjis as well as

---

4. Paris, Fayard, 2009.

the president would no longer have any legitimacy. Present Islamic institutions are the only guarantee of immunity for the clerics who are governing Iran now and have enriched themselves in the process. This aspect of the Iranian nomenklatura is never discussed and yet it is one of the fundamental requirements for a peaceful evolution of the regime.

Secularization

In the past the Ottoman Sultan Abdulhamid II (1876-1908) attempted to steer a pro Islamist course as the Ottoman Empire crumbled: this resulted in complete failure. Erdogan has most probably learned from this episode. He has chosen unity over religion when religion might have caused division and fragmentation of society.

The Pahlawis dreamed of establishing a modern Iran. They took their inspiration from the Kemalist revolution. This imperial dream came to an end with the establishment of the Islamic Republic in 1979 and the role it gave the clergy. Iran, proud daughter of greater Persia, then experienced a period of Middle Ages.

Marcel Gauchet's concept of "exit from religion" cannot be applied to Muslim societies. In those societies there is no confrontation between state and church: society is founded on Islam. But to describe Iran as a theocracy would be a mistake. Khomeini's republic failed to create such a system. Also, a debate on secularism as is recurrent in France, cannot take place in countries where Islam is the state religion or the majority religion. Iranian society is becoming secularized: but this is very different from French "laïcité."

Secularization would seem easier to accomplish in Sunni Muslim countries where there is no clergy. But in fact, in those countries religion is managed by the state. Imams are paid their salaries by the government. They are often discredited in the eyes of the people. Those religious figures who make use of the freedom afforded by the places of worship oppose the government and advocate a fundamentalist version of Islam. There are also many Imams who are trained abroad or are self-proclaimed Imams attached to a radical form of Islam. All these factors which characterize the Sunni Muslim world go against secularization.

In Iran, one could theoretically imagine a reaction on the part of the clergy to prevent secularization or at least slow it down. But in fact, the contrary is happening. A majority of clerics is prepared to go along with secularization if only in the hope of securing their own future. The institutions of the republic make it possible and recent history—Iran reliving a kind of Middle Ages—makes it desirable. Still, the possibility of a confrontation between the high clergy represented by the Supreme Leader of the Revolution and the secular government represented by the president of the republic and the popularly elected parliament cannot be excluded.

The reason why this conflict has not already erupted is in part because the Islamic republic as envisioned by its founder has been a failure. The revolution did not bear any political, social or economic fruit, which explains the post Islamic phase Iran is experiencing now. Imam Khomeini's utopia: rejecting everything to with the modern world and the West has failed.

Certain facts also have to be taken into account. The Islamic revolution represented a break with the historical tradition and with Shiite religious dogma. The religious and cultural authenticity of the regime was seriously affected by the reign of terror which accompanied its implementation and the systematic violence perpetrated against ordinary people. These elements go against tradition, culture and Shiite dogma. But of course it was a revolution, as bloody as both the French and the Bolshevik preceded it.

The reason why part of the clergy immediately opposed Ayatollah's Khomeini's regime does not stem only from the bloody repression against many clerics. From the beginning, there was doctrinal opposition to the Islamic republic. For part of the clergy, the Prophet must be viewed in his dual roles: as a messenger of God, the Prophet is holy and so is his word. His teachings must be obeyed by every Muslim. But as a political leader of his people, Muhammad the Prophet does not have a sacred dimension, he is a historical figure. Muslims owe obedience to the Prophet but not to the political leader. This understanding of the dual—religious and political roles applies to the Supreme Leader.

Individualism and democratization are two central tenets of modernity. Both these concepts are closely tied to secularization. These parameters are at work in today's Iran. Individualism means that faith is no longer a communitarian phenomenon: it now belongs to the private sphere. This is particularly the case among Iran's educated class who are open to the world and most of all to the West: they reject any communitarian dimension to faith. Olivier Roy's comment that "religion has become secularized, not in the French sense of "laïcité" but in the sense that faith has now become a personal matter" applies to Shiite Iran.

Another illustration of growing individualism in Iranian society is to be found in people's attitude to business. Sociologist Max Weber's ideas on the link between religion and capitalism[5] apply in countries such as Iran and Sunni Turkey. Even though part of the economic sector is controlled by religious foundations or groups such as the Revolutionary Guards in Iran and the army in Turkey, both countries have long had a thriving private sector and market economy. Besides individualism, secularization implies democratization.

To discuss Iranian democracy or democratization does not mean forgetting the long reign of terror at the beginning of the republic, the repression of demonstrations or the attacks against human rights. The Islamic republic has an imperfect form of democracy, where its representatives are elected by popular vote. During its thirty year history there has been political change, and voters were able to choose between reformers and conservatives. Even Mousavi's supporters in the West presented him as a democrat declaring the elections democratic, before the second round.

Iran is not surrounded by a wall to keep its citizens from leaving or traveling and returning home. The only obstacle to travel is money. Even though it cannot be said that there is an organized opposition, civil society has a voice, as the demonstrations showed after the second round of elections and after Montazeri's death. The

---

5. *L'éthique protestante et l'esprit du capitalisme.*

intelligentsia, women and youth use whatever forms of freedom the state will allow to claim autonomy as individuals and citizens.

The 'exit from religion', which I have rejected as not applicable to Iran, does not mean that religion must leave the public sphere. Even in countries as secular as France or the United States, religion is far from absent from the political debate or decision making: even more so in Iran as it progresses toward complete secularization.

In the move toward secularization in Iran, religion, even though it will remain in the public sphere, will no longer control its organization. This evolution has been clear since the death of the founder of the Islamic republic. Its pace increased because of Mahmoud Ahmadinejad's reelection and its consequences for the role and the authority of the Leader.

The Shiite high clergy can support this evolution and be a part of it. The road to modernity entails change in the fabric of society, such as individualism and democratization: these changes will have repercussions on the entire Muslim world, especially since they are already taking place in Sunni, conservative-Islamic Turkey under Erdogan. In the old Ottoman Empire, change was initiated by the head of state and the ministry of religious affairs, with the support of Sufi communities. The fact that the Shiite clergy is powering this new orientation will allow a 'leap forward' in time ... a second rebirth.

The shock wave of the Arab Spring has hardly been felt in Iran, where the 'democratic' aspects of political life partly serve as an explanation. Since 2009, demonstrators take to the streets and even if the security forces repress them, the degree of freedom they have is exceptional in Muslim countries. In Iran the wall of fear did not have to come down, it already had done so! That is why there were more than a million people in the streets in February 2011, in spite of the ban on demonstrations.

Before the Storm

Politicians sometimes can also run a high pitched fever. Ali Akhbar Rafsanjani chose to give up the presidency of the Assembly of Experts a position he held since 2007, rather than be defeated and become the reason for a dispute. He felt that "The Islamic Republic had lost the trust of the faithful." His replacement was a conservative ayatollah Mohammad Reza Mahdavi Kani, age 80 and a fleeting interim prime minister after the 1979 revolution. The son of the Supreme Guide Mojtaba heads military intelligence and took part in the witch hunts against those that the regime considers "lukewarm." The religious clerics are not exempt as in Qom where fundamentalists have upset the courses given by the great "independent" ayatollahs, such as Vahid Khorasani and Shobeiri Zanjani. On May 25, 2011, after having cancelled his visit to the holy city of Qom several times, the president aware of their opposition refused to meet with any member of the upper clergy.

Today the president of the republic himself is at the center of the storm with the struggle for power intensifying with the coming elections. The successor to Ahmadinejad is the issue and whether Esfandiar Mashaei will be the next president. Once again the Guide has decided to attack the president's closest advisor. Mashaei is accused of "witchcraft and associating with jinnis." Some twenty people that were part of the president's entourage (assistants, councilors) were arrested for the same reasons.

On June 1, 2011, 165 out of 290 members of the Iranian parliament complained to the courts about the fact that Mahmoud Ahmadinejad appointed himself oil minister at a time when after thirty-five years Iran would have the presidency of OPEC, a position that would allow the president to acquire more international exposure. The members of parliament considered this to be an unconstitutional decision that went hand in hand with the president's intention to control a strategic ministry with colossal oil revenues. This conflict came ahead of several others that demonstrate the kind of struggle that is taking place within the highest reaches of political power.

It is useful to examine how the conflict was resolved in a four part scenario:

One: the Council of Guardians stated that the president's decision was illegal…the president rejected the council's opinion.

Two: in the course of a meeting (executive, legislative and judiciary) presided by the Guide, the representatives of all three branches approved the decision handed down by the Council of Guardians.

Three: Faced with the president's refusal to comply, parliament decided in early June 2011 to bring legal action against Mahmoud Ahmadinejad for breaking the law.

Four: the president is forced to appoint a new oil minister.

On April 20 the Supreme Guide Ali Khamenei vetoed the firing of the intelligence chief that the president had selected. In a show of rebellion toward the country's highest authority Mahmoud Ahmadinejad symbolically retired from public life to remain...silent for two weeks. The ultra conservatives in such a context were attempting to isolate the president. Besides the struggle for influence among the various factions in Teheran the wind of revolt that swept the Arab countries had implications for Iran's role in the region.

Addressing the Iranian people on May 29, 2011, the Supreme Guide Ali Khamenei issued a warning. Possibly referring to the presidential elections of 2009 he called for "friendship and moderation," stating that "no one is authorized to interfere with the elections." The parliamentary elections of 2012 and the presidential contest of 2014 may be one more step in the separation of the mosques from the state. With Ahmadinejad leaving office, secularized Iran will have reached a turning point. It will be a day of reckoning among Iranians and Persia's return to the region and the community of nations.

Both factions are facing one another today. On one side the Supreme Guide counting on the higher religious leaders who have the support of the heads of the Revolutionary Guards. On the other is the president and his clan.

Solutions to a Latent Conflict

Khamenei offered his support and validation during the first round of the presidential vote. He always feared what he calls "deviationist movements" meaning those behind the protest of June 2009 while he also knows that Ahmadinejad is close to the end of his term. The first vice president of parliament, Mohamed Reza Bahonar confirms the feeling of members of parliament on June 2, 2011: "We have reached the conclusion that the Guide was ready to take a position and put an end to this government; but apparently he prefers to allow it to continue its work quietly until the end of the term so that the tenth government has a natural ending."

Perhaps the Supreme Guide will repeat the operation that had been so successful when he had Mahmoud Ahmadinejad elected: to thrust a completely unknown individual onto the presidency. In a sense it turns the page without betraying the past, a way to ensure the survival of the religious oligarchy in a country that is becoming increasingly secularized.

Another Shock Wave

Ten years after 9/11 one would think that the theories about the "clash of civilizations" or the "axis of evil" belonged to the past along with George W. Bush and the neo-cons.

Yet during the annual ambassadors conference (in September 2011) the French president issued a warning to Iran regarding a possible "preventive attack" against its nuclear sites should it continue to harbor ambitions of that kind. He didn't name the countries that could be tempted by such an action. It was an isolated statement, an expression of strength and influence following the Libyan crusade and solidarity with Israel... Nicolas Sarkozy added nevertheless that "a preventive attack on Iranian locations would set off a major crisis that France wants absolutely no part of." Hassan Tajik the director general of European affairs at the Iranian foreign ministry reacted: "Iranian defensive activity is entirely based on deterrence. Any comment based upon mistaken information can create instability within the region." Who could be interested in setting on fire a region that is already smoldering?

Following the events in several Arab countries, the people went through a time of euphoria while the future never looked so uncertain. For the near future many questions remain open. In the spring of 2009 with the mobilization of youth Iranian democrats had reason to hope. Contrary to countries that were able to free themselves from the heavy hand of dictatorship, Iran is a country going through an evolution that began with the death of the Imam Khomeini. I have previously described in another book my understanding of what was happening in Iran and the relationship between power and religion using the accountant's saying: "First in, first out" for the changes in the Arab Muslim world.[1] For the past thirty years Persia has been marching toward its rebirth into a secularized society where the people are emphatically calling for a separation between Mosque and State.

Two years after the "Arab Springs" there is hope for the start of a new era. The dictatorships were falling. Cell phones and social networks effectively helped inform and mobilize public opinion. Very quickly the limits of those movements became apparent in spite of the enthusiasm they unleashed. Without the neutral attitude on the part of the army and the decision of the military to push out Ben Ali and Mubarak, neither Egypt nor Tunisia would have experienced a peaceful resolution to the crisis. If the tyrant was brought down in Libya it was only due to the intervention of NATO, the weaponry provided by the West and finally the "discrete" presence of French and British commandos on the ground despite a UN resolution against any such action.

A dictator's departure doesn't necessarily mean the end of a totalitarian regime or the dawning of freedom. Democracy progresses step by step through the difficult exercise of free elections. But democracy cannot be imposed by decree. For it to be effective it requires political parties, leaders and programs electoral lists and a whole form of education.

While the Islamists were the movers of the "Arab Springs" other groups of citizens (the unemployed, youth, intellectuals, professionals) who were not the originators of those revolts were also involved. The consequences of a chosen strategy and the fear it inspired accompanied the movements. But the Islamists did not take the lead or attempt to take over. Contrary to the Iranian revolution of 1979 no Islamic republic has yet been proclaimed. The final objective

---

1. Op. cit.

of those movements close to the Muslim Brotherhood is not power for the sake of power. They intend to have a deeper and longer influence on their respective societies. They know that the forces that yesterday were holding up the previous regimes, the army first and foremost, wouldn't accept to see them—the Muslim Brotherhood— take over completely. In Egypt time marches on and the demonstrators of Tahrir Square have learned that the army is reluctant to give up power even when it doesn't sit in the front rows. Proof is in the attack on the Israeli embassy in Cairo that the Egyptian military didn't prevent but was the pretext they chose to reintroduce the state of emergency in effect since 1980 that had only been lifted a few months before.

Who shall govern Tunisia, Egypt or Libya tomorrow? These situations as well as the actors are all very different so it is far too early to imagine what those countries will be like in the future. From a geostrategic standpoint a double revolution is taking place: the emergence of a restructured Maghreb and even more a new configuration for the Mediterranean coastal countries beyond the Arab Muslim world. In such a context of true or simply surface democracy the future will hang on important elections.

In Cairo the Muslim Brothers represent a "quiet power." Their strategy is based on time and caution. Their objective being to have a strong group in parliament that translates what they represent for the country without seeking the presidency which could be interpreted as a challenge by the military. They want the Islamization of Egypt and the ability to influence the future of the Gaza Palestinians or that of their Jordanian and Syrian brothers. At the same time the Brotherhood serves as buffer against the jihadists and the Salafists. This also reassures Washington about Egypt's future since the Brotherhood will not seek to reverse the peace treaty with Israel. Yet the exasperation of the Egyptians hoping to see the end of the "transition" is targeting the relations between Cairo and Jerusalem as the reason for their difficulties. The street backed the Palestinians while the Egyptian regime was fighting Hamas as though it were an ally of Israel. That trend should be reversed.

In Tunisia almost 55 percent of the voters have registered for parliamentary elections among them 45 percent of the women. This is viewed a success since the ISIE (Instance supérieure indépendante pour les elections) was starting from scratch in organizing the voting. As a first in the Arab world the electoral lists must be fair: the Ennahda Islamist Party that was banned nine months before the elections of October 2011 had four out of its twenty-six lists headed by women. During the campaign the leadership kept a low profile even though the party was thought to be ahead to avoid frightening those who feared an Islamist political force. The near term will be one of apprenticeship: government coalitions will have to be created and be able to stand together. During the vote former party leaders who had called for the reelection of Ben Ali or certain groups such as the ambassadors were declared to be ineligible to participate. This exclusion from public life cannot be permanent.

As Ennahda admits on the Islamist side while all are not organized in political parties many "conformist or democratic" movements will become major players in the future. Some as Ettahrir which is not yet recognized are active in several Arab countries and call for the Caliphate. During the campaign a few "bearded ones" attacked artists groups that became the focus of aggressive behavior and violence. The reason for the anger of the Islamists was the documentary by Nadia al-Fani: *Neither Allah, nor master.* In today's Tunisia it's not a good idea to announce that you are an atheist and don't believe in God.

Even after having been liberated from Qaddafi, Libya doesn't fit the description as a nation-state. The country remains fragile and has only one asset with its oil reserves, it is torn between clans, tribes, South vs. North and East vs. West, without forgetting the disputes among war leaders that each want to carve their place in the country's new leadership. After some fifty years of dictatorship, fellow travelers and leaders of the former regime are still in charge. Islamist groups close to Al Qaeda fought on the rebel side. Abdelhakim Belhaj the current military leader in Tripoli is an Islamist and former jihadist who was imprisoned by Qaddafi as were the 5,000 former members of the LIFG (Libyan Islamic Fighting Group) anointed by Osama

Bin Laden in 2007 that joined the revolt. There are many other more or less structured Islamist factions that helped bring down the regime. As a harbinger of problems to come one of the demands of the Islamists before they gave up their weapons was the proclamation of a "Constitution that recognizes the importance of religion." Teheran welcomed the victory of the CNT as "the victory of the revolution of the Muslim people of Libya" and invited its leader to visit Iran "as soon as possible."

If the agitation was limited in Algeria some unknown factors remain. It becomes necessary to go beyond events and avoid speculating. The spectacular attack on the Cherchell military academy in August 2011, which was the deadliest in many years, was claimed by Al Qaeda in the Islamic Maghreb because of the Algerian regime's support for Qaddafi. Relations between Algeria and Libya were poor since the 1970s. The Libyan leader declared himself the "protector" of the Tuareg rebellions in Mali and Niger. His interventions in the Southern Sahara and his pro-Polisario positions in the Western Sahara were considered provocations by the Algerians. During the civil war, Tripoli was said to have delivered weapons to the Islamists in northern Mali on the Algerian border.

With the evolution of the Maghreb and Egypt, the questions regarding the future of Syria, and of the Mediterranean coastal areas is in the balance. In all those countries Islam represents an alternative. Turkey is the model, the economic, military and political power to which Europe has closed its door. Even though many Islamist movements proclaim themselves close to the Turkish Islamic conservative system, Ankara had to take into account the consequences of the "Arab Springs." The Turkish street is increasingly vocal in claiming an Islamist identity, showing greater solidarity with the Palestinians, and opposing a past relationship with Israel. Syria used to be the entry point for Turkey into the Arab world. Ankara's support for Syrian Sunnis and the Muslim Brotherhood in particular, its recent opposition to Bashar al-Assad has paradoxically led to Turkey's isolation in the Middle East even though Erdogan in his trips to Somalia and Egypt is attempting to gain influence among Arab Muslims.

A second bloc is attempting to take shape within the Arab Muslim world. The failure of the "Arab Spring" in Bahrain was the result of the intervention of Saudi and Emirate troops. The Cooperation Council of the Gulf that includes the Sunni monarchies in the region (Saudi Arabia, Bahrain, United Arab Emirates, Kuwait, Oman, Qatar) has invited Morocco and Jordan to join. Then there is Turkey.

This restructuring of the Arab Muslim world has given the Teheran, Damascus, Beirut axis renewed vigor…creating the impression of a historical turning back to the 1980s. With the significant difference that Iraq must be added to that Shia group. Both the Iranians as well as Iraqi Premier Nuri al-Maliki have accused the hand of foreigners, and specifically of Al Qaeda behind the Syrian revolt. If Bashar al-Assad can still count on the Alawites, a minority group among the Shia, on the army and the security forces but given the blindsided repression, he must also account for the distancing of the Druse and Christians. The majority Sunni front is growing in its opposition to the Assad family.

We live in a changing and less than monolithic world. Nothing has been played out in the Arab Muslim countries. In spite of the apparent stability and unchanging conservatism, the Gulf monarchies will also in due course, find what may be called the "domino effect" even if it may not be in the revolutionary kind. They cannot ignore the changes that have taken place with lasting effects for all other Arab countries. Sooner or later heed the call for democracy from their peoples and King Abdullah's decision which had to be drawn from the religious leaders and the conservatives, to allow Saudi women the right to vote and run in municipal elections in 2015: a revolution for women in the kingdom. The minority Shia in the Emirates with the notable exception of Bahrain where they are the majority will show how much the monarchies can change under the watchful eye of Teheran in a reminder of the antagonism and cleavage between Arabs and Persians, Sunni and Shia.

While the fall of the Berlin Wall symbolized the end of the Cold War and the East-West antagonism, new blocs with potential clashes have appeared some twenty years later. The evolution of the Middle

East is tied to the solution of the Israeli Palestinian conflict. Since none can be found the most extreme reactions will continue. Jerusalem attributes the attacks in southern Israel in August 2011 to the Committees of Popular Resistance (CPR.) This movement includes those disappointed in al Fatah, Hamas, the Palestinian Islamic jihad or members of the al Aqsa Martyrs Brigade.

Mahmud Abbas issued an "historic appeal" for Palestine's entry into the UN that would de jure imply recognition of the Palestinian State. Obama ran for reelection and could not agree to a position that would alienate the Jewish vote. The Arab Muslim world is more fragmented than before the "Arab Springs." Groups of countries are facing off in Africa as in the partition of Sudan with the Muslim North, Egypt, Eritrea, Somalia and the Christian animist South with Ethiopia, Kenya and Uganda all redefining a geopolitical reality based on ethnic and confessional criteria. The evangelists are present not only to proselytize but with their political agenda. The fear of Salafism is real not only in the Middle East but also in the Maghreb and Muslim sub-Saharan Africa. At the Algiers book fair the authorities, seeking to limit that group, had banned 500 religious books published in Saudi Arabia and Egypt. The Indo-Asian world is not immune either Religious and extremist groups are multiplying and becoming more active attacking the symbols of democracy in Pakistan, India and Kashmir. A new deadly attack was attributed to the movement Harkat-ul-Jihad al-Islami in New Delhi against the High Court of Justice two months after the triple attack in Mumbai.

The return of religion and the emergence of political Islam are not restricted to the Muslim world. While traditional religions were dominant in the West, religion was a guidepost in a time of crisis. Once the credibility of every institution is questioned (political parties, labor unions, churches…abstention during elections) part of public opinion takes refuge in populism. There is no confessional voting. The rise of populism is found in a society where religious practice has been constantly reduced along with the influence of the churches. The religious factor, the strength of the churches provided a path in the name of certain values, to reject the most extreme positions even though it would take the Vatican's condemnation of

Maurras to stop certain Catholics from being attracted to what we call the "extreme right." The Dreyfus Affair and the thinking of Charles Maurras left their mark on pre-war France and his ideas influenced several generations. Xenophobia, impressions of decadence, the drive toward decentralization, those were part of the doctrine of the founder of Action française, a nationalist who singled out foreigners by calling them "métèques" as they were described in ancient Athens. Maurras wasn't yet a monarchist at that time.

Today Europe's societies are liberal or social democratic so there are fewer right-left antagonisms. The splits are found in the ideas of conservatives and reformers. As far as management is concerned whoever is in power matters little since the space to maneuver is limited due to the requirements of the economy and globalization. Policy choices are very similar except for certain debates that take on an ideological connotation such as the 35 hour work week in France. In Western Europe the Churches no longer can swing elections one way or another. There are Catholics in all political parties and the era of Christian political parties or labor unions has passed as have left wing Christians in a context where Catholicism was seen as closer to right wing politics. Yet this movement that has inherited the social Catholicism of Marc Sangnier[2] or Jacques Maritain[3] also gave rise to politicians such as Jacques Delors and a few others. The time when politicians described themselves as left wing Christians has definitely passed.

The commitment is a personal one and religion just like faith today belongs to the individual's personal sphere. Yet the need for spiritual as well as philosophical research is more widespread than it used to be using means of expression that are markedly different. There are no longer towering personalities such as François Mauriac who would introduce himself as a Catholic intellectual. Upon his return from Stockholm where he was awarded the Nobel Prize for literature France's most celebrated writer at the time had set up with other left leaning Catholics a "friendship" circle the Centre France-Maghreb. That initiative came as a reaction to the uncompromising

---

2. September 25, 2011.
3. September 23, 2011.

attitude of Marshal Alphonse Juin toward the Moroccan nationalists as resident general of France in Morocco. Juin castigated the "Christian consciences" that "were giving surprising support to the enemies of our country." Mauriac responded in the conservative daily *Le Figaro*: "The religion of the heart has more power over men than the religion of force." The Christian intellectual Mauriac would support peace in Algeria as well as independence for the former colony in his column in the Paris weekly *L'Express* which he dedicated to his faith.

A bit similar to the Muslim world where Islamism was under fire, the former Eastern European countries that joined the European Union had favored atheism. The Churches were being persecuted and viewed as institutions that were the enemies of communism and groups that were resisting the political leadership. Those same countries today have given rise to political parties that call themselves Christian. They take a position using the doctrine of the Catholic Church as a reference even when that means contradicting European principles and rights that they had to subscribe to in joining the EU.

The power of the Churches depends upon the strength that their institutions represent in historical terms, the influence they have over public opinion and the closeness they enjoy to the regime in power. The weight of the Orthodox Church in Russia turns it into the key institution in the country as for example the Grand Rabbinate of Israel even though the country identifies itself as secular and the ultra-Orthodox are a minority. The more fundamentalist and doctrinaire fringes whether they are Orthodox, Evangelical, Jewish or Catholic exercise a political influence. They often behave as a lobby. In Spain today, a country with a strong Catholic tradition, the clergy is at the forefront of the struggle over all issues that it considers ethical (opposition to same-sex marriage, right to life ...) even when it means appearing as an ally of the Spanish right wing and opposed to the socialist government that was in power at the time. Yet once it returned to power the Popular Party wouldn't cancel any of the reforms made by José Luis Zapatero.

The Religious Right and the Tea Party represent one facet of America. Their influence is negligible when it comes to doctrine or religion. Seeing themselves as the heirs to the Boston Tea Party insurgents of the War of Independence and of the founding fathers that were opposed to taxation imposed by the British Crown, they have found in the economic crisis of the United States an issue that unites those who are disappointed in the American Dream and upscale Republican voters. They reject the Obama stimulus plan and its 447 billion dollar price tag that will mean higher taxes. As Hubert Védrine says Obama can win reelection "above all if he faces an extreme Republican candidate."[4] The former French minister of foreign affairs feels that the world is changing and the challenge is to know how "the West will manage the transition from having a monopoly ...to sharing power with new countries." While he views a second Obama term necessary for "Middle East peace" he remains realistic about the Arab Springs: "The democratization of the Arab world is a long and frustrating process [...] there can be clashes between Islam and the West but the true battle against fundamentalism will be won inside the Arab world."

A path that Iran is showing us today with the return of Persia.

---

4. September 2011.

Biographies

Mahmoud Abbas (born 26 March 1935) is the Chairman of the Palestine Liberation Organization (PLO) since 2004 and became President of the Palestinian National Authority in 2005 as the Fatah candidate. Elected to serve until 2009, he unilaterally extended his term for another year and continues in office even after that second deadline expired. Hamas announced that it would not recognize the extension or consider Abbas as rightful president.

Abdallah, King of Saudi Arabia (Abdullah bin Abdulaziz al-Saud) (born in 1924) is the Custodian of the Two Holy Mosques, and King of Saudi Arabia. He ascended to the throne on 1 August 2005 upon the death of his half-brother, King Fahd.

Omar Abdel Rahman (born 3 May 1938), known in the United States as **"The Blind Sheikh,"** a blind Egyptian Muslim leader who currently serving a life sentence at the Butner Medical Center. Formerly a resident of New York City, Abdel-Rahman and nine others were convicted of seditious conspiracy, which requires planning a crime, not that it necessarily be attempted. His prosecution grew out of investigations of the World Trade Center 1993 bombings.

Abdulhamid II (22 September 1842–10 February 1918) was the last Sultan of the Ottoman Empire to exert effective control. He was deposed in 1909 followed by the Young Turk Revolution who ushered the return to constitutional rule.

Abdullah II, King of Jordan (born 30 January 1962) is the Reigning King of the Hashemite Kingdom of Jordan, he ascended the throne on 7 February 1999 upon the death of his father King Hussein.

Madani Abessi (born in 1931). President of the Islamic Salvation Front in Algeria. As its leader he became the voice of a large part of the dispossessed Algerian youth.

Michel Aflak (1910–Paris, 23 June 1989) A Syrian medical doctor and political philosopher, sociologist and Arab nationalist who played a significant role in the development of Ba'athism and its political movement. He took refuge in Iraq and died in Baghdad revered by Saddam Hussein as the founder of the Ba'ath Party.

Ali Mohsen al-Ahmar (Born 20 June 1945) A general of the Yemeni army, he serves as President Saleh's chief military adviser. Helped recruit Islamist radicals to fight in Afghanistan during the Soviet-Afghan War. In March 2011 he said he would protect the anti-government Yemeni protesters, along with other top Yemeni army commanders, in a move that was later condemned by President Saleh as mutiny.

Madeleine Albright (born in 1937) was the first woman to become the United States Secretary of State, appointed by President Clinton in 1996. She is currently a Professor of International Relations at Georgetown University. In May 2012, she was awarded the Presidential Medal of Freedom by President Barack Obama. Secretary Albright also serves as a director on the Board of the Council on Foreign Relations.

Alexis II (1929–2008) 15th Patriarch of Moscow and all Russia, as the primate of the Russian Orthodox Church. Elected Patriarch of Moscow 18 months prior to the fall of the Soviet Union, he became the first Russian Patriarch of the post-Soviet period.

Zine al-Abidine Ben Ali (born 3 September 1936) was the second President of Tunisia from 1987 to 2011. He was appointed prime minister in 1987, and assumed the presidency on November 1987 in a bloodless coup d'état that ousted President Habib Bourguiba, who was declared incompetent. Fled the country during the initial Arab Spring.

Ygal Amir (born May 23, 1970) the Israeli assassin of Prime Minister Yitzhak Rabin of Israel (the assassination took place in Tel Aviv in November, 1995). He is currently serving a life sentence for murder.

Benigno Aquino. Filipino politician who served as Speaker of the National Assembly of the Second Philippine Republic from 1943 to 1944. His grandson Benigno S. Aquino III is the current president of the Philippines.

Corazon Aquino (1933–2009) was the 11th president of the Philippines and the first woman to hold that office (first female president in Asia). She led the 1986 People Power Revolution, which toppled Ferdinand Marcos and restored democracy to the Philippines. She was named "Woman of the Year" in 1986 by *Time* Magazine.

Swami Aseemanand is a former Rashtriya Swayamsevak Sangh (RSS) activist from India who is accused of planning terror attacks on Ajmer Sharif, Mecca Masjid, 2006 Malegaon blasts and 2007 Samjhauta Express bombings. The Central Bureau of Investigation (CBI) arrested Aseemanand on November 19, 2010, for his involvement in the Mecca Masjid bombing. On 24 December 2010 he was handed over to the NIA. In his confession before Metropolitan Magistrate Deepak Dabas in the Tis Hazari courts on December 18, 2010, he confessed that he and other Hindu activists were involved in bombings at various Muslim religious places as they wanted to answer every Islamist terror act with "a bomb for bomb" policy.

Catherine Ashton (born 20 March 1956) is a British Labor politician who in 2009 became the High Representative of the European Union for Foreign Affairs and Security Policy and Vice-President of the European Commission. She became a Privy Councilor in May 2006 and was the Leader of the House of Lords in June 2007.

Bashar al-Assad (born in 1965). President of Syria and Regional Secretary of the Syrian-led branch of the Arab Socialist Ba'ath Party. His father ruled Syria for 29 years until his death in 2000. In 1994, he entered the military academy and, took charge of the Syrian occupation of Lebanon in 1998. He was elected in 2000 and 2007, unopposed each time. During the Syrian uprising, activists and protesters have called for his resignation.

Hafez al-Assad (6 October 1930–10 June 2000). President of Syria for three decades. He served in the Syrian air force, before rising through the ranks of the Syrian-led branch of the Arab Socialist Ba'ath Party, and seizing power in the 1970 Corrective Revolution. He purged the party, introducing Alawite sectarian rule of Syria, placing its members in leading positions in every sector of Syrian society.

Rifaat Ali al-Assad (born 22 August 1937). Younger brother of the former President of Syria, Hafez Assad and Jamil Assad, and the uncle of the incumbent President Bashar al-Assad, all of whom come from the minority

Alawite Muslim sect. He is perhaps best known for allegedly personally overseeing the Hama massacre of 1982.

Mustapha Kemal Atatürk (19 May 1881–10 November 1938) was an Ottoman and Turkish army officer, revolutionary statesman, writer, and the first President of Turkey. He is credited with being the founder of the Republic of Turkey and enforcing a secular constitution.

Martine Aubry (born in 1950). French politician, and First Secretary of the Party Socialist since 2008. She also held the posts of Minister of Labor and of Social Affairs. Her father, Jacques Delors, served as Minister of Finance and President of the European Commission.

Rami Ayyad was martyred for his faith in Gaza.

Tarik Aziz (born 28 April 1936) was the Foreign Minister (1983–1991) and Deputy Prime Minister (1979–2003) of Iraq and a close advisor of former President Saddam Hussein. They were activists in the 1950s, in the Iraqi Ba'ath Party.

José Aznar (born in 1953). Prime Minister of Spain from 1996 to 2004. He is on the board of directors of Rupert Murdoch's News Corporation and is also a member of the Club de Madrid.

Michele Bachmann (born in 1956). American Republican member of the United States House of Representatives, from Minnesota's 6th congressional district since 2007. She is the first Republican congresswoman from the state. Previously served in the Minnesota State Senate and was a candidate for the Republican nomination in the 2012 U.S. presidential election.

Bagaza (born in 1946) was President of the Republic of Burundi (1976-1987) was an Officer and former Chief of Staff General of the Burundian army. He took power after a coup against Michel Micombero, who had overthrown the monarchy in 1966.

James Baker (born in 1930). American lawyer, politician and political advisor, who served as the Chief of Staff to Presidents Reagan and Bush. He also served as Secretary of the Treasury and Secretary of State in those administrations. Honorary chair of the James A. Baker III Institute for Public Policy at Rice University in Houston, Texas.

Ghassem Ravan Bakhch is the head of Basij militia, the "Hojatoleslam."

Abulhassan Banisadr (born in 1933). Iranian politician, economist and human rights activist who served as the first president of Iran from 4 February 1980 after the 1979 Iranian Revolution and the abolition of the monarchy until his impeachment on 21 June 1981 by the Parliament of Iran. Prior to his presidency, he was Minister of Foreign Affairs in the Interim Government.

Hassan al-Banna (October 14, 1906–February 12, 1949). A schoolteacher and imam, best known for founding the Muslim Brotherhood, one of the largest and most influential 20th century Muslim revivalist organizations.

Ehud Barak (12 February 1942) is an Israeli politician. Served as prime minister from 1999 to 2001, leader of the Labor Party until January 2011 and holds the posts of Minister of Defense and Deputy Prime Minister in Binyamin Netanyahu's government. He served in the Israel Defense Forces until 1995.

Marwan Barghouti (born 1958). Politician and a Palestinian military leader. Marwan Barghouti has been incarcerated since 2002 in a high security prison in Israel, sentenced to five life sentences.

Antoine Basbous. A Lebanese political scientist working in France, specializing in the Arab world and Islam. He is the founder and director of the Observatory of Arab Countries. From 1975 to 1987 he was a journalist in Beirut, at the Maronite Phalange newspaper, then in Paris. His book, *The Arab Tsunami* (2011), deals with all the changes of the Arab Spring.

Gary Bauer (born May 4, 1946) is an American politician notable for his ties to several evangelical Christian groups and campaigns

Abdul Aziz bin Abdullah bin Baz (November 21, 1910–May 13, 1999), Saudi Arabian Islamic scholar, one of the most respected Muslim scholars of the twentieth century. He was the Grand Mufti of Saudi Arabia from 1993 until his death in 1999.

Israel or Yisrael Beiteinu Beitenou. Nationalist political party in Israel describing itself as "a national movement with the clear vision to follow in the brave path of Zev Jabotinsky," the founder of Revisionist Zionism.

Abdelhakim Belhaj. Libyan politician and military leader. He is the leader of the conservative Islamist Al-Watan Party and former head of Tripoli Military Council. He was emir of the Libyan Islamic Fighting Group, a now defunct guerilla anti-Qaddafi group. Belhaj has also been associated with Al-Qaeda in Libya.

Ali Belhadj (Born in 1956) was a teacher of Arabic and an Islamist activist in the 1970s before becoming the vice president of the Algerian Islamic Salvation Front (FiLS). In 1991, he was arrested and jailed on charges of threatening state security and remained in jail throughout most of the Algerian Civil War, he was released after serving a 12-year sentence in 2003 under the condition of abstaining from all political activity. Abdelkahar Belhaj was considered to be a high ranking senior leader in Al Qaeda in the Islamic Maghreb.

Ahmed Ben Bella (25 December 1918–11 April 2012). Algerian soldier and revolutionary, one of the founders of the FLN (National Liberation Front), who became the first president of Algeria from 1963 to 1965.

Ahmed Benchemsi. Moroccan journalist. Founder and was the publisher and editor of TelQuel and Nishan magazines.

David Ben-Gurion (16 October 1886–1 December 1973). First prime minister of Israel and a major Zionist leader and Executive Head of the World Zionist Organization in 1946. He headed the Jewish community in Palestine, and formally proclaimed the establishment of the State of Israel May 1948, being the first to sign the Israeli Declaration of Independence. Known as "Israel's founding father."

William Bennett (born July 31, 1943). American conservative pundit, politician, and political theorist who served as U.S. Secretary of Education from 1985 to 1988. He was also Director of the Office of National Drug Control Policy under George H. W. Bush. In 2000, he co-founded K12, a for-profit online education corporation which is publicly traded.

Omar Hassan al-Bashir (born 1 January 1944) is the President of Sudan and head of the National Congress Party. He came to power in 1989 in a coup d'état. A controversial figure worldwide, he is accused of genocide, crimes against humanity and war crimes in Darfur in 2008. He is the first sitting head of state indicted by the International Criminal Court.

Chadli Benjedid (born April 14, 1929) was the third president of Algeria from February 9, 1979 to January 11, 1992.

Éric Besson (born in 1958). French politician and Minister of Industry and Energy under the Minister of Economy, Finance and Industry, Christine Lagarde. From 2009 to 2010, Minister of Immigration and Integration, in the government of François Fillon. He left the Socialist Party in 2007 to found The Progressives, a social democratic party affiliated to Nicolas Sarkozy's Union for a Popular Movement (UMP).

Georges Bidault (1899–1983). French politician. During World War II, he was active in the French Resistance. After the war, he served as foreign minister and prime minister on several occasions before he joined the Organisation armée secrète (OAS). He was allowed to return to France in 1968 after an amnesty.

Leonardo Boff (born in 1938). Theologian, philosopher and writer, known for his active support for the rights of the poor and those who are marginalized. Currently serves as Professor Emeritus of Ethics, Philosophy of Religion and Ecology at Rio de Janeiro State University.

Robert Brasillach (31 March 1909–6 February 1945). French author and journalist, best known as the editor of *Je suis partout*, a nationalist and anti-Semitic newspaper. Inspired various fascist movements and supported Jacques Doriot. After the liberation of France in 1944 he was executed for advocating collaborationism. His execution remains controversial because it was for "intellectual crimes," rather than military or political actions.

Fernand Braudel (1902–1985). French historian and the leader of the Annales School of historiography in the 1950s and 1960s, he exerted enormous influence on historical writing in France and other countries. He can also be considered as one of the founders of World Systems Theory.

Ofer Bronchtein is the Chairman of the Forum for Peace and Reconciliation in the Middle East, works for the political reconciliation of Palestinian and Israeli intellectuals.

Yasen Buyukavit (born 1 September 1940). The 25th Chief of the Turkish General Staff of the Turkish Armed Forces, from 28 August 2006 to 28 August 2008.

Dalil Boubakeur is a Mufti, and the current rector of the Paris Mosque.

Houari Boumediene (23 August 1932–27 December 1978) served as Algeria's Chairman of the Revolutionary Council from 19 June 1965 until 12 December 1976, and from then on as the second President of Algeria until his death on 27 December 1978.

Habib Bourguiba (3 August 1903–6 April 2000). Tunisian statesman, the founder and first President of the Republic of Tunisia from July 25, 1957 until 7 November 1987. He is often compared to Turkish leader Mustafa Kemal Atatürk because of the pro-Western reforms enacted during his presidency.

Abdelaziz Bouteflika (born 2 March 1937). Algerian politician and fifth President of Algeria since 1999. He presided over the end of the bloody Algerian Civil War in 2002, and ended emergency rule in February 2011 amidst regional unrest. He has also served as president of the United Nations General Assembly.

Boutros Boutros-Ghali (born 14 November 1922). Egyptian politician and diplomat who was the sixth Secretary-General of the United Nations (UN) from January 1992 to December 1996. An academic and former Vice Foreign Minister of Egypt, Boutros Boutros-Ghali led the UN through several world crises, including the breakup of Yugoslavia and the Rwandan Genocide.

Agostino Casaroli (1914–1998). Italian Catholic priest and diplomat for the Holy See, who became Cardinal Secretary of State. He was the most important figure behind the Vatican's efforts to deal with the persecution of the Church in Soviet bloc countries after the Second Vatican Council.

Giuseppe Castiglione (1688-1766). Italian Jesuit, missionary to China and painter at the imperial court. He was one of the favorite artists of the emperors of the Qing Dynasty. Castiglione was appointed architect in 1747.

Manal al-Charif (born in 1978). Human rights activist for Saudi women. In 2011, she began a movement for women's right to drive. To promote her campaign, she published a video of herself driving on Youtube and Facebook. She was taken into custody by Saudi officials, who, before releasing her on bail, imposed the following conditions: an obligation to go to subsequent interrogations, a ban on driving, and being forbidden from talking to the media.

Louis-Ferdinand Céline (27 May 1894–1 July 1961) was the pen name of the French novelist, pamphleteer and physician **Louis-Ferdinand Destouches**, known for his anti-Semitic writings.

Lien Chan (born in 1936). Politician in Taiwan. He was Premier of the Republic of China from 1993 to 1997, Vice President of the Republic of China from 1996 to 2000, and Chairman of the Kuomintang (KMT) from 2000 to 2005. Upon his retirement as chairman in August 2005, he was given the title Honorary Chairman of the Kuomintang.

Hugo Chavez (born 28 July 1954). Currently the president of Venezuela since 1999. He was formerly the leader of the Fifth Republic Movement political party from its foundation since 1997 and became the leader of the United Socialist Party of Venezuela in 2007. He has focused on implementing socialist reforms in the country inspired by Cuba.

Malek Chebel (born in 1953). Algerian anthropologist and philosopher of religion. Essayist, author of specialized books on the Arab world and Islam, and creator of "Islamic Enlightenment" (2004), he lectures often in many European and African countries, and is undertaking a wide investigation of European Islam. He is known for his thoughts on Islam, its culture, its history, its intellectual life, its eroticism. He has taken a public position in favor of a liberal and reformed Islam, including the positive aspects of political modernity.

Pierre Claverie (born in Bab El-Oued May 8, 1938, and assassinated on 1 August 1996). A priest Dominicain French from Algeria who became bishop of Oran.

Jean-Marie Colombani (born in 1948) in Dakar, Senegal, is a French journalist, and was the editor of *Le Monde* from 1994 until 2007.

Costa-Gavras (born 1933). Greek filmmaker, who lives and works in France, best known for films with overt left-wing political themes, most famously the fast-paced thriller, *Z* (1969). Most of his movies were made in French.

Mohammed Darif is a University of Mohammedia professor who studies Islamic terrorism.

Ahmet Davutoglu. Foreign minister of Turkey. He is also a political scientist, an academic and an ambassador at large and was formerly chief advisor to the prime minister.

Léon-Étienne Duval (November 9, 1903–May 30, 1996). French Cardinal of the Roman Catholic Church. He served as Archbishop of Algiers in Algeria from 1954 to 1988, and was appointed cardinal in 1965.

Jean-Claude Duvalier, nicknamed **"Baby Doc"** (born in 1951). Former president of Haiti from 1971 until his overthrow by a popular uprising in 1986. He succeeded his father, François Duvalier, upon his father's death in 1971. After assuming power, he introduced cosmetic changes to his regime and delegated authority to his advisors, while thousands of Haitians were killed or tortured, and hundreds of thousands fled the country. He maintained a notoriously lavish lifestyle (including a state-sponsored $3 million wedding in 1980), and made millions from his involvement in the drug trade and from selling body parts of dead Haitians.

Laurent Dispot (born in 1950) is a French journalist and writer. One of the committee members at the magazine *La Règle du Jeu*. He previously wrote for many papers, *le Matin de Paris* and *Globe Hebdo*. With Pierre Hahn, Guy Hocquenghem, and Françoise d'Eaubonne, he is the co-founder of the FHAR (Homosexual Front for Revolutionary Action), created in Paris, from 1971 to 1973.

Keith Elisson (born August 4, 1963). U.S. Representative from Minnesota's 5th congressional district since 2007 and a member of the Democratic-Farmer-Labor Party. He is the first Muslim to be elected to the

United States Congress. He is also the first African American elected to Congress from Minnesota.

Necmettin Erbakan (29 October 1926–27 February 2011). Turkish engineer, academic, politician, who was the Prime Minister of Turkey from 1996 until 1997. Turkey's first and only Islamist prime minister. In 1997 he was pressured by the military to step down and was later banned from politics by the constitutional court.

Recept Erdogan (born 26 February 1954). Prime Minister of Turkey since 2003, he is chairman of the ruling Justice and Development Party (AK Parti), which holds a majority of the seats in the Grand National Assembly of Turkey.

Roger Marie Élie Étchegaray (born in 1922). Basque Cardinal of the Roman Catholic Church. Étchegaray served as Archbishop of Marseille (1970-1985) before entering the Roman Curia, where he served as President of the Pontifical Council for Justice and Peace (1984-1998) and President of the Pontifical Council *Cor Unum* (1984-1995). He was appointed cardinal in 1979.

Freddy Eytan (born January 1947). Israeli diplomat, former ambassador, writer and journalist.

Laurent Fabius (born in 1946) is a French Socialist politician. He served as Prime Minister from 17 July 1984 to 20 March 1986. At age 37 he was, so far, youngest prime minister of the Fifth Republic and currently France's Foreign Minister since 16 May 2012.

Jerry Falwell (August 11, 1933–May 15, 2007). American evangelical fundamentalist Southern Baptist pastor, televangelist, and a conservative political commentator. He was the founding pastor of the Thomas Road Baptist Church, a megachurch in Lynchburg, Virginia. He founded the Lynchburg Christian Academy (now Liberty Christian Academy) in 1967, Liberty University in 1971, and cofounded the Moral Majority in 1979.

Norah Abdallah al-Faiz also spelled Noura al Fayez, is the first woman to attain the highest governmental rank in Saudi Arabia.

Farouk I of Egypt (11 February 1920–18 March 1965), was the tenth ruler of the Muhammad Ali Dynasty and the last King of Egypt and the Sudan, succeeding his father, Fuad I of Egypt, in 1936. Overthrown in the Egyptian Revolution of 1952 and forced to abdicate in favor of his infant son Ahmed Fuad, who succeeded him as Fuad II of Egypt but never reigned. He died in exile in Italy.

Salam Fayyad (born in 1952). Independent Palestinian politician. Minister of Finance since March 17, 2007, appointed Prime Minister of the Palestinian Authority 15 June 2007.

Francisco Franco y Bahamonde (1892–1975). Spanish general, dictator and the leader of the Nationalist military rebellion in the Spanish Civil War. The authoritarian head of state of Spain, from October 1936 (as a unified nation from 1939 onwards) until his death in November 1975. He came to power adopting the principles of the far-right Falange movement for propaganda purposes, since he belonged to no political party before becoming Head of State.

Francis Fukuyama (born in 1952). American political scientist, political economist, and author. He is best known for his book *The End of History and the Last Man* (1992. Fukuyama is a Senior Fellow at the Center on Democracy, Development and the Rule of Law at Stanford University.

Rashid al-Ghannushi (born 1941). Tunisian Islamist politician who co-founded the Ennahda Movement, currently the largest party in Tunisia. He has been called the party's "intellectual leader."

Pierre-Marie Gerlier (1880-1965). French Cardinal of the Roman Catholic Church. He served as Archbishop of Lyon from 1937 until his death, and was made cardinal in 1937.

Gabrielle Giffords (born in 1970). American Democratic party member of the House of Representatives. She represented Arizona's 8th congressional district from 2007 until her resignation on January 25, 2012, to recover from her wounds after being shot. A "Blue Dog" Democrat, her position on health care reform and illegal immigration made her a target of various conservative groups.

Bouabdallah Glamhallah (born February 14, 1934). Algerian politician. Headed the cultural section and editor of the daily *Echaab*. In 1980 he was a Director at the Ministry of Education. In 1990 he served as Secretary General of Ministry of Education before running Koranic schools in Tiaret and devoting himself to teaching and religious education. Since 25 January 1997, he is Minister of Religious Affairs and Habous.

Richard Goldstone (born 26 October 1938) is a South African former judge who issued key rulings that undermined apartheid. He headed the influential Goldstone Commission and became a well-known public figure in South Africa, attracting widespread international support and interest.

Archbishop Jaime Gonçalves took on the responsibility of peacefully resolving the conflict that lasted for 16 years in Mozambique after a long struggle for independence from Portugal. Jaime, with the assistance of the Community of Sant'Egidio, an international Catholic lay movement that played the role of mediator, successfully brokered peace, an African peace lasting over 15 years.

Sylvain Gougenheim (born in 1960). French medieval historian. In 2008, his book *Aristotle at Mont Saint-Michel* radically questions the idea that the Muslim world played an important role in the transmission of science and Greek philosophy to the West during the Middle Ages. For him, the Arabic language is also not conducive to the development of rational thought.

Alain Gresh (born in 1948). French journalist. He published several books on the Middle East and Islam. Editor of the monthly *Le Monde Diplomatique* until December 2005, he became its deputy director from January 2008. The long-time companion of Tariq Ramadan, they are the co-authors of *Islam in Question*.

Henri Guaino (born March 11, 1957) was a special advisor to the former French president Nicolas Sarkozy from 2007 until his defeat in 2012. Guaino was responsible for writing the so-called "Dakar Speech" which Sarkozy gave in 2007 that was criticized for being condescending towards the African continent.

Claude Guéant (born 1945). French civil servant. Former Chief of Staff to Nicolas Sarkozy, he served as Minister of the Interior from 27 February 2011 until 15 May 2012. He is a member of the Union for a Popular

Movement (UMP). He studied law in Paris, then attended Sciences-Po and the ENA administration school. After graduating from ENA, he became chief of staff of the prefect of the Finistère department.

Abdullah Gül (born 29 October 1950). President of the Republic of Turkey since 2007. He previously served as prime minister and as Minister of Foreign Affairs. He is the first openly devout Muslim President in the modern history of Turkey.

John Hagee (born April 12, 1940). American founder and senior pastor of Cornerstone Church in Texas. He is also the CEO of Global Evangelism Television and of J. Hagee Ministries which telecasts his national radio and television ministry, also the founder and National Chairman of the Christian-Zionist organization Christians United for Israel, incorporated on February 7, 2006.

Ismail Haniyeh (born 29 January 1963) is a senior political leader of Hamas who became prime minister after the elections of 2006. President Mahmoud Abbas dismissed him, but Haniyeh continues to exercise authority in the Gaza Strip, and is still recognized by the Palestinian Legislative Council.

King Faycal of Saudi Arabia - Faisal bin Hussein bin Ali al-Hashemi (20 May 1885–8 September 1933) was for a short time king of the Arab Kingdom of Syria or Greater Syria in 1920, and king of Iraq from 23 August 1921 to 1933. He was a member of the Hashemite dynasty.

Theodore Herzl (May 2, 1860–July 3, 1904). Ashkenazi Jewish Austro-Hungarian journalist and the father of modern political Zionism and of the State of Israel.

Fouad Ali al-Himma (born in 1962). Moroccan politician who was Minister for the Interior from 1999 to 2007, alongside Chakib Benmoussa, Minister of the Interior.

Brice Hortefeux (born 1958). French politician. He was Minister of the Interior, and of Overseas Territories. He was previously Minister for Labor, Labor Relations, the Family, Solidarity and Urban Affairs and Minister-Delegate for Local Government at the Ministry of the Interior and a Member of the European Parliament.

Wolf Huber (1485-1553). Austrian painter, printmaker, and architect, a leading member of the Danube School.

Samuel Huntington (1927–2008). Influential American political scientist whose works covered many areas of political science. He gained wider prominence through his *Clash of Civilizations* (1993, 1996) thesis of a post-Cold War new world order.

Michael James Nazir-Ali (born in 1949). The 106th Bishop of Rochester in the Church of England; he retired in September 2009 to become director of the Oxford Centre for Training, Research, Advocacy and Dialogue. He holds dual citizenship of both Pakistan and Great Britain.

Lionel Jospin. Socialist Party candidate for President of France in the elections of 1995 and 2002. He was narrowly defeated in the final runoff election by Jacques Chirac in 1995. He ran for President again in 2002, and was eliminated in the first round behind both Chirac and the far-right candidate Jean-Marie Le Pen. He then announced his retirement from politics.

Tony Robert Judt (1948-2010). British historian, essayist, and university professor who specialized in European history. Judt moved to New York and served as the Erich Maria Remarque Professor in European Studies at New York University, and Director of NYU's Erich Maria Remarque Institute. A frequent contributor to the *New York Review of Books*. In 1996 Judt was elected a Fellow of the American Academy of Arts and Sciences and in 2007 a corresponding Fellow of the British Academy.

Saif al-Islam (born 25 June 1972). Son of dictator Muammar Qaddafi and former Libyan political figure. He publicly turned down his father's offer of the country's second highest post and held no official government position. Despite this, during his father's reign, he was the second most widely recognized person in Libya and was at times the "de facto" prime minister. An arrest warrant was issued for him by the International Criminal Court for charges of crimes against humanity against the Libyan people, for allegedly torturing and killing civilians. He was arrested in November 2011 and is still detained.

Rebiya Kadeer (born in 1946). Uyghur human rights activist from Xinjiang, China. Kadeer is the leader of the Uyghur self-determination movement in her capacity as President of the World Uyghur Congress, a group that advocates for greater autonomy for Uyghurs in China and fights against what they consider to be the oppressive policies of the Chinese government. She lives in the United States.

Abdel Kader (1907-1948) was a nationalist and Palestinian fighter. During the War of 1948, he directed the Jaysh al-Jihad al-Muqaddas until his death April 8, 1948, during Operation Nahshon.

Yahia Kahn (1917–1980). A senior army commander who was the third President of Pakistan, and the military dictator from 1969 until the dissolution of East-Pakistan, in December 16, 1971.

Mehdi Karoubi (born in 1937). Influential Iranian reformist politician, democracy activist, leader, and chairman of the National Trust Party. He presided over the parliament from 1989 to 1992 and 2000 to 2004, and a presidential candidate in the 2005 and 2009 presidential elections.

Ayatollah Mohammad Reza Mahdavi Kani (born in 1931). Iranian cleric, conservative politician, writer and current Chairman of the Assembly of Experts, which elects and supervises the Supreme Leader of Iran.. He is also the current leader of Combatant Clergy Association. Previously, he was Acting Prime Minister of Iran from 2 September 1980 when Prime Minister Mohammad-Javad Bahonar was assassinated until 29 October 1981.

Gilles Kepel (born in 1955). French political scientist, specialist of Islam and the contemporary Arab world. He is a Professor at Sciences Po Paris and member of the Institut Universitaire de France. He graduated in Arabic and philosophy, with two doctorates in sociology and political sciences. Dr. Kepel also taught at New York University in 1994 and Columbia University in 1995. Appointed to the Philippe Roman chair in History and International Relations at the London School of Economics in 2009–2010. He contributes regularly to *Le Monde*, the *New York Times*, *La Repubblica*, *El Pais*, and several Arab medias.

Grand Ayatollah **Ali Khamenei** (born in 1939). Supreme Leader of Iran, a Twelver Shi'a marja, he also served as the President of the Islamic Republic of Iran from 1981 to 1989. In 2010, *Forbes* named him 26th on the list of the "World's Most Powerful People." Holding absolute power in his country, he has been described as one of only three people having "important influence" during the history of the Islamic Republic of Iran.

Abdul Qadeer Khan (born in 1936). Pakistani nuclear scientist and a metallurgical engineer, considered the founder of HEU based gas-centrifuge uranium enrichment program for Pakistan's integrated nuclear bomb project. Founded and established the Kahuta Research Laboratories in 1976, he was both senior scientist and Director-General until his retirement in 2001. Apart from participating in the nuclear bomb project, he made major scientific contributions, including integrated applications, as one of Pakistan's top scientists.

Ayatollah Khatami (born in 1943). Iranian statesman. Minister of Culture and Islamic Guidance, was Iran's president from 2 August 1997 to August 3, 2005. During his presidency, Khatami built diplomatic relations with many countries, including those of the European Union and Asia. In domestic policy he advocates free speech and tolerance, but fails to change the institutions, or revive the economy because of conservative opposition in parliament.

Ayatollah Khomeini (September 1902–3 June 1989). Iranian religious leader and politician, and leader of the 1979 Iranian Revolution which saw the overthrow of Mohammad Reza Pahlavi, the Shah of Iran. He held the title of Grand Ayatollah and is officially known as Imam Khomeini inside Iran and internationally.

Grand Ayatollah Hossein Vahid Khorasani. Iranian Twelver Shia Marja who moved to Iraq and studied in seminaries of Grand Ayatollah Khoei until he moved back to Iran in 1972 and currently resides and teaches at the Seminary of Qom, Iran. He is also the father in law of Sadeq Larijani.

Nasser al-Kidwa (born 1959). United Nations (UN) Deputy Special Representative of the Secretary-General for Afghanistan in the UN Assistance Mission in Afghanistan, he is a Palestinian diplomat and was the Permanent Observer from the Palestinian National Authority at the UN.

Kiril, Patriarch and former Metropolitan Bishop (born in 1946) became Patriarch of Moscow and all the Rus' and Primate of the Russian Orthodox Church in 2009 after having been Archbishop of Smolensk and Kaliningrad since 1984. He is Chairman of the Orthodox Church's Department for External Church Relations and a permanent member of the Holy Synod beginning in November 1989.

Irving Kristol (January 22, 1920–September 18, 2009). American columnist, journalist, and writer known as the "godfather of neoconservatism." As founder, editor, and contributor to various magazines, he played an influential role in the intellectual and political culture of the last half-century.

Yves Lacoste (born 1929). French geographer and geopolitician, born in Fez, Morocco. In 1976 he established the French geopolitical journal *Hérodote*. He is the author of a *Geopolitical Dictionary* (1993) and the French Institute for geopolitics. In one of his known works, *La Géographie du sous-développement*, Lacoste suggests a spatial explanation for underdevelopment.

Jack Mathieu Émile Lang (born 1939). French politician and member of the Socialist Party, he served as France's Minister of Culture from 1981 to 1986 and 1988 to 1992, and as Minister of Education from 1992 to 1993 and 2000 to 2002. He was also the Mayor of Blois from 1989 to 2000 and served until 2012 in the National Assembly from the sixth district of Pas-de-Calais.

Louis-Joseph Lebret (1897–1966). French Dominican social scientist and philosopher who sought to "put the economy at the service of man" and advanced the notion of the "human economy." He was also responsible for introducing concern for development to the Catholic Church. He was aware of the challenges posed to the Church and the Western by underdevelopment and pushed the argument for an increased solidarity with poor countries.

Marine Le Pen (born 1968). Lawyer and French right-wing politician she is the president of the Front National (FN), the third largest political party in France, since 16 January 2011. She is the youngest daughter of the French politician Jean-Marie Le Pen, former president of the FN and currently its honorary chairman, and Marion Maréchal-Le Pen's aunt.

Monica Lewinsky (born in 1973). American woman with whom United States President Bill Clinton admitted to having an "improper relationship" with while she worked at the White House in 1995-96. The affair and its repercussions (which included Clinton's impeachment) became known as the Lewinsky Scandal.

Avigdor Lieberman (born in 1958). Israeli politician, originally from Moldova, founder and leader of the far-right Yisrael Beiteinu ("Israel our Home") Party. Foreign Minister and Deputy Prime Minister of Israel since March 31, 2009. He was at the top of the list of candidates during the Israeli elections of 2006 and 2009.

Dov Lior (born 1933). Israeli rabbi, currently the Chief Rabbi of Hebron and Kiryat Arba in the southern West Bank. He heads the "Council of Rabbis of Judea and Samaria."

Amin Maalouf (born 25 February 1949 in Beirut). Lebanese-born French author. Although his native language is Arabic, he writes in French. His works have been translated into many languages. Awarded Prix Goncourt in 1993 for his novel *The Rock of Tanios* and has also been awarded the Prince of Asturias Award for Literature in 2010. Elected to the Académie Française on 23 June 2011.

Mounir al-Majidi. Director of the private secretariat of King Mohammed VI of Morocco.

Nouri al- Maliki (also known as **Jawad al-Maliki** or **Abu Esraa**), (born in 1950). Prime minister of Iraq and secretary-general of the Islamic Dawa Party. His government succeeded the Iraqi Transitional Government. He also holds in his second Cabinet since December 21, 2010, the positions of Interior Minister, Defense Minister, and National Security Minister.

Robert Malley (born 1963). American lawyer, political scientist and a specialist in conflict resolution. He is currently Program Director for Middle East and North Africa at the International Crisis Group and a former Special Assistant to President Bill Clinton for Arab-Israeli Affairs (1998–2001). Malley is considered an expert on the Israeli-Palestinian conflict.

Manhigut Yehudit. Movement started by Moshe Feiglin and Shmuel Sackett to give the State of Israel "authentic Jewish values." The movement opposes religious coercion, seeks Jewish identity as prescribed by the

Tanakh (Bible) and authentic Jewish teachings to become Israel's official culture.

Charles Martel (686–741). Frankish military and political leader, who served as Mayor of the Palace under the Merovingian kings and ruled *de facto* during an interregnum (737–43) at the end of his life, using the title Duke and Prince of the Franks He is remembered for winning the Battle of Poitiers in 732, in which he defeated an invading Moorish army. This victory is traditionally credited with halting northward Islamic expansion in Western Europe. He was also the grandfather of Charlemagne.

Esfandiar Rahim Mashaei (born in 1960). Top adviser, and close confident of Iranian President Mahmoud Ahmadinejad. Currently Ahmadinejad's Chief of Staff, he served as the head of the Presidential Center from 2009 to 2011, and was First Vice President of Iran for one week in 2009 before he was removed from that post by Supreme Leader Ayatollah Ali Khamenei. He has been widely criticized by Iranian conservatives for alleged "deviant" tendencies.

Charles Maurras (1868–1952). French author, poet, and critic. Leader and principal thinker of *Action Française*: monarchist, anti-parliamentarian, and counter-revolutionary movement. As a political theorist, he had a major intellectual influence in early 20th-century Europe, his views anticipated some of the ideas of fascism.

François Mauriac (1885–1970) was a French author; member of the *Académie Française* (1933); laureate of the Nobel Prize in Literature (1952). He was awarded the Grand Cross of the *Légion d'honneur* (1958). Mauriac was opposed to French rule in Indochina, and strongly condemned the use of torture by the French army in Algeria.

Abbas Malekzadeh Milani. Iranian-American historian and author. Milani is a visiting professor of Political Science and the director of the Iranian Studies program at Stanford University. He is also a research fellow and co-director of the Iran Democracy Project at Stanford University's Hoover Institution. Milani has found evidence that Persian modernism dates back over 1000 years.

Rabbi Melamed. Already mentioned in the Hebrew Bible as a teacher or tutor. In the Talmudic period, he becomes almost exclusively a tutor or schoolmaster of children, the word is often followed tinokot (infants, children) and has an Aramaic equivalent, "makre dardeke." The melamed was designated by the community, and his work was highly regulated.

Aaron David Miller (born March 25, 1949). Analyst, author, and negotiator, he is on the U.S. Advisory Council of the Israel Policy Forum, and was an advisor to six secretaries of state. He worked within the United States Department of State for twenty four years and left in January 2003 to serve as president of Seeds of Peace, an international youth organization, founded in 1993.

George Mitchell (born August 20, 1933). Senate majority leader (1989-1995). Senator from Maine; took a leading role in negotiating peace in Northern Ireland. Appointed special envoy to the Middle East by President Obama. Author of the *Mitchell Report* (2001), stressing need for Israel to halt the expansion of the settlements and for Palestinians to prevent violence. He resigned in 2011.

Mohammed Morsi (born August 1951). Fifth and current President of Egypt since 30 June 2012. Morsi was a Member of Parliament in the People's Assembly of Egypt from 2000 to 2005 and a leading figure in the Muslim Brotherhood. He became Chairman of the Freedom and Justice Party, in the wake of the 2011 Egyptian revolution and stood as its candidate for the 2012 presidential election.

Mohammed Mossadegh (1882-1967). Prime Minister of Iran from 1951 until being overthrown in a coup d'état in 1953. His administration introduced a wide range of social and political reforms but is most notable for its nationalization of the Iranian oil industry, which had been under British control since 1913.

Emmanuel Mounier (1905–1950). French philosopher and the guiding spirit in the French Personalist movement, and founder and director of *Esprit*, the magazine which was the organ of the movement. A child of peasants, Mounier was a brilliant scholar at the Sorbonne. In 1929, when he was only twenty-four, he was influenced by the French writer Charles Péguy, to whom he ascribed the inspiration of the personalist movement.

Mohammed Moussaoui (born 1 April 1964 in Figuig, Morocco) is the president of the French Council of Muslim Faith. As of 2008 he is a French citizen.

Mir-Hossein Mousavi (born in 1942). Iranian politician, Prime Minister of the Islamic Republic of Iran from 1981 to 1989. Candidate in the presidential election of 2009, supported by major "reform" parties he was defeated by Mahmoud Ahmadinejad. The ballot was challenged by hundreds of thousands of people protesting for several weeks, Mir Hossein Mousavi is considered the leader of the revolt that led to dozens of deaths and executions.

Rupert Murdoch (born in 1931). Managing director of Australia's News Limited, inherited from his father, in 1952. He is the founder, Chairman and CEO of global media holding company the News Corporation, the world's second-largest media conglomerate.

Murphy Nicholas Xavier Pakiam (born in 1938) is the third metropolitan archbishop of the Roman Catholic Archdiocese of Kuala Lumpur, Malaysia. Former president of the Catholic Bishops' Conference of Malaysia, Singapore and Brunei; and the publisher of the Catholic weekly newspaper, *The Herald*.

Grand Ayatollah **Hussein-Ali Montazeri Najafabadi** (1922–2009) was a prominent Iranian scholar, Islamic theologian, Shiite Islamic democracy advocate, writer and human rights activist. One of the leaders of the Iranian Revolution in 1979, and for a time the designated successor to the revolution's Supreme Leader Ayatollah Khomeini, with whom he had a falling-out in 1989 over government policies that Montazeri said infringed on people's freedom and denied them their rights. Montazeri spent his last years in Qom, and remained politically influential in Iran, especially to the reformist movement. He was widely known as the most knowledgeable senior Islamic scholar in Iran and a *Grand Marja* (religious authority) of Shi'ite Islam.

Mullah Omar (born in 1959) is the spiritual leader of the Taliban. He was Afghanistan's de facto head of state from 1996 to late 2001, under the official title "Head of the Supreme Council." He held the title Commander of the Faithful of the Islamic Emirate of Afghanistan, which was recognized by only three nations: Pakistan, Saudi Arabia and the United Arab Emirates.

Ali Ben Bongo Ondimba (born in 1959). President of Gabon since October 2009. During his father's presidency, he was Minister of Foreign Affairs from 1989 to 1991 and represented Bongoville as a Deputy in the National Assembly from 1991 to 1999; subsequently he was Minister of Defense from 1999 to 2009. The candidate of the Gabonese Democratic Party in the August 2009 presidential election, following his father's death. According to official results, he won the election with 42% of the vote.

Jaime Ortega (born in 1936). Latin Rite Archbishop of the Archdiocese of Havana and a Cardinal of the Catholic Church. He is the second Cuban elevated to Cardinal.

David Ownby (born 1958). Associate Professor of the Department of History at the University of Montreal. His areas of specialization, among others, is the history of China

Rick Perry (born in 1950). Governor of Texas since 1998. Perry also served as Chairman of the Republican Governors Association. In 2011, Perry announced that he was running for the Republican nomination for President of the United States in the 2012 presidential election. On January 19, 2012, Perry announced he would be suspending his campaign but gave his support to Mitt Romney.

Trevor Phillips, OBE (born in 1953), chairs the Equality and Human Rights Commission (EHRC) a former television executive and presenter. He became head of the Commission for Racial Equality.

Meir Porush (born 11 June 1955). Israeli politician and a former member of the Knesset for the ultra-Orthodox Agudat Yisrael faction of United Torah Judaism.

Jean-Pierre Raffarin (born 1948 in Poitiers), is a French conservative politician and senator for the Vienne department. He served as prime minister of France, resigning after France's rejection of the referendum on the European Union draft constitution.

Akbar Hashemi Rafsanjani (born in 1934). Influential Iranian politician and writer, and the fourth President of Iran. He was a member of the Assembly of Experts until his resignation in 2011. Currently, he is Chairman of the Expediency Discernment Council of Iran.

Said Ramadan (1926-1995). Son-in-law of Hassan al-Banna, and the founder and a major figure in the Muslim Brotherhood. He moved to Saudi Arabia where he founded the World Islamic League, a charity and missionary group. His son, Tariq Ramadan, is prominent in international Islamic affairs and academia. Said Ramadan's US connections included Malcolm X and Dawud Salahuddin.

Raja Rao (November 8, 1908–July 8, 2006). Indian writer of English-language novels and short stories, whose works are deeply rooted in Hinduism. Raja Rao's semi-autobiographical novel, *The Serpent and the Rope* (1960), is the story of a search for spiritual truth in Europe and India. It established him as one of the finest Indian stylists and won him the Sahitya Akademi Award in 1964. For the entire body of his work, Rao was awarded the Neustadt International Prize for Literature in 1988.

Clotilde Reiss (born 31 July 1985). French student who was accused of being an agent of the French Secret Service. Her arrest in Iran on espionage charges on 1 July 2009 generated considerable diplomatic controversy. She holds a master's degree from Sciences-Po Lille. At the time of her arrest she was teaching in Isfahan and writing a master's thesis about teaching history and geography in Iranian schools.

Mohsen Rezaï (born in 1954). Iranian politician, economist and former military commander, currently the Secretary of the Expediency Discernment Council of the Islamic Republic of Iran. Before that, he was the Iranian Revolutionary Guard Corps Chief Commander for 16 years.

Andrea Riccardi (born in 1950). Founder, in 1968, of the Community of Sant'Egidio Since 1981 he is professor of history of Christianity and Religions at the University of Rome III. In 2009, he agreed to serve on the jury prize for conflict prevention. On 16 November 2011, he was appointed Minister of International Cooperation and Integration in the new government formed by Mario Monti.

Pat Robertson (born March 22, 1930). U.S. media mogul, television evangelist, ex-Baptist minister and businessman who politically aligns himself with the Christian Right in the United States. He is the founder of numerous organizations and corporations, and hosts TV programs.

Sir William Rowan (1789–1879). British military commander. Born in the Isle of Man, Rowan was commissioned into the 52nd Light Infantry in 1803. He fought at the Battle of Waterloo and took part in the charge of the 52nd Light Infantry. After the war he was in charge of the First arrondissement of Paris. In 1828 he became Military Secretary to Sir John Colborne, Lieutenant Governor of Upper Canada.

Yitzhak Rabin (1 March, 1922–4 November, 1995). Israeli politician, statesman and general. He was the fifth prime minister of Israel, until his assassination. In 1994, Rabin won the Nobel Peace Prize together with Shimon Peres and Yasser Arafat.

Tariq Ramadan (born 26 August 1962 in Geneva, Switzerland). Swiss academic and writer. He is also a Professor of Contemporary Islamic Studies in the Faculty of Oriental Studies at Oxford University. He advocates the study and re-interpretation of Islamic texts, and emphasizes the heterogeneous nature of Western Muslims.

Jean-Paul Roux (5 January 1925–29 June 2009). French Turkologue and a specialist of Islamic culture. A graduate of the Institut national des langues et civilisations orientales, at the École du Louvre. He was Director of Research at CNRS from 1957 to 1970, the Science Secretary for the Department of Oriental Languages and Civilizations from 1960 to 1966, and a teacher of Islamic art at the École du Louvre.

Mark Rutte (born in 1967). Dutch politician and leader of the People's Party for Freedom and Democracy (VVD). He has been the prime minister of the Netherlands and Minister of General Affairs since 14 October 2010 as head of the cabinet. When he was sworn in on 14 October 2010, he became the first liberal prime minister in the Netherlands in 92 years.

Nayef bin Abdulaziz al-Saud (1933–16 June 2012). Crown Prince of Saudi Arabia, as well as First Deputy Prime Minister, from 2011 to 2012. He was also Minister of the Interior from 1975 to 2012.

Leopold Sedar Senghor (1906–2001). One of the most influential African intellectuals of the 20th Century. He was a poet, politician, and cultural theorist who served as the first president of Senegal (1960–80). He was also the first African elected as a member of the *Académie Française*. Before the independence, he founded the political party called the Senegalese Democratic Bloc.

Abraham Serfaty (1926–18 November 2010). Internationally prominent Moroccan dissident, militant, and political activist, who was imprisoned for years by King Hassan II of Morocco, for his political actions in favor of democracy and development during the Years of Lead. He paid a high price for such actions: imprisoned for fifteen months living underground, seventeen years in jail and eight years of exile.

Gilad Shalit (born in 1986). Israeli soldier of the Israel Defense Forces who was abducted inside Israel by Hamas militants in a cross-border raid via underground tunnels in June 2006, held for over five years in violation of international humanitarian law, and released on 18 October 2011 as part of a prisoner exchange deal.

Kenneth Starr (born in 1946). American lawyer and federal judge best known as the independent counsel appointed to investigate the suicide of Vince Foster and the Whitewater real estate investments of Bill Clinton. That investigation was expanded into the Monica Lewinsky scandal. Clinton was found to have lied about the affair and was about to be impeached. Starr now serves as president of Baylor University in Waco, Texas.

Igor Stechine. During the first two presidential terms of Vladimir Putin, Stechine was a deputy chief of administration and Deputy Prime Minister for Energy. He has always been a close associate of Putin and one of the most influential members of the former government, even though he is not part of the present government.

Ahmed al-Tayyeb (born in Fez in 1928). A well-known Moroccan writer of poetry and drama. He is considered one of the great voices of contemporary Moroccan theater.

Emmanuel Todd (born 16 May 1951). French historian, anthropologist, demographer, sociologist and political scientist at the National Institute of Demographic Studies (INED), in Paris. His research examines the different types of families worldwide and how there are matching beliefs, ideologies and political systems, and the historical events they influence.

Mohamed Tozy (born 1956). Moroccan political scientist, university professor and writer in the fields of the sociology of religion and political systems of the Arab world—especially the politico-religious area and Islamism in contemporary Morocco. He is also frequently asked to be an expert consultant by international organizations.

Rania (born **Rania al Yassin** on 31 August 1970) is the Queen consort of Jordan as the wife of King Abdullah II of Jordan.

Franz Josef Strauss (6 September 1915–3 October 1988). German politician, chairman of the Christian Social Union, member of the federal cabinet in different positions and long-time minister-president of the state of Bavaria. His last two decades were also marked by a fierce rivalry with CDU chairman Helmut Kohl.

Prince Talal Ben Abd-al Aziz (1933–16 June 2012) was the Crown Prince of Saudi Arabia, as well as First Deputy Prime Minister, from 2011 to 2012. He was also Minister of the Interior from 1975 to 2012.

King Hassan II of Morocco (July 9, 1929–July 23, 1999) was King of Morocco from 1961 until his death in 1999. The eldest son of Mohammed V, Sultan, then King of Morocco (1909–1961) and his wife Lalla Abla bint Tahar (1909–1992).

King Mohammed V of Morocco (10 August 1909–26 February 1961) was Sultan of Morocco 1927–1953 under the name Sidi Mohammed ben Youssef, exiled from 1953–55, then again recognized as Sultan upon his return, and King from 1957 to 1961. He was a descendant of the Alaouite Dynasty.

King Mohammed VI of Morocco (born 21 August 1963). The present king of Morocco, acceded to the throne on 23 July 1999 upon the death of his father, King Hassan II.

Mohamed Hussein Tantawi Soliman (born October 31, 1935). Egyptian Field Marshal and statesman. He is the commander-in-chief of the Egyptian Armed Forces and, as Chairman of the Supreme Council of the Armed Forces, was the de facto head of state from the ouster of Hosni Mubarak on February 11, 2011, to the inauguration of Mohamed Morsi as President of Egypt on June 30, 2012. Tantawi has served in the government as

Minister of Defense and Military Production since 1991 and was also Deputy Prime Minister in January–February 2011.

Shah of Iran. Title of the ruler of certain Middle Eastern and Central Asian countries, especially Persia (modern Iran) and on the Indian subcontinent; it derives from the Persian word *shah*, meaning "king."

Omar Suleiman (born 2 July 1936). Former Egyptian army general, politician, diplomat, and intelligence officer. A leading figure in Egypt's intelligence system beginning in 1986, Suleiman was appointed to the long-vacant vice presidency by then-president Hosni Mubarak on 29 January 2011.

Shenouda III (3 August 1923–17 March 2012). 117th Pope and Patriarch of the Church of Alexandria. His long episcopate lasted more than 40 years from 1971 until his death. He was a conservative figure within the Church; and was also respected within the Muslim community.

Cyril John Radcliffe (1899–1977). British lawyer, appointed by the British government to draw in five weeks (with the help of two Hindus and two Muslims) the borders during the partition of India 17 August 1947, two days after independence from British Raj that gave birth to India and Pakistan.

Ali Abdullah Saleh (born 21 March 1942). Yemeni politician. He served as President of the Yemen Arab Republic (North Yemen) from 1978 until 1990; after the unification of North and South Yemen in 1990, he became President of Yemen from 1990 to 2012.

Ali Ahmad Saleh is the eldest son of Yemeni president Ali Abdullah Saleh, and was widely expected to succeed his father even though he would never have been elected. He is also associated with a vast amount of corruption throughout the capital. During the 2011 protests when his father left for medical treatment in Saudi Arabia, Ahmed was informally placed in charge of the elite Republican Guards. Under his authority, the security forces killed over 100 people in less than 5 days in Sanaa.

Jules-Géraud Saliège (1870–1956). French Cardinal of the Roman Catholic Church. He served as Archbishop of Toulouse from 1928 until his death, and was elevated to the cardinalate in 1946 by Pope Pius XII.

Fahd bin Abdulaziz al-Saud (1923–1 August 2005). Custodian of the Two Holy Mosques. He was king of Saudi Arabia, from 1982 to 2005.

Prince Sultan bin Abdulaziz al-Saud (30 December 1930–21 October 2011) called *Sultan al-Khair* was the Crown Prince of Saudi Arabia, from 2005 to 2011.

Luiz Inácio Lula da Silva (born in 1945). Popularly known as "Lula," served as the 35th President of Brazil, from 1 January 2003 to 31 December 2010. Founding member of the Workers' Party in the 2006 election, he was re-elected to a second term as president, which ended on 31 December 2010. Often regarded as the most popular politician in the history of Brazil and, during his presidency, one of the most popular in the world thanks to his social programs. Lula played a prominent role in recent international relations developments, including the Nuclear program of Iran and global warming, and was described as "a man of bold ambition, seeking to alter the balance of power among nations."

Jaime Sin (1928-2005). Roman Catholic Archbishop of Manila known for his instrumental role in the People Power Revolution, which toppled the regime of Ferdinand Marcos and brought in Corazon Aquino as president of the Philippines.

Ayatollah Abbas Vaez Tabasi. Influential member of the Expediency Discernment Council and the Assembly of Experts of the Islamic Republic of Iran. Vaez-Tabasi is the head of the Astan Quds Razavi Foundation. The foundation runs "auto plants, agricultural businesses, and many other enterprises, and it is worth an estimated $15 billion."

Henri Teissier (born on 21 July 1929 in Lyon). French-Algerian Catholic Bishop and Archbishop Emeritus of Algiers.

Henri Tincq. French journalist. He was the religion expert at *Le Monde* daily from 1985 to 1998, after working at the Catholic newspaper *La Croix*. He now contributes regularly to the online magazine *Slate French*. Author of a dictionary of religions, he became interested in the history of the popes.

Theodoor "Theo" van Gogh (1957–2004). Dutch film director, film producer, columnist, author and actor. Van Gogh worked with the Somali-born writer Ayaan Hirsi Ali to produce the film *Submission*, that criticized the treatment of women in Islam and aroused controversy among Muslims. On 2 November 2004 he was assassinated by Mohammed Bouyeri, a Dutch-Moroccan Muslim.

Mohammed al-Utaibi. One of the 134 Saudi citizens who have been held in the Guantanamo Bay detention camps in Cuba.

Hubert Védrine (born in 1947). French Socialist politician. Diplomatic adviser of President Mitterrand, he served as secretary-general of the presidency from 1991 to 1995, then as Foreign Minister in the government of Lionel Jospin from 1997 to 2002. All three men agreed in their strong opposition to unilateral action by the United States in Iraq.

Odon Vallet (born in 1947). Doctor in Law and History of Religions. He is also a religious French scholar.

Xavier de Villepin graduated from the renowned French business school HEC, and later from the Harvard Business School. He took part in the French Resistance in 1944. He was also a French senator. In 1993 Villepin was elected chairman of the French Senate Committee on Foreign Affairs, Defense, and Armed Forces. He resigned from the committee in 2002 following the appointment of his son Dominique de Villepin as Minister of Foreign Affairs.

Pinhas Wallerstein is second in command of the Yesha Council, the main representative body of the colonists on the West Bank.

Vernon A. Walters (1917–2002). United States Army officer and diplomat. Most notably, he served from 1972 to 1976 as Deputy Director of Central Intelligence, from 1985 to 1989 as the United States Ambassador to the United Nations and from 1989 to 1991 as Ambassador to the Federal Republic of Germany during the decisive phase of German Reunification. Walters rose to the rank of lieutenant general in the U.S. Army and is part of the Military Intelligence Hall of Fame.

Geert Wilders (born in 1963). Dutch right-wing politician and founder of the Party for Freedom, the fourth largest political party in the Netherlands. Wilders is the Parliamentary group leader of his party in the Dutch House of Representatives. Best known for his criticism of Islam, he also states, "I don't hate Muslims, I hate Islam." Wilders' views regarding Islam have made him a deeply divisive figure in the Netherlands and abroad.

Christian Wulff (born in 1959). German politician and lawyer. He served as President of Germany from 2010 to 2012. A member of the Christian Democratic Union, he served as Prime Minister of the state of Lower Saxony from 2003 to 2010. He was elected President in the 30 June 2010 and forced to resign in a corruption scandal on 17 February 2012.

Liu Xiaobo (born in 1955). Chinese literary critic, writer, professor, and human rights activist who called for political reforms and the end of communist single-party rule in China. He is currently incarcerated as a political prisoner in China. Liu has served from 2003 to 2007 as President of the Independent Chinese.

Ahmed Yassin (1937–22 March 2004). Founder of Hamas, an Islamist Palestinian paramilitary organization and political party. He also served as the spiritual leader of the organization. He was assassinated by an Israeli helicopter gunship.

Yaakov Yossef (born 18 October 1946). Israeli rabbi and former politician who served as a member of the Knesset for the Shas Party between 1984 and 1988.

Susilo Bambang Yudhoyono (born in 1949). Indonesian politician and retired army general officer, President of Indonesia since 2004. He won the 2004 presidential election, defeating incumbent President Megawati Sukarnoputri. Widely known in Indonesia by his initials "SBY," he was sworn into office on 20 October 2004, together with Jusuf Kalla as vice president. He ran for re-election in 2009 with Boediono as his running mate, and won with an outright majority of the votes in the first round of balloting; he was sworn in for a second term on 20 October 2009.

Thierry Zarcone (born in 1958). French historian. His research focuses on the intellectual and religious history of the Turkish and Iranian cultures. Especially interested in Sufism and Freemasonry, he co-directs, with Ekrem Ishin and Arthur Buehler, the *Journal of the History of Sufism*, founded in 2000. He is also a consultant since 2000 with the Office for Democratic Institutions and Human Rights Organization of the OECD.

Muhammad Zia-ul-Haq (1924-1988). Fourth Chief martial law administrator and the sixth President of Pakistan from September 1978. Distinguished by his role in putting down the Black September insurgency against King Hussein in Jordan in 1970, he was appointed Chief of Army Staff in 1976. After widespread civil disorder, he planned and overthrew ruling Prime Minister Bhutto in a bloodless coup d'état on July 5, 1977, and became the state's third military ruler to impose martial law. Zia's idea of religious conservatism in Pakistan became the main tenet of his military government. Throughout the 1980s, Zia managed to consolidate more and more power in his hands, gradually putting down all opposition groups in Pakistan. Bhutto was tried and executed in 1979. Zia-ul-Haq was killed in a suspicious airplane crash on 17 August 1988.

Index